ECONOMICS OF BRITISH INDIA

ECONOMICS OF BRITISH INDIA

By

JADUNATH SARKAR, M.A.

FOURTH EDITION

Enlarged, re-written, and brought up to date

GYAN

Published by

Gyan Publishing House
5, Ansari Road
Daryaganj, New Delhi-110002
Phone: 011-47034999, 9811692060
E-mail: books@gyanbooks.com

Distribution Network
gyanbooks.com
India, USA, Canada, UK, Australia, France

ISBN : 978-81-212-6826-4 (PB)
First Published, 1909

2nd Impression 2022

Printed at: Gyan Press, Delhi.

ECONOMICS OF BRITISH INDIA
Author: JADUNATH SARKAR

ECONOMICS OF BRITISH INDIA

BY

JADUNATH SARKAR, M.A.,

Professor, Patna College.

FOURTH EDITION,

Enlarged, re-written, and brought up to dáte.

1917.

First edition (143 pp), *March, 1909.*
Second edition (304 pp.), *March, 1911.*
Third edition (336 pp.), *March, 1913.*
Fourth edition (384 pp.), *April, 1917.*

In this edition the book has been thoroughly revised, the statistics brought up to date, and a chapter on the economic effects of the war on India added. So rapid is the economic transformation of India going on before our eyes and so fast is the literature on various aspects of it growing up, that a general account of the subject requires to be mostly re-written every six years, and not only have new facts to be noted but even the old conclusions have to be greatly modified in the light of the new facts. Such a restudy has been attempted in the present edition. Throughout the book I have taken 1913-14, the last year of peace, as the standard of comparison and the basis of study. But the changes effected by the war have been duly noted in various places and studied together in the last chapter (X), which is altogether new; and the statistics of 1917 as far as available have been supplied. Among the more important additions are the inquiry into High Prices, the Report of the Royal Commission on Indian Currency (1914), recent developments of co-operation and our war finance and tariff changes.

PRINTED AT THE KUNTALINE PRESS, 61, BOWBAZAR STREET, CALCUTTA BY P. C. DASS AND PUBLISHED FROM M. C. SARKAR & SONS BY S. C. SARKAR, 90-2, HARRISON ROAD, CALCUTTA.

CONTENTS.

ECONOMICS OF BRITISH INDIA.

CHAPTER I.

THE LAND.

Physical features of the country and their economic influence.

The Indian Empire including Burma contains over $1\frac{3}{4}$ million square miles of territory, (exceeding by 12,000 square miles the whole of Europe *minus* Russia), and a population which in 1911 numbered 315 millions, being one-fifth of the human race and more than double the population of the Roman Empire. Of these $244\frac{1}{4}$ millions live in British territory. The British Isles in 1911 had a population of 46 millions, and Japan 47 millions.

Of the entire British Indian population

19.5 per cent. live in the United Provinces;

18.6 p. c. in the Bengal Presidency;

16.9 p. c. in the Madras Presidency;

14.1 p. c. in Bihar and Orissa;

9 p. c. in the Punjab and the N. W. Frontier Province taken together;

8 p. c. in the Bombay Presidency;

and a much smaller proportion in the other divisions.

The average density of population in British India is 224 to the square mile. The population is thickest in the Gangetic plain and the two coast-strips of Southern India, which enjoy abundant rain-fall on a fertile soil. Some of the most densely crowded districts are the following:—

Howrah,	1850	persons	per square	mile.
Muzaffarpur,	937	,,	,,	,,
Darbhanga,	875	,,	,,	,,
Saran,	853	,,	,,	,,

The average for the districts of North Bihar taken together is 646 per square mile, (Census of 1911), though this area is essentially rural with very few towns. England and Wales with their enormous town-population have only 618 inhabitants per square mile.

India may be **physically divided** into three well-defined regions:—

A. THE HIMALAYAS.

The Himalayas have a length of 1,500 miles and an average breadth of 200 miles. Their southern off-shoots at the north-western and north-eastern frontiers run down to the sea and completely shut India out from the rest of Asia by land.

Their economic aspects:—

(*a*) Their double walls *catch the* vapour-laden *clouds* driven north from the Ocean by the monsoon winds. The moisture either falls as rain or is frozen into snow and then descends in glaciers, feeding the rivers throughout the year. These hills, therefore, *supply rain-water* to the Indian plains. At Cherapunji in Assam the annual rainfall is about 460 inches. Kashmir is one vast reservoir supplying all the water of the five rivers that fertilise the Punjab plains.

(*b*) The forests covering the southern slopes of the Himalayas retain much of the rain-water among the network of their roots and their floor of dead leaves, by preventing too rapid a surface flow. Throughout the dry season this water slowly trickles down and thus saves our rivers from absolutely drying up. The hills, therefore, store and *regulate the supply of water* to the plains in an equable flow all the year round.

(*c*) The *forests* on the hill-side *yield timber* for Railway sleepers, *fuel*, and *beams* for buildings to all the northern plains. Tea, potato, and certain English fruits thrive greatly on the Himalayas. The indigenous products are barley, oats, millets, borax, honey, and, in a few places, rice; but their total value is not much.

(*d*) The *water-power* of the hill torrents and waterfalls is now used mostly in turning a few old-fashioned mills. But it is of great potential importance, as it can generate an enormous quantity of electricity. Several such schemes have been already set on foot, chiefly in connection with the hill stations, and we may look forward to the rapid development of hydro-electrical installations in the next generation. A vast project for generating power from the Jhelam falls in the Uri gorge of Kashmir, was completed in 1908.

Outside the Himalayas we have the Cavery hydro-electrical works in Mysore and the Tata works at Lonvala in the Western Ghats.

(*e*) Their chief disadvantage is the *cost and difficulty of transport*, which, added to the fact that the hill region can grow food for only a small population, has always caused a *scarcity of labour* in them.

B. THE NORTHERN RIVER-PLAINS.

They stretch between the Himalayas and the Vindhyas, and include three great river-systems,—the Indus, the Ganges, and the Brahmaputra, with their tributaries. This is the most fertile and densely populated region of India and is inhabited by nearly 60 per cent. of the entire Indian population. The slope is so gentle that though Lahore is 1220 miles from Calcutta, yet the elevation of the plain between them never exceeds 800 feet (except near the hills).

Economic aspects of the Indian rivers :—

(*a*) As *water-carriers and fertilisers* :—Their water is employed in irrigation, either directly as when they step over their banks, or artificially by means of canals. The silt which they carry down from the hills spreads a very fertile layer on the soil which they overflood.

(*b*) As *land-makers and land-destroyers* :—The fall

in elevation is very rapid in their upper courses among the hills, and as they dash through gorges with rocky walls rising many thousand feet on both sides, huge boulders are broken into fine sand. On reaching the plain the fall is very gentle* and the slowly moving rivers deposit their load of sand on their two sides or at their mouths.

The silt carried down by the Indian rivers every year is of an enormous quantity. Lower Bengal is "the gift of the Ganges", just as Sind is "the gift of the Indus." The whole of the Bengal Delta, 50,000 square miles in area, has been created by the Ganges, *i.e.*, it has been raised from the ocean-bed to its present height by the annual deposit of Ganges mud for many ages. At Ghazipur the Ganges discharges every year 6,368 million cubic feet of silt, and the quantity deposited at the combined mouths of the Ganges and the Brahmaputra must be at least six times as large as this. Similar extension of land is going on at the mouths of the Indus, the Godavari, and the Kistna.

But the Indian rivers, especially in their lower courses, are great destroyers, too. Every year they eat

* The INDUS is 1800 miles long, of which 860 miles are passed in the hills with a fall of 14000 feet, while in the remaining 940 miles (passed in the plains) the fall is only 2,000 feet.

The GANGES, 1550 miles long, has a fall of 12,776 feet in its first 180 miles situated in the hills, while in the 1,370 miles of its course lying in the plains its bed sinks only 1,024 feet. At the head of the Bengal Delta the fall is 4 inches per mile, and below Calcutta from one to two inches only.

away their banks at this place or that, swallowing up fields, houses and cities; (at present Dera Ghazi Khan and Rohri are undergoing this fate).

Moreover, every now and then the rivers in the soft soil of Bengal or Sind suddenly desert their beds and thereby cause the ruin and abandonment of many old capitals and commercial cities. In an alluvial tract there is no means of confining a vast river to the same channel for ever.

The Brahmaputra, for example, is a terrible menace to Northern and Lower Bengal. It is like a big drain into which a smaller drain, the Ganges, falls *at the same level.* The natural result is that the bigger volume of water moving down the Brahmaputra forms a solid wall forcing back the water and silt of the Ganges. Hence the Ganges is year by year becoming more sluggish; it is more quickly depositing silt along its course, raising its bed, and blocking up the mouths of its tributaries. Thus the natural drainage of many parts of Bengal is becoming obstructed, and marshes and stagnant pools are being formed where there were fresh flowing streams before. The mass of water in the Lower Ganges, already depleted by the huge canal systems of Northern India, is being still further reduced by the falling off in the supply from its now sluggish tributaries. One day a gigantic convulsion of Nature will take place; the tributaries of the Ganges unable to find a free way to their main stream, will take advantage of an earthquake or subsidence of the soil to burst their banks and transfer their waters to the Brahmaputra, carving out new channels for themselves by destroying fields and hamlets on their way. The Teesta river did it in 1787. These natural operations are on too stupendous a scale to be prevented by man.

(*c*) As *highways*:—The Ganges has been well called "the great high-way of Bengal." It is navigable for a thousand miles above its mouth (to Cawnpur and even beyond). The Ganges-borne trade of Calcutta was worth 40 *crores* of Rupees in 1891. The Indus is navigable for 800 miles above its mouth (to Dera Ismail Khan). Until recently the Brahmaputra, (navigable for 800 miles up to Dibrugarh), was the only highway of Assam, and very large steamers have plied on it, carrying goods worth 6 crores of Rupees annually (1900).

These rivers supply the easiest and cheapest means of transport. India being the land of small producers and petty dealers, a man has only to hire a boat or two to carry all his produce or merchandise to the market. He can consult his own convenience during the journey, and his goods will be perfectly safe under his own eyes. The Ganges, particularly, has many rich and populous cities and shrines on its banks, and has been the commercial artery of Northern India from time immemorial. But (1) large steamers cannot ply on it, and (2) the frequent changes in its bed caused by the deposit of sand make water-transport uncertain and unprofitable except for boats of light draught. (3) The huge quantities of goods dealt with by modern commerce cannot often be transported by river, at least not so cheaply or quickly as by rail.

CROPS: The Northern Plains yield two harvests and sometimes three in the year. *Rice* is the chief crop of Bengal and Bihar. In Lower Bengal the other distinctive crops are *jute, plantain* and *cocoanut.* [*Bamboo*, too, is of first-rate importance to the people.] Proceeding westwards from Bengal, the crops are (1) *wheat*, (2) *barley*, (3) *millets*, and (4) *potatoes*. Besides these main cereals, *pulses, sugar-cane, oilseeds, tobacco*, spices, and an immense variety of edible *vegetables* and fibrous plants grow both in Bengal and in the Upper Provinces of the Gangetic Plain. The jungles produce (1) lac, (2) *tassar*, (3) silk, (4) timber, (5) millets, and (6) the *Mohua* plant, whose flower is eaten and when distilled yields a spirit which is the chief drink of the wild tribes.

C. THE SOUTHERN TABLELAND OR DECCAN.

Its average height is from 1000 to 3000 feet. The land gradually rises as we advance south, till it culminates in the plateau of Coorg (4000 feet above sea level). Three mountain-walls support the tableland, *viz.*, in the north the Vindhyas with their eastern continuation, the Kaimur range; in the east the Eastern Ghats; and in the west the Western Ghats. The last two converge in the Nilgiri Hills (rising to a height of 7000 feet), and then, beyond the gap of Palghat, they run southwards to Cape Comorin in a single chain, called the Travancore Hills.

At the northern end of the Deccan the two large rivers, Narmada and Tapti, flow into the Arabian Sea. But from Surat southwards the Western Ghats form an impenetrable barrier and all the other rivers of the plateau flow eastwards into the Bay of Bengal.

The rainfall on the table-land is scanty (about 30 inches in the year.) But the two coast-strips on the west and the east are extremely fertile and well-watered by the monsoons, especially the deltas near the Madras coast, which rival Bengal in the richness and close succession of their crops, and the abundance of rice and cocoanut. Irrigation canals have utilised the waters of the Madras rivers from the days of Hindu rule, and greatly increased the agricultural wealth of the land. Many parts of the tableland are *subject to drought*, as the rainfall, small in the best seasons, varies greatly from year to year. Consequently famines occur here frequently. From time immemorial the people have followed the system of storing the precious rain-water at various places by damming up valleys and thereby forming artificial lakes and tanks, the water of which irrigates lands on a lower level. Agriculture is entirely dependent on artificial irrigation. There are four great *forest* regions in the Deccan.

The most valuable crop of the Deccan is *cotton*, to which the black soil of Malwa, Khandesh, and Berar is remarkably suited. *Wheat* is grown only in the northern valleys. The other agricultural products are *pulses, jawar* and *bajra; pepper* and *spices* abound in the south; and *rice* is extensively grown in the Madras Delta, C.P., and the Malabar coast-strip only. Sugar-cane and tobacco are also cultivated in certain parts. The minerals of India are mostly to be found in the Deccan plateau and its hill spurs, Chota-Nagpur and the Central Provinces. They are of immense value, though inadequately worked as yet. Among them are *coal* (in Chota Nagpur), lime, iron, manganese, and mica (fast rising into importance), diamond (now closed), and gold (flourishing in Mysore).

Economic influences of land and climate. The Deccan plateau in spite of its agricultural poverty, is rich in minerals; and manufacturiug industries dependent on mineral substances must be established within easy reach of it. The chief disadvantages here, however, are scarcity of water and difficulty of transport. The mines are all situated in far inland places, many hundred miles away from the sea, with no navigable river or canal close to them. The railway is the only means of transporting their output to the populous northern plains and the ports of embarkation. But the broken nature of the country adds to the cost of railway construction, and the scantiness of the local population throws this cost entirely on the mines. Thus the price of the output is unduly raised for the manufacturer and consumer. Modern metal factories cannot be worked on the tableland, though the raw materials are plentiful there. A heavy cost has to be incurred before they can be taken from the pit to the factory. The absence of water-power in India's vast plains and plateaus and her unequal distribution of coal—of which 90 p. c. is concentrated in the Raniganj and Jheria fields,—have hitherto rendered industrial production very laborious and costly in most of her provinces.

The semi-tropical climate of the most populous and fertile tracts of India stands in the way of her resources being developed as economically and efficiently as in European countries. Division of labour between nations is "chiefly determined by climate and by Nature herself... The countries of the world most favoured by Nature...are evidently those whose soils bring forth the most common necessaries of life of the best quality and in the largest quantity, and whose climate is most conducive to bodily and mental exertion, and these are *the countries of the temperate zone;* for in these countries *the manufacturing power* especially *prospers,* by means of which the nation attains to the highest degree of mental and social development and of political power." (*List,* 131). "Labour requiring the agency of fire can only be given abundantly in cold countries; labour requiring suppleness of body and sensitiveness of touch, only in warm ones...The production of great art is limited to climates warm enough to admit of repose in the open air, and cool enough to render such repose delightful. The labour which at any place is easiest, is in that place cheapest." (Ruskin's *Munera Pulveris*, ch. iv.)

But India is immensely rich in raw materials. In variety of products and climate, she is rather a continent than a single country. There is hardly any object of Nature with which her soil is not already gifted, or which she cannot grow. She has, therefore, the natural capacity of supplying all her own needs and of producing almost all articles of civilised life. She can be self-sufficient in industry and agriculture at the same time, if we take care to develop the two in those regions which are specially suited to each, and land transport is cheapened between her tropical parts (growing raw materials) and her temperate regions (where alone factories can be efficiently worked). This may happen in the distant future. So, we must combat the orthodox economic theory that it is the natural function of India (like other tropical countries) to produce raw materials only and to get manufactures from the colder countries of Europe by exchange. The United States was long regarded as destined by Nature to be a producer of raw materials only. But by properly utilising her immense variety of climate and natural resources, she has become a first-rate manufacturing country also. India has the same continental vastness and variety as the United States, and can attain to a similar industrial growth by education and proper guidance.

RAINFALL AND ITS DISTRIBUTION.

The air currents that govern India's welfare and the life of her peasantry come mainly from the Ocean in the south. The scanty rainfall of the cold weather is, however, greatly dependent on storms that originate in the higher atmosphere north-west of India, especially that of Persia and Central Asia.

We have two *monsoons* or seasons of strong wind-currents, *viz.*, (*a*) the *North-Eastern* monsoon, from the middle of December to the end of March, during which the wind is comparatively dry and only 10 per cent. of the annual rainfall is received. These winds often produce light rain and storms in the plains of Upper India and heavy gales and snowfall in the western Himalayas. This *cold-weather rain* is very *important for* the *Punjab.* From March to May we have storms and moderate rainfall in North-Eastern India. This *hot weather rain* is very *useful to Assam.*

(*b*) The *South-Western* monsoon, from June to September, bringing vapour-laden clouds from the Ocean and yielding heavy rain (90 *per cent.* of our annual rainfall). In October the wind-currents begin to retreat south-wards from India and the rainfall soon ceases.

During the monsoons the trade-winds blowing northwards over the Indian Ocean are divided. One portion, (the *Bombay current*), strikes the Bombay coast and waters the Deccan and Central India; another, (the *Bengal current*), of much smaller volume, rushes up the Bay of Bengal and gives rain to Bengal and the Gangetic Plain; while a third (the *Burma current*), disburdens its moisture over the Irawady Valley.

The Bengal current, as it advances northwards from the head of the Bay of Bengal, is arrested by the Assam and Manipur Hills and deflected westwards over the Northern Plain, distributing rain all the way from Bengal to the Punjab.

The Bombay current, when arrested by the long line of the Western Ghats, yields copious rain (about 100 inches in four months) to the coast-strip and the adjacent hill districts. That portion of it which is forced across the Ghats, moves *eastwards* over the Peninsula, but with little rain-giving power left in it. At the same time the Bengal current is blowing in an opposite direction over the plains of the north, the two currents being separated by an imaginary line drawn through Agra, Allahabad and Hazaribagh. The *northern* portion of the Bombay current passes over Guzerat and Western Rajputana, giving little rain, and at last mingles with the Bengal current in Eastern Punjab. From this union, Eastern Punjab and Eastern Rajputana get moderate rain.

The Bombay current begins to give rain early in June, two weeks before the Bengal current.

For the success of Indian agriculture two things are necessary in the monsoons: (*a*) The rainfall *must not vary* greatly from year to year; or else the young crops would be either washed away or burnt up. (*b*) The rainfall *should be intermittent* during these three months; *i.e.*, there should be intervals of fine weather between every two periods of rain, in order to allow the soil to be softened, the seed to send up sprouts, the shoots to grow, and the ears to ripen, without their being either scorched up by continuous sunshine or rotten by unbroken rainfall. Hence, even if the rainfall is normal in amount but concentrated in two or three weeks, cultivation will be as thoroughly spoilt as if no rain had fallen.

Of the provinces of India, Guzerat, the western portion of the Northern Plain, and the Deccan are subject to very great variations from the normal rainfall, and to consequent risk of famine. The other provinces are more secure, especially Burma and Bengal, where the normal rainfall is in excess of the needs of cultivation and consequently even a large deficiency of rain cannot do harm to the chief crops. It is only in the districts whose normal rainfall is just sufficient for the crops, that agriculture is precarious, for there even a slight shortage of rain means ruin to the peasant. In Central India the S. W. monsoon also often fails if the N. E. monsoon of the preceding cold weather had failed. (*Ind. Emp.* i. 144-146).

The following table (*Cd.* 8157, p. 125) of the rainfall in the different parts of India is useful, as it shows the crops which Nature has meant for each of them. Rice requires about 60 inches of rain if it is to be grown without the help of irrigation. For wheat a lighter rainfall suffices, while the hardy millets grow in tracts that receive little rain from the sky, and hence their chief home is the dry Peninsula and Rajputana.

DIVISIONS OF INDIA	Normal rainfall in inches.
Excessive Rainfall—	
Lower Burma	123
WEST COAST (southern half or Malabar)	127
WEST COAST (northern half or Konkan)	109
Assam	98
Bengal Delta	92
Eastern Bengal	85
Heavy Rainfall—	
Western Bengal	59
Orissa	57
Chota Nagpur	53
Central Provinces, East ...	53
Bihar	50
Moderate Rainfall—	
Upper Burma	42·2
Central Provinces, West / Central India, East ...	45·1
Central India, West	34·8
Madras coast, North	40·3
United Provinces	39·4
Berar	31·10
Guzerat	33·6
Bombay Deccan	31·9
Nizam's Dominion, North ...	35·7
Mysore	36·5

Scanty Rainfall—

Madras Deccan	...	...	24
Rajputana, East	...	...	24
Punjab, East and North		...	23
Rajputana, West	...	...	12
Punjab, South-West	...	. ...	9
Sind ...	...	...	6

The Provinces of India: their Physical features and Economic aspects.

The MADRAS Presidency consists of two *coast regions*,—the short and narrow western strip along the Arabian Sea, and the very broad and long eastern plain along the Bay of Bengal,—which are well-watered, fertile and highly cultivated and grow abundance of rice, pepper, spices and cocoanut, and a third region, the table-land between the two coasts, which is dry, treeless and sterile like the Deccan plateau generally.

The BOMBAY Presidency with Sind contains widely different varieties of soil and climate. Among its divisions, Gujrat and the Tapti Valley (in Khandesh) are very rich in productivity and population; the Konkan or western coast-strip (north of the Malabar coast-strip belonging to the Madras Presidency) has plenty of rainfall and grows rice and plantain in abundance; the Deccan Plateau is dry and barren, "yielding to much labour a bare measure of subsistence"; the Bombay Karnatik or the South Maratha Country has many well-watered fields and large forests and is agriculturally better off than the Plateau.

BENGAL, as reconstituted in 1912, consists of the lower valleys and deltas of the Ganges and the Brahmaputra with some hill tracts in the north (*viz.*, Jalpaiguṛi and Darjiling) and in the south-east (*viz.*, Tippera and Chittagong). "It is a vast fertile alluvial plain, intersected in its southern portion by an infinity of rivers, creeks and channels." A belt of dense jungles, made up of forests, creeks and swamps, (named the Sundarbans) separates its cultivated plain from the Bay of Bengal. The average density of population of the Presidency is 551 to the square mile. "Bengal is thus more densely populated than any of the other Indian provinces or any European country except Belgium and England." It has practically a monopoly of jute cultivation and is the largest producer of rice and tobacco, with fair quantities of sugar and oil-seeds, but no wheat or cotton.

BIHAR consists almost entirely of fertile alluvial plains, yielding large crops of rice, pulse, potato, wheat, maize, sugar-cane and tobacco, besides vegetables of all sorts. Jute cultivation is extending in its north-eastern parts. *Chota Nagpur* is a mountainous region rich in minerals and forests. Nearly two-thirds of the cultivated area of the province of Bihar and Orissa are devoted to rice. Of India's annual coal output of $16\frac{1}{4}$ million tons, $10\frac{1}{2}$ millions come from Bihar and $4\frac{1}{2}$ millions from Bengal, while the rest of India supplies only $1\frac{1}{3}$ million tons or 8 per cent. of the total.

The UNITED PROVINCES of Agra and Oudh consist of portions of the Himalaya and Vindhya ranges and the great Gangetic plain (which latter covers more than half the area of the province). This plain is very densely peopled, fertile and closely cultivated. In most places of it canals have secured an assured water supply. The rocky tracts are infertile, thinly peopled, and in the southern border (*i.e.*, Bundelkhand) liable to famine. The northern hills (*i.e.*, the Himalayas) are rich in forests. The province is the second largest producer of wheat in India, and first as regards maize, gram and sugar-cane. Rice, millets, oil-seeds, cotton and tobacco also are extensively grown here.

The PUNJAB and the N. W. Frontier Province taken together are one-fifth hilly and four-fifths plain country gently sloping to the south-west. The plains *east* of Lahore have just sufficient rainfall to make cultivation possible without irrigation in favourable seasons, but failure of harvest is sure if there is the least shortage of rain. The population here is large, 300 to the square mile, with many large cities and much trade and manufacture. The plains *west* of Lahore, on the other hand, have a scanty rainfall and a thin population (100 per square mile), and in them cultivation is possible only with the aid of irrigation. But British engineering skill has covered this tract with extensive canals, protecting it from drought and famine and enabling a large and growing population to colonise it. This province is the largest grower of wheat (11 million acres) and second in respect of gram and sugar-cane. But about a million and a half acres are also devoted to each of the following crops —millets, oil-seeds, cotton and maize, while half a million acres are under rice.

In the CENTRAL PROVINCES and Berar, which consist of uplands and plain country, rice, wheat and the millets grow equally well, while this division is first in cotton and oil-seeds. The area devoted to each of these five crops ranges from 3 to 5 million acres. The population is sparse, but the forests are valuable and the mineral deposits very promising.

BURMA, leaving out the northern and western hills and highlands, is one vast plain, consisting almost entirely of a rich alluvial deposit and fertile in the highest degree, with abundant rainfall. Rice is by far the predominant crop, 10 million acres out of a total of 13·74 being under rice, while moderate quantities of tobacco, oil-seeds and millets are also grown. Wheat and cotton are unknown. But Burma has the richest petroleum deposits in India; timber is one of its main sources of wealth, and there are some gem mines also. Nearly two-thirds of the total area of the province is forest. [Based upon *Code 220* of 1913.]

The distribution of our chief crops (1911).—

RICE is grown in nearly one-third of the entire cultivable area of India. It is the staple crop in regions of heavy and assured rainfall, such as Bengal, Bihar, Madras and Burma, which four provinces contain between them nine-tenths of the total rice-area of India. Elsewhere fairly good quantities of it are grown, but only with the aid of irrigation. Half the total rice area of India lies in Bengal and Bihar together (38 million acres), while Madras and Burma together supply another 38 per cent. (20 million acres).

WHEAT is cultivated extensively in Upper India, namely, the Punjab, the United Province, the Central Provinces and Central India; while moderate quantities are grown in Bihar and Bombay also; but hardly any in Burma, Bengal or Madras. The area under wheat has been extending since 1901 owing to the steady demand for the grain in foreign markets.

The two larger MILLETS *jawar* (called *cholum* in Madras) and *bajra* (Madrasi name, *cumbu*) are, after rice, the most extensively eaten food-stuffs in India, especially among the lower classes in Southern India and C. P., and to a much less extent in Bihar, U. P. and the Punjab. So also is *Ragi* (or *marua*), a smaller variety of millet. The stem of *jawar* is the chief cattle fodder of a large part of the country. Another important food of the poor is maize (*mako* or *bhutta*) which grows mostly in Bihar, the U. P. and the Punjab (about 1½ million acres in each).

Among the *pulses*, gram or chick pea (*boont* or *chhola*) is very important, it being the most extensively consumed food for horses, besides being eaten by large numbers of men in Upper India in the form of pulse soup (*dal*). The chief growers of it are the U. P. (7 million acres) and the Punjab (4¼ mil. acres), while Bihar and the C. P. each devotes a little short of a million acres to this crop.

Sugar-cane, is grown mainly in the U. P. (1⅛ mil. acres), the Punjab (⅓ mil. acres) and Bengal and Bihar (¼ mil. acres each).

Jute grows mainly in the swamps of Bengal (2¾ million acres), while N. E. Bihar supplies the remaining quarter of a million acres devoted to this crop in India. Its cultivation is small in Assam at present, but rapidly extending there. No other province grows it, except in negligible quantities.

Tobacco grows everywhere in India, Bengal, Madras and Bihar being engaged in its cultivation to the extent of 3, 2 and 1 hundred thousand acres respectively, and the U. P. and Burma coming up close behind the last.

In 1911, the C. P. and Bombay devoted about 4½ million acres each, Madras 2½, the Punjab & N. W. F. Province together 1½, and the U. P. a little below a million acres to *cotton*. (*Code 220* of 1913).

The **Staple Crops** of the different provinces in 1913 will be found in the following table compiled from *Code 8157*. (Areas cropped more than once have been counted as many times as they were under different crops).

Cropped area in *millions of acres* (1913):—

Province.	Rice.	Wheat.	Millets 3 kinds.	Oil-seeds.	Jute.	Total cropped area.
Bengal ...	19·7	0·14	—	1·8	2·7	28·7
Bihar ...	16	1·34	1·15	2	0·3	31·8
Assam ...	4·7	—	—	0·3	0·1	6·4
					Cotton	
U. P. & Oudh...	6	6·4	4·5	0·78	1·5	39·4
Madras ...	10·6	—	11·5	3·17	2·7	38·3
Punjab & N. W. F. Province...	0·8	9·5	4·37	1·3	1·8	30
Bombay & Sind	3	1·9	14·4	1·4	4·4	30·7
C. P. and Berar	5	3·2	4	2·2	4·7	25·8
Burma ...	10·4	—	0·77	1·5	0·3	14·7
TOTAL ...	77	22·6	41·1	14·6	15·8	24·7

The lesser crops, *area in acres* (in 1913):—

	Sugar-cane.	Tobacco.	Tea.
Bengal	216,500	319,000	156,000
Bihar	263,000	115,000	2,000
Assam	37,800	8,000	367,000

The lesser crops, *area in acres* (in 1913):—(*contd.*)

	Sugar-cane.	Tobacco.	Tea.
Bombay and Sind ...	63,400	97,000	—
Madras	83,600	207,000	26,800
Punjab & North-West Frontier	442,000	55,000	9,800
United Provinces & Oudh ...	1,389,300	75,000	8,000
Central Provinces & Berar ...	20,000	26,000	—
Burma	15,000	95,000	1,700
TOTAL ...	2·5 mil.	1 mil.	572,000

From the above we see that the U. P. contain far more cultivated land than any other province; this portion of India is *first* in *sugar*, *second* in *wheat*, and *third* in *millets.*

BOMBAY is *first* in *millets*, a good *second* in *cotton*, *third* in *oil-seeds.*

BURMA is *fourth* in *rice* and *oil-seeds* and *fifth* in *tobacco.*

MADRAS ranks as *first* in *oil-seeds*, *second* in *millets* and *tobacco*, and *third* in *rice*, *cotton* and *tea.*

BENGAL is *first* in *rice*, *jute* and *tobacco*, and *second* in *ea* . Bihar is *second* in *rice* and *jute* and *third* in *oil-seeds*, *sugar* and *tobacco.* Assam is *first* in *tea* and *third* in *jute.*

The CENTRAL PROVINCES (with Berar) are *first* in *cotton*, *second* in *oil-seeds*, and *third* in *wheat*.

The PUNJAB is easily *first* in *wheat*, *second* in *sugar*, and *fourth* in *cotton*.

The relative importance of the different crops to each province will be seen from the following table.

The percentage of its total cropped area which each province devoted to the different kinds of produce in 1913 :—

	Rice.	Wheat.	Millets.	Oil-seeds.	
Bengal ...	68·6	—	—	6	Jute. 9·4
Assam ...	73·4	—	—	4·7	1·6
Bihar ...	50·3	4·2	3·6	6·3	1
Bombay ...	9·7	6·2	47	4·5	Cotton 14·3
Madras ...	28	—	30	8	7
Punjab ...	2·6	32	14·6	4·3	6
U. P. ...	15·2	16·2	11·4	2	3·8
C. P. ...	19·3	12·4	15·5	8·5	18·2
Burma ...	70·7	—	5·2	10·2	2
India ...	31·1	9·2	16·6	6	6·4

India's total out-turn of her chief agricultural exports is given below:—

	Produced (1913)	Exported (1913)	Proportion of expor to production
Rice *in million tons*	28	2·45	9 per cent.
Wheat *in mil. tons*	8·42	1·2	14·2 p. c.
Raw Cotton *in mil. lbs*	2319	1190	51 p. c.
Raw Jute *in mil. lbs*	3557	1720	48·3 p. c.
Tea *in mil. lbs*	307·25	289	94 p. c.

Our principal crops and the conditions of their growth.

RICE is by far the most important crop of India. It is the staple food of most parts of India. This grain is eaten by the Bengalis, Assamese, Uriyas, Madrasis, Biharis, and all but the poorest Marathas and its use is extending to the other races of India. One-third of all our cultivated lands is under rice, one-eleventh under wheat, one-sixth under millets, and one-sixteenth under cotton. (1913.) Then, again, rice forms 60 p. c. of the total value of food grains exported from India, wheat 30 p. c. and barley only 3·5 p. c.

Rice grows only in a hot and damp climate. It requires about 36 inches of water, and consequently where the annual rainfall is below 60 inches the rice-field must be irrigated artificially.

In most parts of India, only one crop of rice is raised in the year. It is sown as the rains set in and harvested in autumn. In Bengal there are two sowings in the same season but not in the same field:—(*a*) the *Aush* or early crop sown in highlying lands in April and reaped in October; and (*b*) the *Aman*, sown in the lower fields in June and harvested in December. In some rich canal-irrigated lands of Madras, three successive crops of rice are raised from the same field in a year.

Rice is sown broad-cast where the soil is poor and the peasants lazy; elsewhere it is first sown on a select bed, and then after a month the young plants are transplanted to the fields of cultivation, this method producing a great economy of seeds and a large increase of out-turn in comparison with equal areas sown broad-cast. The usual yield of an acre under transplanted rice is 30 *maunds* of paddy.

WHEAT is always grown in the cold weather. It is greatly benefited by the heavy dews, and requires light rain only. Sown late in October, it ripens in the irrigated areas in five months, and in Bombay and C. P. in four months. The latter variety requires little rain, while in the case of the former any deficiency of rainfall may be supplemented by canal water. The yield per acre is 15 to 20 *maunds* for the former and 10 *maunds* for the latter. "Wheat in India is harvested in April to June."

The MILLETS, *Jawar*, *Bajra*, and *Ragi* (or *Marua*) are the cheapest kind of food grains and are eaten by the poorest people. They are the staple crops of the dry area. In the Deccan, *Jawar* is grown in rotation with cotton. One variety is sown in June and harvested in October, in areas with about 35 inches of rainfall per annum. Another variety,—sown in October, reaped in March,—requires some rain in the sowing season. *Jawar* is also a valuable fodder crop, one acre often yielding 375 *maunds* of green fodder. The yield of grain per acre is about 8 *maunds*, besides one or two subordinate crops grown mixed with the *Jawar*. *Bajra* flourishes on sandy soil.

The PULSES (*dal*) are only second in importance among our food-stuffs, because they are an even more necessary addition to our principal food (rice or bread) than butter is to bread in a European's meal. One advantage of the pulses is that they are a second crop of the year, grown in rotation with some principal grain. Sometimes they are sown mixed with wheat, barley or oil-seed. The leaves of the pulse *Arhar* are the most effective of green manures.

The pulses require little rain or watering, and are grown only in winter, (sown in October, reaped in Sarch). The out-turn of gram is 7½ to 10 *maunds* per acre.

SUGAR-CANE is essentially a tropical plant and requires a great deal of water but a well-drained soil. It takes a year to ripen. The yield of *gur* or unrefined sugar ranges from 1½ to 3 tons per acre, while in Java the out-turn of *refined* sugar is 3½ tons and in Hawaii 4 tons per acre. In 1913 India produced 2¼ million tons of raw sugar (*gur*) from 2·5 million acres devoted to this crop.

COTTON is a tropical plant, taking five to eight months to ripen according to its different varieties. In the former kind the fibre is coarse and shorter, but its cultivation is less liable to injury from defective rainfall. The other or late-ripening variety requires a deep moisture-holding black soil (as in the Deccan) or a prolonged rainy season like that of the Gangetic Plain, but cannot bear the severe cold of northern winters. Its fibre is longer, finer and more valuable. The quality of Indian cotton has rapidly deteriorated owing to the mixing up of seeds and the absence of manuring. Even the long-staple Egyptian cotton, though it has been grown with profit in Sind, is less hardy and steadily declines, and the staple becomes shorter year by year. The indigenous varieties of the cotton plant, while producing a short and coarse type of fibre, require a shorter period of growth, give a larger yield, and are less susceptible to changes of weather and rapid deterioration than the long-stapled foreign cottons. Moreover, the Indian mills as a whole were hitherto accustomed to consume short staple only, and hence the Indian producer of long-stapled cotton could find no ready or remunerative market locally. This disadvantage is now being partly removed, but only in our largest centres of trade.

Experiment has shown that two varieties of long-stapled American cotton (technically called *Cambodia* and *Buri*) can be acclimatised without deterioration and grown under normal circumstances in many parts of India, esp. Sind, Madras, C. P. and parts of Bombay and U. P. In 1912 Madras alone yielded *Cambodia* worth 1½ crores of Rupees and the C. P. a tenth of that sum.

The total area under cotton in British India increased from 9·6 million acres in 1900 to 15·8 mil. acres in 1913, (or, adding the Native States, from 14·5 to 25). The average yield per acre is about 1¼ *maunds* of fibre and 3¾ *maunds* of seed. [Cotton seed is of great commercial importance. In 1913 we exported 5·6 million cwt. of it, valued at a million and a half pounds sterling.]

The yield per acre of *Cambodia* is 4 or 5 times that of the indigenous varieties.

TEA is grown at all heights from 300 to 7,000 ft. above sea-level. In North-Eastern India it requires a well-distributed rainfall of 100 inches. The gardens chiefly occupy alluvial land, but deep sandy loams with a free sub-soil are most suited to tea. The leaves begin to be plucked when the plants are three years old.

In manufacturing tea, the leaves are first withered artificially by passing over them dry heated air which removes their moisture. They are then rolled and twisted in order to let the juices escape. The next process is oxidation by mixing them with damp cool air. Finally the leaves are rolled a second time, dried, sifted, and packed ready for sale.

In 1915, India produced 372 million lbs. of tea. Our total export of tea that year reached 338 million lbs., and three-fourths of this quantity were taken by England. We supply 60 p. c. of all the tea consumed the British Isles.

JUTE grows on river-banks and other lowlying lands, where the young plants can remain partly submerged in water for some time. On higher lands it requires plenty of manuring and irrigation during the whole period of its growth. Sown in April, the green stalks are cut in September and steeped in water for three weeks, after which the loosened bark is stripped off by hand, and the fibre is separated from the stem and washed clean. An acre usually yields 15 *maunds* of clean fibre, but a good crop may be double of that amount. (Compiled mainly from *Ind. Emp.*, iii. ch. 1.)

Irrigation.—The problem of Indian agricultural improvement is mainly a problem of water supply. Eastern Bengal, Lower Bengal, Assam, Burma, and the two coast-trips of the South, enjoy heavy rainfal and are naturally secure from famine. Other tracts o good rainfall have to be protected by irrigation work in order to *ensure the necessary* supply of *water* durin the growth of the crops. Such is the case in Norther Punjab, the Madras Delta, and the U. Provinces Thirdly, on the Deccan plateau and certain parts o Malwa, the Central Provinces and Guzrat, cultiva tion is extremely precarious because the (moderat normal) *rainfall* is *liable to great variations.* This area about one million square miles, is exposed to grea *risk of famine.* But the configuration of the groun and the nature of the soil do not in every cas permit the construction of canals. Lastly, in Sind South Western Punjab, and Western Rajputana, th annual rainfall is nominal, and here cultivation i always impossible without irrigation. (*Ind. Emp.*, iii 316-28.)

The Madras Presidency is distinguished by th variety and extent of its irrigation works, ranging fron the great canal system of the deltas of the Godavari Krishna, and Cavery rivers, to the 60,000 tanks whicl are more or less dependent on the local rainfall,— whereas the irrigation works of Northern India draw their supply of water from large rivers fed by th melting of the snow on distant mountain ranges Tank irrigation is the system most prevalent ir Southern India. Most of these tanks or storage work are of ancient Hindu origin.

The above facts prove the importance of irrigation to India,—an importance which has been recognised by our kings and farmers from very ancient times, and has led to splendid achievements by the British. Three methods of watering fields are practised in India :

(*a*) From *wells*, 13·86 million acres or nearly 30 p. c. of the total irrigated area. [Of these 7 million acres are in the U. P., 3¾ mil. in the Punjab, and 2 million acres in Madras and Bombay taken together. Absent from Bengal, but very prevalent in Bihar, three-fourths of a million acres.]

(*b*) From *tanks*, 6·3 million acres, mainly in Madras, Bengal, Bihar and C. P., and to some extent in Mysore, Hyderabad, Rajputana, Bombay, and Upper Burma.

(*c*) From *canals*, 20·44 million acres, or 44 p. c.

Of the total cropped area of India about 19 p. c. is irrigated, namely 8·2 p. c. from canals, 5·6 p. c. from wells and 2·5 p. c. from tanks. The comparative importance of irrigation to each province will be seen from the following table :—

	Area ordinarily irrigated, in *millions of acres.*	Proportion of total cropped area irrigated.
Sind	3·44	75 p. c.
Punjab & N. W. F. P. ...	12·36	41·2 "
U. P.	11·56	29·3 "
Madras	9·85	26 "
Upper Burma	0·94	17 "
Bihar	4	12·7 "
Bengal	2·1	7·5 "
Total for India ...	46·83	19 "

All the above figures refer to 1913. (*Cd. 8157*, p. 129.)

Artificial irrigation has been practised in India since the dawn of history. (See *Arthashastra* ii. ch. 24). Some large canals were constructed by the Muhammadan rulers in Northern India, and by Hindu princes in Madras (*e.g.*, the *anicuts* or dams across the Cavery River). The British Government about 1840 began a wise policy of canal construction, which has been vigorously carried on to our own days. Each famine has driven home the lesson that canals alone form the insurance against famine, and the public expenditure on irrigation works has greatly increased since 1905. The results have been equally good to agriculture and public finance, as the following statistics (*Code 8157*, p. 146) of the working of the State irrigation department in 1913 will show:—

Productive major works only.—

Province.	Capital outlay *in mil. £.*	Area irrigated *in mil. acres.*	Percentage of net revenue on total capital outlay.
Punjab excluding N. W. F. P. ...	13·62	6·87	12·18 p. c.
U. P. & Oudh ...	6·48	3	8·09
Madras ...	5·61	2·14	9·83
Bihar and Or. ...	3·58	0·809	2·13
Bombay & Sind ...	2·66	1·3	4·78
Burma ...	1·27	0·28	5·16
All Br. India ...	36	14·74	8·62

Some of the Punjab canals are extremely profitable, *e.g.*, the Lower Chenab Canal, (which irrigates 2¼ million acres) yielded 42 p. c. net return on capital. The three great canals of Madras, (the Cavery, the Godavari, and the Krishna, which between them water 1¾ million acres), earned 20, 20·7 and 17·6 p. c. net revenue respectively (1913). Besides the *Productive* Canals which yield more than the interest on their capital cost, there is a second class, called *Protective* Canals, which are undertaken as an indirect protection against famine, though they are not directly remunerative,—the net revenue yielded by them being a little less than 1 p. c. of their total capital outlay. The first class is financed from the Public Debt (or surplus revenue), and the latter from certain taxes set apart under the name of 'Famine Insurance Grant.'

Both the above classes are called "major" works, while there is a third class called "minor" irrigation works, which are constructed and maintained out of the ordinary revenue.

The totals. for 1914 are: capital outlay on all three classes 42·66 million £, area irrigated by the state 25·6 million acres, net receipts on capital outlay on productive major works 8·97 p. c., on protective major works 0·59 p.c., and on minor works 4·52 p. c. (*Cd. 36* of 1916.)

In the Punjab a grand scheme, called the Triple Canal Project, is nearing completion. It comprises the Upper Jhelum Canal, the Upper Chenab Canal, and the Lower Bari Doab Canal. It will water two million acres at an outlay of seven million sterling. When completed, the Triple Project will help to "convert the Punjab from the Indus on the west to the Jumna on the east into a vast irrigated tract permanently insured against famine." Another irrigation scheme, called the Sutlej Valley Project, not yet undertaken, aims at throwing open to cultivation three million acres in what is now the great desert south of the Sutlej River, at a capital expenditure of 6 million sterling. (*Code 220* of 1913, pp. 319-320.)

Forests.—Forests play a most useful part in the economy of Nature: (1) they store the rain water in the soil, prevent its too rapid surface flow, minimise its evaporation (which inside a forest is only one-half of that which proceeds outside), and send it down slowly but regularly during the rest of the year. (2) By communicating moisture through their leaves, they reduce the temperature of the air. (3) They supply a vast amount of grazing to cattle, and also timber for building and fuel. (4) Many minor forest products, such as turpentine, gum, rubber, lac, tanning materials (bark), cardamoms, and *Sabai* grass (for paper making)—have great commercial value, and their importance will increase with the industrial development of the country and the increasing ability of the people to utilise them in modern ways.

But ignorance and neglect led to many forests being denuded in consequence of the increase of population during Indian rule and even in the early British period. At last in 1878 Government began a regular system of conservation and replanting, which has saved our remaining forests from destruction and greatly improved their trees and produce. At present (1913) forests cover 22·7 p. c. of the total area of India,—63 p. c. of Burma, 46 p. c. of Assam, 19 of C. P., 14 of Madras, 10 of Bombay, 8·6 of the Punjab, 13·5 of Bengal, and only 3·4 p. c. of Bihar & Orissa. *(Cd. 8157).*

Indian forests have been divided by law into three classes:—

(a) *Reserved*, which are permanently maintained and strictly controlled by the State;

(b) *Protected*, in which State control is laxer and less exclusive, and to which the neighbouring population have free access for many purposes;

(c) *Unclassed*, which are given over to the public use with slight restrictions by Government.

The forest areas of the different provinces were thus classified in 1913—

	Reserved sq. miles.	Protected sq. miles.	Unclassed sq. miles.	Net forest surplus of 1913 £
Burma ...	27,332	...	114,111	476,000
C. P. & Berar	19,684	...	...	82,000
Madras ...	18,863	...	802	84,000
Bombay ...	11,857	385	...	167,000
Assam ..	4,381	...	18,401	12,000
Bengal ...	4,871	1,711	4,030	65,000
U. P. ...	4,121	33	39	121,000
Punjab ...	2,165	5,203	946	29,000
All India ...	96,297	8,390	140,925	1,050,000

The most valuable products of the Indian forests are teak wood (79 *lakhs* of Rupees worth exported in

1913), myrobalans (57 *lakhs* worth exported, but not all from the State forests), lac (nearly 2 *crores* worth exported), rubber, sandal and ebony. The home consumption includes bamboos (very useful to millions of poor people), sandal, fuel, grass, building timber (esp. *sal* and *sisu*) and teak wood. Nor should elephants be forgotten.

Minerals.—Our mineral deposits are among the richest in the world; but as, with the exception of the old Bengal Iron and Steel Co. of Barakar and the newly started Tata Iron and Steel Works, we have no metal industry conducted on modern advanced lines, nearly all our metal ores go abroad for manufacture. The out-turn of our few old fashioned metal works has no power to compete with foreign manufactures. Hence India's import of *wrought* metallic ware is steadily advancing, inspite of her increased production of *raw* ore. In 1913, we exported only 1½ *crores* of Rupees worth of raw minerals, excluding coal, salt, petroleum, and saltpetre, while we imported 33½ *crores* worth of metals and metal manufactures, excluding railway materials (10 *crores*) and instruments (1·8 *crores*).

Our imports *in crores of Rupees.*	1913	1915
Hardware and cutlery, excluding apparatus & instruments	3·94	2·38
Machinery	7·75	4·77
Unwrought and wrought metals ...	22·02	11·15
Total metals and metal manufactures ...	33·7	18·3

Even in raising the ore our methods are primitive, laborious, and inefficient, partly from the ignorance and partly from the smallness of capital of our mine-owners. Except in a few big concerns (owned and conducted by Europeans), such as the Kolar Goldfields and some of the Bengal collieries, the mines do not go deep enough, the quarrying is performed by hand, and no labour-saving machine or power is employed. Our labour supply, though cheap and admittedly skilled in mining, must under these adverse conditions be very inefficient and costly when compared with the output. For instance, the average Indian miner employed underground, raised 167 tons of coal per annum in 1911, while a miner in England raises about 317 tons. The deeper strata that have been now reached (esp. in our coal mines), will make the use of machinery indispensable in future.

The distribution of our minerals (1913).

Coal.—Half the total output for all India comes from the *Jharria* fields, one-third from the *Raniganj* and 5 p. c. from the *Giridih* fields. The other coal-mines of Bengal and Bihar are in *Daltonganj* (70,000 tons), *Rajmahal*, *Ramgarh-Bokaria*, and *Sambalpur*,—which last three yield a few thousand tons only. Ninety-four per cent. of our total coal production belongs to Bengal and Bihar. Outside these two provinces, the most important mines are those in the Nizam's Dominions, which yielded half a million tons, or 3 p. c. of India's output, in Assam (311,000 tons) and C. P. (250,000 tons in 1915). The *Mohpani* mines of C. P. yielded 52,000,—the *Khost* and Sor Range of Baluchistan, 41,000 tons,—the *Salt Range* of the Punjab, 30,000 tons,—and the *Bikanir* mines, 14,000 tons in 1911. The native States together produced 744,000 tons in 1915.

Gold.—Mostly from the Mysore gold-fields (at Kolar and other places), which contributed 93·3 p. c. of the total, and about 3 p. c. from the Hutti mine in the Nizam's Dominions. The only gold produced in British India comes from the Anantapur district, Madras.

Petroleum.—98 p. c. from Burma, less than 2. p. c. from Assam, and a trifling amount from the Punjab.

Manganese.—From the Central Provinces (80 p. c.), Madras (12 p. c.), Bombay (5 p. c.), and the remainder from Bihar, Mysore and Central India.

Saltpetre.—From U. P. (40 p. c.), Bihar (37 p. c.), and Punjab (20 p. c.).

Mica.—From Chota Nagpur, Madras, and Rajputana. India turns out more than half the world's supply.

Iron.—Orissa (Maurbhanj), Central Provinces, and Chota Nagpur.

Salt.—In 1911 India produced $33\frac{1}{8}$ million maunds of salt, of which 88 p. c. was derived from sea-water and lakes, and 12 p. c. by mining and quarrying.

(*a*) By evaporation of sea-water :			
Madras ...	...	11·28 mil.	mds.
Bombay & Sind	...	12·74 ,,	,,
Burma ...	...	0·714 ,,	,,
(*b*) By evaporation of the Sambhar and other lakes in Rajputana ...	...	4·5 ,,	,,
(*c*) Rock-salt from the Salt Range in the N. W. F. Province and the Punjab mines	...	4 ,,	,,

Our annual production of minerals (1913.)

	Value of output in millions sterling.	Quantity of output.	Number of labourers employed.	Exported abroad.
Gold ...	2·29	595,761 oz.		2·3 mil. £
Coal ...	3·79	16·2 mil. tons	133,000	£461,424
Petroleum ...	1·034	277 mil. gallons		
Salt (all kinds)	0·472	1·3 mil. tons		
Saltpetre ...	0·2	14,462 tons		£205,598
Manganese ore	1·21	815,047 ,,		
Mica ...	—	—		53,891 cwt. =£302,564
Ruby, &c. ...	0·055	278,706 carats		
Wolfram ...	0·127	1,688 tons		
Total ...	9·63	—	181,260	5 mil. £

Transport.—(*a*) *Rivers.*—In the northern plains, rivers have formed the chief path for the carriage of goods from time immemorial, and large cities, shrines, and commercial centres have flourished on their banks.

(*b*) *Navigable canals.*—There is very little traffic on the Indian canals, which were constructed primarily for irrigation only. They do not pass through large cities and important trade marts, nor do they connect with the sea and the great rivers. Besides, they often afford a roundabout route. The Indian boatman likes to pass by towns and villages where he can buy his daily provisions and get down on the bank and cook his meals, and also to take his own time in moving on. These things are impossible on a canal, especially on one with locks to be crossed. The railway often offers a shorter and cheaper route for goods. Hence, the numerous irrigation canals of India are not much used for navigation. The Madras canals are well adapted to boat traffic, as they flow through a flat and populous country; but the navigation on them barely pays the working expenses. In Bengal, the Orissa and Midnapur canals (connecting Cuttack with Diamond Harbour) have attracted little traffic. There are certain canals constructed for navigation only *e.g.*, the Buckingham canals, north of Madras, (262 miles), the Orissa Coast and Hijili canals, from north of Chandbali to west of Diamond Harbour, (135 miles), and the Calcutta and Eastern canals, between the Ganges and the Brahmaputra, (47 miles of canals and above 1000 miles of connected river channels). They carry on a good deal of traffic, which just suffices to meet the annual expenses and the interest on the capital spent on their construction. (*Ind. Emp.*, iii. 355). In short, on most of the Indian canals the traffic is purely local, while the railway is popular for long distance transport. Navigable canals can succeed only in the deltas of Lower Bengal, where railways would entail a prohibitive expenditure on bridges. (*Cd. 220* of 1913, p. 316.)

(*c*) In Muhammadan times our only highways

were the military roads connecting the provincial chief towns with the capital, *e.g.*, the road built by Sher Shah (1540 A.D.) from Bihar to Rohtas in the Punjab, the Imperial Mughal roads (*shah-rah*) from Delhi to Lahore, Kabul, Bijapur, Ahmadabad, Patna, etc.* Over hard soil the roads were well kept, and their remains excited the admiration of Elphinstone and Burnes, early in the 19th century. In low lands they were effaced every year by rain and flood. None but the smallest rivers had bridges. There were no *pucca* feeder roads running from these few highways to the villages and marts. Indeed, an agricultural country like Bengal or Madras, that depends for its crops on the annual flood, cannot maintain *high* roads except by ruining its agriculture or spending a fabulous amount on bridges and culverts. So necessary is the annual flood, that in Bengal village-roads have to be breached to admit the water, and I have seen the opposite banks of an old village-tank cut, in order to let the river flood sweep through it and reach the fields beyond.

Land transport is conducted mainly by primitive and slow *bullock-carts*. But in the pre-British days even carts could make trips only on the Imperial highways. The Indian carrier, therefore, used *ponies, oxen, buffaloes, donkeys* and *camels* to carry his packages of goods. Each animal could transport only a small quantity. But the *Bunjaras* or professional grain-carriers formed

* For details about these roads, see my *India of Aurangzib, Topography, Statistics, and Roads*, 1901.

large parties and successfully supplied the armies of Aurangzib and Cornwallis with food during long campaigns. Each man loaded his pair of bullocks, and a whole party of them, sometimes numbering 10,000 men, organised under a leader, would accompany an army over roadless tracts. The camel is used as a beast of burden in the Punjab and Rajputana, the mule in most places of Northern India, and ponies, donkeys and even sheep in the hills.

(*d*) *Railways.*—First opened in August 1854. In March 1915 we had a total open length of 35,285 miles, of four different gauges: the *standard* (in which the rails stand 5 feet 6 inches apart), 17,827 miles, the *metre* (3 ft. $3\frac{3}{8}$ in. apart), 14,552 miles, the *special* or *narrow* gauge (2 feet 6 inches apart), and the *light railway* gauge (2 feet apart), 2,906 miles for the last two.

India has, no doubt, a greater proportionate mileage of railway than any other country outside Europe, but the chief defects of the Indian railways are the variety of gauges and the comparative absence of bridges over large rivers. Consequently the transhipment of goods is frequently necessary in long journeys and this results in increase of freight and the risk of breakage and theft.

The economic effects of Railways—

(1) Saving time to pilgrims, who number several millions of men every year. As they are mostly of the labouring class, this gain in time means increase in their earnings.

(2) Helping the quick and cheap migration of the surplus population, and hence increasing the labour supply where needed. The railway alone can feed a large population of labourers assembled for construction work at places where the local food supply is insufficient. [Hence equalising wages.]

(3) Securing good prices for the surplus agricultural produce by extending its market. For instance, kitchen vegetables from Patna, and sheep and goats from Buxar, are carried 350 miles away to Calcutta. Fish from Saraghat and Katihar reach Darjiling. The local producers are enriched, while the consumers have to pay less than if they had to depend on their neighbourhood only. The surplus produce is no longer wasted or sold for a trifle at the place of its growth.

(4) Equalising prices within a certain distance of the line. Natural produce has been cheapened in the big cities, and manufactures and imports have been cheapened in the villages served by the railway. Owing to the badness of the Indian roads, "the cultivator in the past probably imported next to nothing from the world outside his village, and to this day he imports very little; but in respect of what he does import he has been a gainer by the reduction in the cost of carriage" effected by railways. (*Morison*, p. 137.) But at the same time the dumping of foreign machine-made manufactures in the villages has taken away the hereditary village craftsmen's bread.

(5) Helping the relief of famine by enabling large quantities of grain to be promptly carried to the affected area.

(6) Moral effect: they act as a solvent on caste, provincial isolation, and the narrowness of mind of the untravelled Indian. (*Ind. Emp.*, iii. 385-388.)

For a comparison between railways and canals as means of famine protection, see *Indian Emp.*, iii. 354, and as means of transport, iii. 362. On the general effects of railways see L. Levi's *History of British Commerce*, 2nd ed., 193, 304-6.

India and England.—From the economic point of view there is the greatest possible contrast between the two countries. (1) Geographically England is an island, so advantageously placed that the hemisphere of which she is the centre contains the largest amount of land on the earth's surface. Thus, Nature has meant England to be the mistress of the world's carrying trade, and the land which can most economically send her manufactures abroad. India is a halfway house between England and Australia; she is close to Persia and Egypt on the one hand, and to Siam, China, and the Eastern Archipelago on the other. This position will be of great advantage to us in distribution when our industries are developed and we begin to export our manufactures. Eastern peoples must necessarily be our best customers (except for raw produce, which they can raise themselves).

(2) The coasts of England are indented with

countless harbours and creeks in which ships can defy the most violent storms; almost every centre of production in the island has a harbour close to it and often the choice of two or three ports. India, on the other hand, is singularly deficient in harbours. Her rocky western coast is "furiously beaten by winds and waves during the monsoon months." Bombay alone affords a tolerably safe refuge to ships. Karachi and Rangoon, though good ports, are situated at the mouths of rivers, and every year a good deal of money has to be spent in dredging away the deposits of sand and keeping the channels open. River-sand long ago closed the historic port of Surat. On the east coast of India there is *not a single* harbour. [Calcutta is 86 miles inland, and is reached by an intricate passage, rendered risky by sandbanks. The pilotage charge is very heavy.]

The eastern coast also slopes away so gently that big ships cannot come within three miles of it. Breakwaters have been constructed at an immense cost to turn Madras into a port, but it is not safe. (*Ind. Emp.*, iii. 272.) All the centres of production are far inland places with no short or natural communication with the sea. Hence our heavy cost and loss of time in transport.

(3) As regards inland communication, England made about 1775 a splendid set of canals connecting her great rivers together and affording short and cheap routes between London, the west, the north, and the south-west. These canals greatly helped her "industrial revolution in the last quarter of the 18th century.'

Indian canals are not so well suited to navigation, and costly land transport is our only resource for moving large quantities of goods.

(4) England is a wet country; the Gulf Stream sends up moist currents of air which always keep the soil damp, and rain sometimes falls nearly every week in the year. But India is a dry land, subject to long periods of rainless weather, and with a soil which (in most places) quickly absorbs the moisture and presents a hard or sandy parched surface.

(5) England's coal mines are near her beds of iron and tin, or (in the case of Welsh coal) close to the seashore. Hence, she easily holds the first place in the cheap manufacture of metal. Moreover, there is abundance of water in her northern districts, the chief seat of her industries. Thirdly, her water-power has been usefully employed in economising labour for small village industries. All these favourable conditions are absent from India.

(6) England is essentially a land of cities: three-fourths of her people live in towns against only one-tenth in India. With us, agriculture is the main industry of the people; and so we have to depend greatly on regular rainfall, *i.e.*, on a precarious natural agency,—while England is predominantly a manufacturing country: three-fourths of her people live by non-agricultural work, against one-fourth in India. Manufacture is more dependent on human skill and effort than on Nature's gifts.

(7) In the cold climate of England, physical exertion is a delight and a means of preserving health; the average duration of life is longer, epidemics are unknown or have been banished by science. In India (except in a few favoured tracts far away from the populous plains), the climate relaxes the fibres of the body; to do strenuous labour is to court premature death; life (except of the vegetating kind) is very short; and "tropical diseases" have found here a congenial home. In the struggle with Nature, man, unaided by science, is not yet more than half victorious.

(8) As is the land, so are the people. The English race is methodical, cool-headed, strenuous and thorough in all they undertake. Their higher minds are self-confident, filled with a divine discontent with things as they are, and

> ——Ever reaping something new,
> That which they have done but earnest of the
> things that they shall do.

The Indian labouring classes (if generalisation be permissible in the case of such a vast and varied population) are slack-nerved, easy-yielding, awed by the stupendous forces of Nature and the might of Fate, and, though generally industrious and sober, apt to be led away by occasional outbursts of impulse or passion, habitually conservative, believing in the wisdom of their ancestors, fond of letting things alone. In their present stage of neglected education, they are essentially mediæval in their thoughts, and as far removed from the abstract "economic man" as can be imagined. Some of their very virtues, such as the domestic habit, patience, content with little, aversion to a spirit of adventure or speculation, and softness of heart, handicap them in the economic struggle with the pushing races of the West.

In the past, particularly in the mediæval Muhammadan period, our thinkers were mostly inclined to sit under the Banyan tree dreaming of metaphysics,

——Annihilating all that's made
To a green thought in a green shade.

To the Indian population their frugality, socialistic spirit and domestic virtue are moral assets of great value. If, even in the economic sphere, the ultimate victory is due to the race and not to the individual (however brilliant), then a nation which recognises it as the duty of every man to marry and of every woman to undertake motherhood, must prove superior to a nation of selfish pleasure-seekers, who deliberately commit race-suicide. When education and sanitary improvements have overcome our heavy untimely death-rate and the development of industries has opened new fields of work at home, India's immense and regularly replenished man-power must be of great advantage to her as a producer.

When we have passed above the harmfully low standard of living which makes sanitation at home and proper physical and mental development impossible,—the very frugality of our people will be a force in our favour. In a country where plain living and high thinking still prevails and expert scientists, foremen, accountants and clerks can be secured on a low pay, the cost of production is naturally lower than where men of equal ability command very high wages. Again, the socialistic spirit of Indian usage and domestic organisation, which will be fully described in the next chapter, exerts a steadying force on the community and tends automatically to correct the evils and sufferings due to outbreaks of individualism on the part of particular persons. Such socialism as still prevails among us is, no doubt, mediæval, uninformed, not scientifically organised. But it has now been recognised in Europe that though individualism may lead to success in the case of one man or even one class,—the future of the race and the abiding good of the community as a whole demand the organisation of the nation on a socialistic basis. For such organisation we have the advantage of already possessing a frame-work, though old and unscientific.

I have described above the natural influence of climate and geography on the Indian character. But under proper education and far-sighted guidance the human brain and the human will can overcome nearly all the obstacles of Nature, and man can triumph over climate.

The resources of modern science are immense and daily increasing, and if they are applied resolutely and systematically, Indians can achieve in the economic as in other spheres practically all that natives of other climes have achieved. In India, as in other lands, man has within himself a boundless potentiality, which it is the duty of statesmanship to develop to the utmost.

In the ancient world Indians did excel in manufacture, agriculture, artistic production, scientific investigation, and even economic organisation. There is no inherent incapacity in the Indian character to do the same now. In our own times there have been examples of the successful organisation of business on modern lines and clockwork regularity by Indians educated in the land who have received no European training or assistance.

CHAPTER II.

THE PEOPLE.

The village system.—Though the Indian population is large (*viz.*, on an average 224 per square mile in British territory), yet almost all the people live in villages, and there is a comparative absence of towns. 24 p. c. of our total population live in places with 2,000 inhabitants or more (1911), whereas in England and Wales 78 p. c. of the population is urban. But if we fix the minimum population for a town at 5,000, then only 10·4 per cent. of the Indian population is urban.

In India cities were created in the past either by the royal residence or the special religious sanctity of a place. Wherever our Muhammadan sovereigns or their provincial viceroys lived, cities sprang up. In a few years the tents were replaced by houses, and when, later on, a defensive wall was added, it became a complete city. Here all the best artisans of the land were concentrated, and here most part of the revenue was spent. Again, the Indian manufacturer of old never thought of going out to seek his customers, he expected them to come to his doors. Hence, every famous centre of pilgrimage, such as Benares, Puri, Kanchi or Mathura, by drawing tens of thousands of visitors every year afforded an excellent market, and induced artisans to settle there. In time, the temple became the centre of a large and flourishing city. "Capitals, ex-capitals retaining some special art or manufacture [and surviving their desertion by the monarch], the colonies of such capitals or ex-capitals, villages grown to exceptional greatness, and a certain number of towns which have sprung up round the temples built on sites of extraordinary sacredness, would go far to complete the list of Indian cities." (Maine's *Village Com.*, 119).

Under British rule commerce and industry are leading to the rapid growth of new cities. Bombay, Karachi, Cawnpore and Howrah, besides many towns in Burma, are the most striking examples of such growth. But the Indian people have not yet been habituated to cities, nor have they developed civic virtues, habits of association extending over the entire city (as opposed to one's own street or ward only), and "the communal soul," which characterise European races. The *village* is, therefore, still the *real unit* of the Indian social organisation. "India is a continent of villages," and this fact determines its economic conditions.

Rural economy.—In several parts of Upper India and the Deccan we have survivals of old village communities, which are "little republics, having nearly everything they can want within themselves, and almost independent of any foreign relations." (Elphinstone's *History of India*, Bk. II., Ch. II). Every village, even when it does not form a regular village-community, is a *self-contained, self-sufficing* whole. It has its own set of hereditary officers and menials, such as the priest, watchman, barber, scavenger, blacksmith, and even its favourite beggar. They exist in all villages, with this difference only that in a "village community" they are paid by the allotment of plots of cultivated land held in hereditary succession and in other villages by an allowance of grain, and secondly, that a village community has two additional officers, the headman and the accountant. The medicine-man (who is both quack and witch-doctor and often a religious mendicant in addition), the midwife, the oilpresser, the carpenter, and the washerman (where such a luxury is maintained), are shared in common by a group of villages. The grain-dealer is a wanderer and does *not* regularly belong to any village.

The horizon of the villagers is extremely limited, and nearly all their simple wants are supplied by their immediate neighbourhood. The markets where they get their necessaries and at which they sell their surplus produce, are very close to them; and the fluctuations of demand and price in the big marts of the world do not touch them at all, or affect them only after many years. The villagers have their own familiar travelling traders who come to their doors in a definite season every year, sell manufactures, or take away the village produce. Villages that supply big cities in their neighbourhood, or stand on important railway lines, are less quiet and more subject to rapid changes of prices and wages. Sometimes we have a group of villages, each of which with its special produce or industry supplements the others, and they together form one self-contained whole.

Such was the picture of still life in our villages so long as society was stationary. But within the last ten or 15 years, the network of railways has spread over the country, (the total mileage open having doubled between 1891 and 1913), and most villagers in the valleys of the Ganges, Indus, Krishna and Godavari now have the railway within a day's journey of their homes. Travel has become more frequent, because easier and cheaper; pilgrimage, litigation and search of more lucrative employment are taking increasing numbers of people away from their native villages and bringing larger numbers of commercial travellers to them. In these, the most populous parts of India, therefore, the villager's horizon has been extended; he is no longer the unsophisticated "country mouse" that his father was. Change, even rapid change, has invaded our rural tracts, and the old generalisation about the immobility of Indian village life is no longer true. This fact will be illustrated in the chapter on Consumption.

The economic effects of the village system— (*a*) Agriculture is almost the only occupation of the people. "It has been estimated that nine-tenths of the rural population in India live, directly or indirectly, by agriculture." (*Ind. Emp.*, iii. 2). The Census of 1901 showed that out of the entire Indian population

52 p. c. were either landlords or tenants,
12 p. c. field labourers,
1 p. c. growers of special products or engaged in estate management,
2½ p. c. partly agriculturists and partly following some other form of employment,
6 p. c. general labourers, but mainly supported by work in the field.

Total 73½ p. c.*

Thus nearly *three-fourths of the entire Indian population depend directly or indirectly on agriculture* for their livelihood.

Industries are absolutely impossible except in our larger towns. Even the system of associated cottage industries practised in Europe a century ago and in Japan to the present day, is unknown in the Indian villages.

(*b*) In the stationary and out of the way villages, the people are extremely conservative and impervious

* We arrive at nearly the same figures if we take the total numbers employed in 1911:

224·7 millions in agriculture and pasture.
1·8 „ fishing and hunting.

226·5 millions out of a total described population of 313·4 millions, *i. e.*, 72·3 p. c.

to new ideas, because of their narrow bounded isolated lives. Economic improvement is almost impossible, and custom reigns supreme among them. (But when the practical benefit of a new method has been clearly *demonstrated before their eyes*, our villagers are ready enough to adopt it). The pursuit of hereditary professions is the rule in villages, and the spirit of ambitious enterprise is wanting, except when easy railway connection with a large town in the district tempts them away to new fields of action.*

(*c*) The village system makes the people home-staying, and prevents any rapid supply or displacement of labour. "The Indian peasant is immobile"; in the Census of 1891 it was found that over 90 p. c. of the inhabitants of every district had been born in that district, 6 p. c. had been born in the districts immediately adjoining it, and only 3 p. c. had come from more distant places. (*Hunter*, 83). It is true that even in England the *fluidity of labour* is much less than we are apt to assume, because "the difficulty of moving the labourer's home limits the field within which he can seek work." (*Cunningham & McArthur*, 108). But in India the evil is aggravated by caste, by climatic, linguistic and social differences between the various provinces, and mainly by the narrow spirit

* "The villagers are ignorant of the outside world, and have no facilities for improving their position. In respect of the most important factors governing their material life, they are helpless." *Morison*, p. 15.

which the self-sufficing life of each village fosters. "The villager looks on the inhabitants of surrounding villages with more or less *distrust*, unless they happen to be of the same caste as himself." (*Dupernex*, 173). Association or concentration of labour on a large scale is impossible without breaking down rural habits.

(*d*) Division of labour being limited by the extent of the market and the possibility of co-ordination of labour in producing the finished article, there is no opening for division of labour in a village, and each labourer has to perform *all* the processes of production. Hence there is a great waste of skill and time. A villager has no incentive to make himself a skilled artisan or to seek a new opening, unless he migrates to a large town. (See *Morison*, p. 8).

(*e*) The markets of the villagers being small, they are entirely influenced by local conditions, and great differences of price have been known to prevail in two villages only a few miles apart owing to the ignorance of the villagers and the difficulty of communication. The contact with the big markets of the world which railway expansion has brought about, tends to equalise prices and limit the range of fluctuation within only a certain distance of the lines.

In short, the village system compels production on a small scale, deepens the effect of custom, checks individual ambition and initiative, and offers resistance to the wave of progress or of any vast economic change.

Peasant-proprietorship—

In India the only *true* peasant-proprietors are to be found in certain villages of Bihar and Benares, where Government made the Permanent Settlement with groups of cultivators, and recognised them collectively as *zamindars*. Their descendants still cultivate the fields of which they are full and inalienable proprietors, their Government revenue is fixed in perpetuity, and they can sell their right of ownership (*malikana*) when they please. In the permanently settled parts of Bengal, the hereditary and absolute rights of certain classes of tenants ("*occupancy ryots*") have been secured by the Bengal Tenancy Act. These men can sell their rights freely, they cannot be evicted at will, and their rent cannot be increased by the *zamindar* unless the rent of the neighbouring tracts is higher or the price of crops has increased. Against every enhancement of rent they have the right to appeal to a law court. They are *in effect* peasant-proprietors. But over the rest of India, where the State lets the land temporarily, the cultivators (both in the *ryotwari* and *mahalwari* tracts) are mere lessees and not at all proprietors, as they are liable to eviction and enhancement of rent at every periodical revision of settlement. Their rent is fixed solely at the discretion of the Settlement Officer (a mere servant of their landlord), against whose decision there is no appeal to any court. In many places their right of sale has been restricted by law. Thus the direct tenants of the

State have no *legal* right to the *three F's* secured by the Irish peasantry, *viz.*, fair rent, fixity of tenure, and freedom of sale, because their own idea of fair rent cannot prevail against the opinion, or even the arbitrary will, of the State landlord's agent, the Settlement Officer. In Madras even the old *mirasdars*,—or families co-sharing a village as its hereditary owners and representing its original colonisers,—had lost their rights under British rule and sunk into tenants at will. But some of their original rights have now been restored.

In the parts of Bihar and Benares where peasant-proprietorship as described above prevails, the descendants of the original grantees (or those to whom they have sold their shares) live in the same village and usually cultivate their lots in common. The harvested and threshed grain is divided among the co-sharers. This results in great economy of labour and is the nearest approach to agriculture on a large scale that we have in India. In Bengal, isolation is the rule; each man cultivates his own field, the limits of which are jealously guarded by means of raised grass-paths called *als* (corresponding to *balks* in England). But sometimes in the lowlying lands near swamps (*bils*) a number of neighbouring owners (or occupancy ryots) work in common, dig up the boundary lines, and divide the harvest in proportion to their respective shares.

Thus we see that in most parts of India "the magic of property" is absent. But land is still greatly in demand, as it is the only investment of the lower classes, and its possession gives the owner a higher position among his castemen. Partly for this reason, but chiefly owing to the pressure of population on the soil, the various agricultural rights of ownership, tenancy, sub-tenancy, etc., are sold at good prices. The Indian peasant-proprietors, like those of other countries, are remarkably hard-working and attentive to their business. But unlike Europe, partition is frequent here and the holdings have a tendency to grow very much smaller with each succeeding generation. Hence our peasant-proprietors are seldom richer than the temporary farmers in their neighbourhood.

Caste and its economic significance—

The *advantages of caste* are : (*a*) It ensures the *possession of hereditary skill* and trade secrets, and the *training* of apprentices. [Machinery and technical schools have greatly reduced the importance of these.]

(*b*) It acts as a trade-guild and a *mutual benefit society*. Each caste forms an association which (1) insists on the proper training of the youth of that craft, (2) *regulates* the *wages* of its members, (3) supplies courts of *arbitration*, (4) punishes social delinquents and keeps up a fairly high standard of morality, and (5) promotes social good feeling by means of dinners, etc. "Caste takes the place of a Poor Law in India" and allows none of its members to starve in ordinary times. (*Hunter*, 247—249). The chief local industries of India in pre-British days were developed under the supervision of caste, (especially at Ahmadabad,

Amritsar, Benares, etc.) Where a certain profession is still confined to a particular caste, its members enjoy a trade monopoly and can raise their wages at will. Recently barbers and midwives have done so at Patna.

(*c*) " It has saved the purer races in India by preventing intermarriage with others physically and mentally inferior, and it has to a certain extent helped to keep the higher races from excess in eating and drinking and insanitary habits." (*Athenæum*, 11 Jan., 1908.) Thus caste has preserved unimpaired certain valuable types of mental capacity and industrial skill.

(*d*) It secures division of labour to some extent, but renders any new distribution of functions impossible, and co-operation, except in fixed grooves, extremely difficult.

All over India, caste is still as strong as before in regulating marriage and dining together *in public*. But in other respects its force for good and evil alike is being rapidly broken by the modern conditions and spirit which British rule has introduced. The good features noted above in (*b*) characterise caste only in its ideal condition, and have almost totally disappeared from Bengal, the most thoroughly modernised province of india. But they are still to be found in Bihar, the United Provinces, parts of the Punjab, and Guzrat. Change is greater at the ports, capitals, and other big towns, and in districts of which the population is predominantly urban and given to travelling. But where the towns are few and the people mostly follow agriculture or village industries and do not emigrate or travel far from home in search of work, the caste organisation continues unimpaired, though many railway lines may cross the district. It is not the railway but the emigration of single families or individuals (as distinct from the transplantation of an entire village or caste-section) to a great distance from the original home, that is the most effective destroyer of caste and local custom. (See Maine's *Vill. Com.*, 39.)

The *disadvantages of caste* are: (1) Emigration or free movement of labour is difficult, and change of occupation is almost impossible. Certain occupations are forbidden to certain castes. This is the general rule, but there is a plasticity in caste too; some lower castes have deliberately changed their ancestral occupations for better ones in historic times. (See *Hunter*, 245.) And a caste revolt against fixed professions has been going on in Bengal for some time past.

(2) Invention or originality is checked, because every workman's social prospects are limited to the customary position of his caste. He cannot rise any higher than the level of his caste-fellows, however much he may distinguish himself. Hence the intellect is not placed at the service of labour in India. There are also many depressed or untouchable castes; the dignity of labour cannot be recognised in such a society.

(3) Caste, unlike European guilds, stands in the way of the infusion of fresh blood into a profession. However worthy or desirable an acquisition a man

may be, he cannot enter a caste, unless he was *born* to it. The strength of a caste can grow by birth only, and not by the assimilation of men from outside. "Caste is a symbol of disunion and weakness. A guild may expand and develop; it gives free play to artistic endeavour. A caste on the other hand, is an organisation of a lower type; it grows by fission." (*Ind. Emp.* i. 343.) In England many an able apprentice rises step by step till at last he marries his master's daughter and enters his business as a partner. In India the ablest servant must remain for ever at the low post ordained for him by his birth; his master may seek his advice, and may even get all his work done by him, but cannot transfer the business to him by making him its avowed head.

(4) Caste stands in the way of the rise of "captains of industry" like the American millionaires, though a few individual workmen may grow rich in their own particular business or by acting as contractors to Government or modern factories. Once a carpenter (or smith), always a carpenter (or smith),—such is the unalterable rule of our society. Hence in our past history, war (which does not stand any sham or false convention) was the only occupation in which genius rose to the highest position irrespective of birth or status. Rapid extension of business, change of profession, and rise from a lower to a higher rank in the scale of labour, are extremely difficult among those communities which observe caste. Hence, the cotton industry of Western India is mainly conducted by

Parsis, the jute industry of Bengal by Europeans, our foreign trade by Europeans, Parsis, and Muhammadans, and the import cloth trade and internal distribution are in the hands of Marwaris,—all of whom are free from caste, and all but the last of whom have no vexatious restriction about food. Caste enables men to attain to a certain amount of success in those small industries which require high or specialised skill and are allied to the fine arts, but it breaks down when we have to organise vast industries, especially factory industries, like those of Europe. (See Bluntschli's *Theory of the State*, p. 118).

(5) Caste causes great material waste. Even a small Hindu household has to keep too many servants, because each caste will do a particular kind of work and no other. There is a frightful waste of fuel and cooked food, because no non-Brahman will eat food cooked by any non-Brahman caste other than his own. And within the same caste one section (*sreni*) often refuses to partake of a meal prepared by another section! Lastly, there is a great loss of skill, because in the absence of a cook of one's own caste, a genius has to waste several hours daily in doing the drudgery of the kitchen, when he might have been more usefully employed in doing the highest kind of work of which he is mentally capable. The economic waste is as great as if a master sculptor were to spend three hours daily in sweeping his own grounds.

(6) Caste distinctions, by preventing the natural

adjustment of the total female population of the country to the total male, are killing off certain sub-castes. The rule of marriage within one's sub-caste (endogamy) also drags down the best members of each caste to the low level of the average.

The joint family: its effects.—In most parts of India the family and not the individual is still the social unit, as was the case in ancient and mediæval Europe. All the members of the family live together under the common head, who rules them with something of patriarchal authority. All the wage-earners pay their earnings into his hands, and he supplies the wants of all, brings up the young, marries them, and starts them in life. This system (1) ensures the education and protection of orphans, and saves Indian workmen from being left helpless in old age or disease, because all the members of a family share the same food even if they have to go half-fed. The joint-family makes work-houses and old age pensions unnecessary in India.

But (2) no member of a joint-family can enjoy or bequeath to his children the entire fruits of his labour. Hence, the keen money-making spirit of western workmen is usually absent from India, and the incentive to exertion is not very strong in any member of such a family.

(3) As the few bread-winners of the family feed all its members, the drones are not roused from their laziness. But in Europe everyman has to work or

he must starve; and even the younger brothers are cast adrift by the eldest when he succeeds to the ancestral property. There stern necessity calls forth every man's latent powers. It is the unendowed "younger sons" who have created England's colonies and world-wide empire as well as her trade and manufacture. But such is not the case in India.

(4) No accumulation of large capital in one hand can continue long in India, because a man's earnings are distributed among his kinsmen. Hence, rich individual firms in many cases cannot last longer than one generation. But a joint-family (especially among the Marwaris and Banias) is often a private joint-stock company also, and the business is smoothly carried on generation after generation as a family property.

(5) This system is inconsistent with modern ideas of domestic peace and individual freedom of action and growth. A joint home is now-a-days usually rendered unhappy by a soreness of feeling which is hardly suppressed and even by open bickerings. The evidence of our old literature shows that the joint-family system did not always create idyllic homes even in the days of our forefathers.

The Indian law of inheritance.—In India the only properties that descend to the eldest son by undivided succession, are certain ancient zamindaries which partake of the nature of sovereignty. But everywhere else *all* the sons have equal rights and *partition* among the heirs *is the rule.* Even a property acquired by a man through his own exertions remains indivisible during his lifetime only, but becomes liable to partition as soon as he dies. "Any direction in a will prohibiting a partition is invalid." (Mayne's *Hindu Law*, 7th ed). In Bengal where inheritance is regulated by the Sanskrit code named the *Dayabhaga* (composed about 1400 A.D.), the law treats the father as the absolute owner, and refuses to recognise any right in the son to a partition during his father's life. But brothers and other collateral members of the joint-family have the right to *dispose of their shares at their pleasure* while the property is still undivided. A widow in an undivided family has the right to succeed to her dead and childless husband's share and *to enforce a partition* on her own account.

The United Provinces, Southern India and the Western Presidency follow the legal treatise *Mitakshara* (c. 1060 A. D.), by which the sons are considered to be joint owners with their father, and to have *by birth* an equal ownership with the father in respect of ancestral immovable property. The result is that the *right to a partition* at any time, between co-sharers, is now *admitted universally.* The son or grandson can enforce a partition of the property in the possession of the father or grandfather, against the consent of the latter, under the *Mitakshara* law. In these provinces we generally find joint holdings managed by the head of the family, though the right of every sharer is recognised. "Under the *Mitakshara*, an absolute discretion [as to the expenditure of the joint income] is vested in the manager [or head], but the family have a right to partition and to an account." (*Mayne*, 370).

Under the Muhammadan law there is an infinite variety of heirs, and partition is effected in the very act of succession. Minute and troublesome subdivision of land and complexity of rights characterise the inheritance of the members of this creed. To buy a Muhammadan's land is often "to buy litigation." There are usually numerous co-sharers, (in one particular case, 66 were represented in court), having microscopic interests in the property, any one of whom can contest the sale and prevent the transfer of the property for years by instituting a lengthy civil suit. The conveyancing of a Muhammadan's real property is often an impossible task, and the land is not a realisable asset. With such a host of co-sharers, constant friction and mismanagement by the managing partner are the usual results, and the estates are saved only by being placed under the Court of Wards.

Unlike the law of primogeniture which obtains in England, the Indian law of inheritance does not favour the concentration of capital or accumulation of large estates in a few hands; it encourages the formation of small holdings and petty cultivation. Secondly, even if an individual builds up in his life-time a business on a gigantic scale, it does not last longer than one generation. Thirdly, "a necessary consequence of the corporate character of the family holding is that whenever any transaction affects that property all the members must be privy to it. A single member cannot sue or proceed by way of execution to recover a particular portion of the family property for himself." (*Mayne*, 379). Then, there is the ruinous litigation which almost always accompanies the partition of property in India. Lastly, where the estate is small and the co-sharers many and dependent on other sources of income, the management is apt to be negligent and wasteful, whereas, if all the other heirs sold their rights to one (as they always do in France and Belgium), the sole owner might have put it to the best use.

Status and custom, and their influence on rents, wages and prices.—Until recently competition had a limited operation in India except at the large sea-ports, which were in constant communication with foreign countries. Even now custom is a powerful factor in villages remote from railways and towns. The place of competition as an economic force was taken by status (*i.e.*, a man's social position as determined by his birth) and custom (or the immemorial practice of ancestors). *Dastur* (or customary usage) was appealed to as a god, and any departure from old ways was condemned by public opinion as an act of impiety. Apart from the stationary character of Indian civilisation and the conservative instincts of our people, there was a third cause of this, *viz.*, the prevalence of natural economy or barter in rural India before British rule. Until recent times in many remote and small villages of North Bengal grain used to play the part of money in the harvesting season, and most things were sold, at so many small cane-baskets of paddy for each. "So long as barter prevails, there are likely to be customary payments of rent, wages, and taxes; but as money is introduced, there may be frequent rearrangements of these payments and they come to be settled by competition." (*Cunningham & McArthur*, 141).

A certain amount of competition has always been known among us, but it operated within very narrow limits, and left most sides of our economic life untouched. Morison writes, "I do not think that competition is a force of less importance in Indian than in European industry,—it is not neutralised by custom. Undoubtedly there is in India a great deal of 'economic friction' impeding the operation of general laws." And again, "Inside the narrow circle of the Indian village, *competition is the rule*, but it is competition between illiterate men, ignorant of the world beyond their village." (pp. 3 and 15). But in many villages there is only one dealer of stores, and hence competition among sellers is out of the question. The same cause operates in regulating the wages of nearly all classes of village servants and artisans. In the purchase of grains, vegetables, fruits, fish and other produce there is a brisk competition, though among local men only.

But whatever might have been the condition of India in the past, the spread of English civilisation, the substitution of money economy, and the extension of communication are rapidly breaking down the force of custom, and competition is now the predominant force everywhere except in a few out-of-the-way districts.

The influence of custom on rents.—It will be shown in the sixth chapter how in most countries of the world custom has a great influence in regulating rent, and also how custom comes to be broken. In India rent was settled by custom (and not by competition among the ryots) in the pre-British days and for nearly two generations after the Permanent Settlement, partly for this reason, but mainly on account of the sparseness of population. In those unsettled times a landlord had often to call upon his ryots to defend him; hence it was his interest to have a large and strong body of tenants. There was plenty of good land lying uncultivated, and landlords competed with one another for attracting cultivators. But within the last fifty years the growth of population has produced the opposite condition, and we now have starving ryots competing for land and offering rack-rent for their only means of sustenance. The force of custom has, thus, been almost entirely broken in many places.

When an estate has remained in the hands of the same family that got it at the Permanent Settlement, there are generally friendly relations between the landlord and his tenants. He feels socially united to them; rack-renting and eviction are unknown. But many of the Bengal estates were sold for default in the first generation after the Settlement of 1793 and many more have been sold for debt since then, and the new owners have very often regarded their lands merely as an investment for their money and have resorted to rack-renting. The Rent Act of 1859 has legalised custom by laying down (1) that no zamindar can enhance the rent of a plot of land beyond the rate prevailing in the neighbourhood, (2) that a twelve years' occupancy by the tenant, creates in him an 'occupancy right' or permanent tenure without any title-deed, and (3) that a tenant has not the right of selling his holding unless the same right is enjoyed in the neighbourhood.

In many parts of Bihar and the U. P. the old customary division of the crop (*batai*) between landlord and tenant still continues, though the system of money rent is rapidly extending.

The influence of custom on wages.—In mediæval India wages did not follow the "iron law," but were determined by custom, and varied according to the labourer's caste or social position and not according to the severity of the task. Labourers were always paid in kind, *i.e.*, received real wages, with a small money allowance added in a few cases. When the population exceeded the demand for labour, the surplus portion did not immediately lower the wages, but swelled the ranks of the unemployed or of beggars. On the other hand, when a sudden decrease of labourers in a particular trade took place, the want could not be supplied by bringing workmen over from any other trade. The surviving labourers enjoyed a monopoly of skill and only got *more work*, but at the old rate of remuneration. Emigration is no doubt now-a-days steadily raising the wages of *common labourers* in the congested parts of India, but even where the emigrants go, as in Assam, the wages are often fixed by local custom or contract and are not subject to the constant variations which result from free and open competition. In modern India, "competition does operate in regulating the salaries of village artisans. All the world over, wages vary much more slowly than the price of commodities, and the wages of an artisan (1) employed by a body of villagers and (2) receiving his wages in kind, must naturally, of all wages, be the most difficult to alter. But when a village artisan is attracted to a town or to public works, the other villagers have to offer better terms in order to keep his successor at his post. Thus custom is broken. Definite alterations, too, have been made by the village elders in the wages of labour, after some great convulsion which disturbed rural economy." *(Morison*, 180—181*)*. All over India *competition* has *raised* the *wages* of the *artisan* class, such as masons, carpenters, smiths, etc. But in some cases the customary remuneration has long remained unchanged such as doctors' fees ; but the reasons are excess of supply and professional etiquette.

The influence of custom on prices.—The prices of agricultural produce was never in the past regulated by custom ; as for other commodities, especially manufactures, their prices are now subject to the law of demand and supply everywhere in India. Even in the villages the fluctuations of prices in the big towns make themselves felt, though after an interval of years Our producers now have the choice of a wider market and can get the best terms if they are sufficiently clever. But, on the whole, the Indian petty dealer and especially the simple villager, are unable to best immediate advantage of higher prices in higher markets, as they are too ignorant, disunited and incapable of holding out. The advantage of such a rise in prices is at first reaped by the middlemen or exporters who are almost always Europeans. For example, the price of hide has been greatly enhanced in Europe, first it took the Indian ryots six or seven years to realise this change, and until recently they were selling ryots hides at the old low prices. It was only in 1910 and the Punjab ryots for the first time held back until surplus wheat in the hope of a rise in Europe, harvest of selling it off at harvest. The knowledge of the now of price in Europe now-a-days rapidly filtrates recently the buying agents of these wholesale exporters to the village producers.

The organisation of Agriculture, Handicrafts and Domestic Industries in rural India.

Agriculture.—(1) Each locality has its agents

rules of land-tenure, which often respect the local customs. Sometimes the tenants possess, by virtue of old usage, the full right of sale, and sometimes they do not. In some tracts metayership is followed, in others money rents or even competition rents prevail. (2) In the organisation of agriculture each village often acts as a self-contained body; it has its own set of artisans and servants, its special brokers, carriers and mart. and its peculiar system of irrigation. (3) In some tracts they use canal water supplied by the State for a special tax on the land; in others each holding has its own well; elsewhere the landlord stores rain-water by embankment and supplies it to the tenants in return for a higher rent. In some villages the community collectively makes its arrangements for irrigation. But speaking broadly, India has been parcelled out into millions of petty farms, and scientific agriculture and the cultivation of a large estate by one management (which result from capitalist farming) are not even dreamt of here.

Handicrafts.—In nearly all the rural parts of India local handicraftsmen supply the few simple wants of the villagers, or the latter resort to a neighbouring town once or twice a year to make their purchases. But certain places in India have been famous for their special handicrafts, which go to all the markets of India, *e.g.*, the pottery of Bidar, the embroidery of Ahmadabad, the printed cloths of Brindaban, the brass-work of Benares, the *huqqas* of Lucknow, etc. These partake of the nature of objects of art, and are manufactured in large villages as well as towns, and usually by hereditary artisans. In some matters of local supply, however, an entire group of villages often depends on a single family or a small cluster of families living in their midst and plying a particular craft. Division of labour is naturally impossible in such small and isolated communities, and no improvement can be effected as each handicraftsman is succeeded by an apprentice trained by himself in the old methods.

The simple crafts of the hamlets are still the most important in the aggregate of all Indian industries. The weaver, the blacksmith, the potter, the oilpresser, the brazier, are members of a community as well as inheritors of a family occupation. Hence they have a sure market for their production, and their trades are regularly taught to the rising generation. *(Hunter*, 701.) But in the course of the present generation mill-woven cloth has penetrated to every nook of India, and the weavers, beaten in the competition with machinery, have mostly abandoned their trade, while a few eke out a scanty living by making towels (*gamcha*) and coarse coating. The blacksmith in most places has lost his chief business of turning out *new* plough-shares, hoes, and big knives (*dao*), which are now imported from foreign countries; but he continues to make the subsidiary articles, as he knows the different shapes of the minor metal utensils of domestic use which different localities prefer. (Machine-made goods are all cast in the same mould and cannot satisfy peculiar local tastes.) The smith now gets higher wages than before for his *repair* work.

Domestic industries.—The few surviving small industries of India are cultivated in the homes of the artisans, and all the members of a family help in their processes, *e.g.*, women and children conduct the easy process of reeling the thread. This arrangement tends to reduce the cost of production and ensures honesty, careful supervision, and the apprenticeship of the son to the father. Cotton spinning, for instance, was a domestic industry among Bengali women in pre-British days, and great fineness and evenness of thread resulted from their hereditary skill. The prevalence of caste among us necessitates the pursuit of industries *at home*. Factories are a very recent innovation here; the Indian workman has for ages been accustomed to take his work to his home and finish it at his leisure; he is averse to congregating in a factory and working for regular hours. The disadvantages of this system are, first, that the decay of any industry ruins whole families without any exception, and, secondly, that any rapid increase of production to meet a new or distant demand is impossible.

Domestic industries are valued in the modern world not as a substitute for, but as supplementary to factory work. They enable every member of a family to earn something, and utilise the labour of those who cannot give their whole time to production or cannot work away from their homes. India, being the land of the caste and *purda* systems, needs domestic industries even more than Europe. The successful introduction of small industries to be carried on at home, will be the salvation of millions, especially of the helpless Hindu widows.

Caste guilds.—(1) A caste is often a trade's union. Most of its members follow the same profession, and are kept in discipline by the *panchayet* or representative heads of the caste. Not only in industries but even in petty trading each caste has its special work. Many of the hundreds of sub-castes or sections into which the Hindus (and in some places the Muhammadans also) are divided, were entirely functional in their origin. Thus, the thread-dyers form one sub-caste, and the thread-spinners another. It is due to caste that the training of apprentices and poor relief are ensured, and each individual workman, so long as he does not disobey the rules of the caste-leaders, is backed by the strength of the whole caste in his struggle with capitalists or purchasers; he is protected against the competition of other members of his craft; he can force his employer to pay his dues and keep the terms of his contract, by preventing any of his fellow-craftsmen from working for such an employer and he is sure of an even distribution of business among *all* the members of the guild by reason of the *panchayet* prohibiting overtime work by any one of the brethren in seasons when employment is scarce. This is a great advantage from the workman's point of view. But a caste-guild also checks individual liberty and accumulation of capital, discourages the spirit of invention and enterprise, and prevents or retards the reform of any old industrial process. It is suited only to the stationary stage of society and is the foe of progress. (*Bombay Gazetteer*, vol. iv, ed. 1879, pp. 106-115; *Hunter*, 245-249.)

City industries.—Many industries were highly developed in India and gained a world-wide celebrity during the Muhammadan period. They were all carried on in cities or in clusters of villages leading a non-agricultural life, which were cities in effect. These manufactures formed India's chief exports till the end of the 18th century. Usually a particular industry had a particular city for its chief seat, *e.g.*, muslin at Dacca, silk at Murshidabad, inlay metal-work at Bidar, shawl weaving at Amritsar, brass-work at Benares, carpet weaving at Mirzapur, horn manufacture and silver filigree work at Katak, and wood-carving and bronze work in certain cities of Madras. In each such town the best workmen of that trade assembled, and their skill was perfected by long specialisation and daily intercourse with other masters. Whole streets were occupied by the members of the distinctive craft of the place and the importance and prosperity of the city depended entirely on them. Their productions commanded the whole Indian market. The European travellers of the seventeenth century have noted the chief industries which they saw flourishing in different Indian cities. Many of these were directly promoted by the patronage of the Emperor of Delhi or his provincial governors. (Constable's ed. of Bernier, 259). After the demand of the rulers had been satisfied, the public made their purchases or gave their orders. Such were the conditions of the embroidery of Ahmadabad, the enamelling of Delhi and Lucknow, and the "India paper" manufacture of Kashmir. The best goldsmiths, too, have lived in cities, but not exclusively in any particular province. Some of these city industries (esp. muslin, silk and shawl weaving) depended for their raw materials on the neighbouring villages. City industries command more distant markets and can meet an increased demand more quickly than rural ones. Yet, even in the cities, we had no factories, except the few work-shops (*karkhanahs*) owned by the Mughal emperors. Every artisan did his work by himself at home, though he had usually to be supplied by the customer with the materials (or a part of the price) in advance. (For the industries of the Mughal times, see my *India of Aurangzib: Statistics, Topography, and Roads*). Inscriptions speak of city guilds in Western India as early as 150 A.D.

Muhammadan guilds and industries:—Islam being a democratic religion, Muhammadan workmen form brotherhoods more quickly and extensively than

Hindu artisans, though a Muslim trade-guild, *when once formed*, has a tendency to become exclusive of other Muslim guilds just like a Hindu caste! (See *Bernier*, 259.) Most large cities of Mughal India had their guilds of workmen, who lived together in the same ward (called *mahalla* in N. India and *pura* in the South), which was often walled off from the rest of the town. Each guild had its special religious processions, festivals, dead saints, and mosques (with schools attached). The guild, by deducting a certain percentage on sales, raised money for communal purposes, such as trade dinners, relief of poor brethren and the building of mosques, besides doing the ordinary duties of a trade's union, *viz.*, (*a*) putting down unfair competition among the members and (*b*) preventing deterioration of the standard of workmanship or materials. A handsome *imambara* at Seroot in the Faizabad District of Oudh was built by the local Muhammadan cloth weaving guild paying a voluntary contribution of $\frac{1}{4}$ of a pice for each piece of cloth woven and thus raising Rs. 6,000. Certain industries of India have been entirely in the hands of Muhammadans, such as artistic book-binding, paper-making, leather-work, silk-embroidery in Benares, fine steel work, damascening, copper-smithy, etc. But most of them are now in decay.

Indigenous organisation of trade and transport.—The internal trade of India, *i.e.*, the work of distribution is entirely conducted by the people of the country. The Vaisyas or trading caste of Manu's time have disappeared. But even now in the different provinces internal trade is mostly confined to certain classes of people, *e.g.*, in Bombay to the Parsis, Gujratis and Marwaris, in the Deccan and Mysore to the *Lingayet* sect, in Madras to the Chetti and Komati castes, in the Punjab to the Khatris, in the U. P. to the Banias, in Bengal and Assam to the Marwaris, who show remarkable hardiness, perseverance and enterprise, and penetrate to every nook of the land in search of new markets. Most of these are petty dealers, who buy from wholesale importers at Calcutta and other big ports through a chain of middlemen and personally sell their wares in their chosen localities. Each village has at least one resident trader, who combines in his own person the functions of money-lender, grain-merchant, cloth-seller (in a few places only), and miscellaneous dealer. This man, called the **Bania** or *Mahajan*, has been condemned as an usurer, but he is a very useful person, and in his absence the whole rural economy would collapse, as "he is the only thrifty person among an improvident population" and he supplies "capital to the land in the minute doses which the agricultural condition of India demands." (*Morison*, 101, *Ind. Emp.*, iv. 523, *Yusuf Ali*, 61-63.)

In every fairly large village a *hát* or "market on circuit," is held twice a week, the stall-keepers visiting different centres in rotation on the days fixed for each. Permanent shops are found only in the biggest villages, which aspire to be towns. In the petty hamlets there is sometimes a resident store-keeper, who combines agriculture with retail trade. He has no regular shop, but keeps his store inside his house and brings out the things as his customers call for them. During the agricultural season he opens his "shop" only after his return from the field. A most important centre of distribution is the *melá* or fair, held once a year on some religious occasion, at which the people of many villages assemble and a brisk trade is carried on. Indeed, "making purchases on the pretext of attending a Ganges bathing festival" has passed into a proverbial expression in Bengal.

Taken collectively the Indian cultivators are at once the chief producers and consumers in the country. They expect the dealer to come to their own doors. Hence, an army of pedlers or travelling salesmen is spread over the country, chiefly in winter, going from village to village with their wares and supplying the local needs for miscellaneous goods, especially metal utensils and European manufactures. Their only occupation is retail dealing among the villagers, and they buy their stores in some provincial chief town. Difficulty of transport is no hindrance to this branch of internal trade, because each pedler's stock is small and can be carried on the head of a coolie or the back of a pack-animal. Increasing numbers of Peshawari Afghans are engaging in this trade, cheap German winter clothing being their specialty.

In Lower Bengal, the land of waterways, we often see trade done in boats. Barges loaded with earthenware, mangoes, jack-fruits, or kitchen vegetables, pass through the rivers and *nullahs*, and the villagers on the two banks buy their stores from them. An enterprising Calcutta publisher even sent a big boat (*budgerow*) load of his books and patent medicines to make a voyage on the Nadia and Murshidabad rivers as a travelling shop!

On the *export* side of our trade we have some very rich wholesale shippers at the chief ports, nearly all of whom are Europeans and a few Parsis. They buy from the villagers either through their agents, or oftener, through a chain of middlemen. Hence, in the harvest season the country is covered with travelling brokers, who buy jute, grain or cotton in small quantities from the ryots and collect them in local centres. A richer class of brokers buy at these centres and accumulate their goods in the district or provincial centres, whence they are taken by the highest class of brokers or the shippers' agents to the ports of embarkation, *viz.*, Calcutta for jute and rice, Rangoon for rice, Karachi for wheat, and Bombay for cotton. Each staple of export has its special district centre, *e.g.*, Sirajganj for jute, Barisal for Bengal rice, Lyallpur for Punjab canal wheat, Hoshangabad for cotton, Rangpur for tobacco leaf, &c. Travelling brokers assemble here for a few weeks in the year at harvest, a brisk business is done and new post offices opened; but when they depart the places return to their normal quiet and obscurity.

In the days before railways the transport of grain and other bulky agricultural produce to long distances was extremely difficult and almost unknown. Hence a famine in one part of the country could not be relieved by importing the surplus crops of another. In ancient times, only costly manufactures and objects of art were transported to distant places. (See *Ind. Emp.*, iii. 301).

Indigenous organisation of banking and agricultural credit.—The trading classes described above were formerly the only bankers of India. Marwari cloth-dealers and the heads of rich temples and monasteries (*maths*) often receive deposits and lend money at interest. In the big towns the bankers are mostly Marwaris or Khatris, and they conduct nearly all moderate financial operations within the country. Their main work is the transmission of money by means of *hundis* or notes of credit, and they have correspondents in many distant parts of India. A Marwari firm is usually a family concern, and is carried on with remarkable efficiency from generation to generation, dishonesty in the officers and bankruptcy of the firm being rare. Much of their capital is locked up in the form of loans to zamindars, and they seldom finance modern manufactures. The new joint-stock banks on European lines which Indian syndicates have been establishing (esp. in Bombay and the Punjab), are diverting many depositors from the Marwari family banks, and the latter are distinctly losing ground in the chief towns.

The village Bania described above is the only rural banker. His high rate of interest is due to the bad security of his debtors. The vast majority of Indian ryots have no ownership in their lands and consequently no credit. All that they can mortgage is the expected harvest, which is entirely dependent on rain and therefore uncertain. The chief obstacle to agricultural improvement in India is the weakness of rural credit. On the other hand, as the price of land has risen, the ryots who happen to possess a permanent (or thirty years') tenure, enjoy a dangerously facile credit. The presence of the Bania enables them to get loans easily, and so tempts them to extravagance for marriage and other unproductive purposes. Banias and sometimes zamindari officers lend money to the cultivators on the security of the next harvest, and the rate of interest in such cases is usually 37½ p. c. Bad debts are frequent, and have to be written off after the ryot has been ruined and turned into a penniless day-labourer.

The money-lending agencies of India may be classified thus:—

I. *Rural Bankers*—

1. The BANIA or *Mahajan*, whose functions are twofold, *viz.*, (*a*) to supply agriculture with capital (which is good), and (*b*) to practise

usury by lending money for unproductive purposes (which is bad).

2. The recently started CO-OPERATIVE CREDIT SOCIETIES, which mainly finance agriculture. The urban societies are comparatively few.

3. The GOVERNMENT, which grants *taqavi* loans to the peasants in years of distress, and recovers the amount in better years. This system has been inherited from the days of the Mughal emperors.

II. *Indigenous Urban Bankers*—

The SETHS or Sahukars, managing hereditary family banks (not joint-stock) with large capital. They—

(*a*) chiefly advance loans on the security of landed estates or ornaments, (this is usury) :

(*b*) finance inland traders or the distributing agency ;

(*c*) sometimes help with capital or loans, *local* manufactures.

III. *Modern Joint-stock Banks at the provincial capitals*—

5. The EUROPEAN BANKS chiefly transact exchange business, assist the foreign trade, and to a lesser extent finance industries and transport agencies.

6. The INDIAN BANKS mainly finance industries and the inland trade, and often grant loans to zamindars, just as the Seths do.

IV. *The Postal Savings Banks*—

7. They help the middle class people of the towns (and a few of the villagers) to save money. But such savings are not capital, as the banker (*viz.* Government) does not employ the deposits reproductively.

V. *Amateur Money-lenders*—

8. Zamindars' officers who practise usury in the villages like the Banias.
9. Temples and monasteries in the cities lend money on the security of house-property and ornaments.
10. Professional men (mainly lawyers) in the district towns, who open "Loan Offices" on a joint-stock, and exclusively practise usury.

Several members of class 4 have become landowners by buying up the estates mortgaged with them. Muhammadans are forbidden by their religion to lend money at interest, and hence the higher and richer classes among them abstain from banking business and sometimes even do not draw the interest on their deposits in the banks! But the lower classes, especially in Bengal, unhesitatingly engage in money-lending when they happen to have the funds. The Peshawari Afghans are as often usurers as pedlers.

Co-operative Credit Societies—

The indebtedness of the peasantry is not peculiar to India. All over the world we find it a normal state of things for the small farmers to be constantly in debt. In the countries where peasant-proprietorship prevails with equal rights of all children, and one heir has to buy out the other heirs, he becomes heavily involved in debt in the very act of succeeding to the property, and has therefore no capital left for making improvements. Moreover, in most civilised countries, owing to the pressure of population on the soil, intensive cultivation has to be practised, which is very costly. Agriculture being a precarious industry, dependent upon the seasons, the peasant in a bad year suffers a heavy loss for no fault of his own, and he must borrow in order to tide over the period of difficulty. Plough-cattle and the better kinds of agricultural implements cost more than the small savings of the average peasant; and he must borrow in order to buy them. Thus agriculture, except in the case of the capitalist farming of England, cannot go on without borrowing.

In India the indebtedness of the peasantry is of a more intense form; in some districts more than half the ryots have to borrow even their seed-grain, and very often three-fourths of the peasantry are in debt and their running account with the *Mahajan* is never closed. The recent increase in the price of agricultural produce, and consequently in the value of land, has enormously increased the peasant's borrowing power. As the Indian peasant is ignorant and improvident, he borrows not according to his need, but according to his capacity. Hence his extravagance and indebtedness have increased with his increased credit. Easy credit leads to reckless borrowing, and the ryot's debt has increased more rapidly than the value of land.

The British Government has tried to remedy the evil by restricting (in the Punjab and Bundelkhand) the peasant's power to sell his land except to members of a *bonâ fide* agricultural tribe. The professional money-lender has thereby been discouraged from lending money to the ryots, as he can no longer buy their holdings in default of payment. This paternal legislation is justifiable only where the peasants are helpless and foolish like children. It has the theoretical disadvantages of reducing the ryot's credit and interfering with the freedom of contract. A better solution of the problem of agricultural indebtedness is the establishment of village land-banks and co-operative credit societies like the Raiffeisen banks of Germany.

Raiffeisen (died 1888), a humble village mayor of Western Germany, applied Schulze-Delitzsch's principles of co-operation in banking among small capitalists from the city to the rural population, (with some important changes). He established his first regular loan society of this type in 1865, and the movement became a great success after 1879. Wollemborg founded similar institutions in Italy.

Raiffeisen's first aim was to substitute for helpless individual peasants a strong associated body. He saw that the credit which the individual could not command, would be accorded to an association framed in such a manner as to inspire public confidence. As his association was based upon *unlimited liability*, it became the direct interest of the members to exact a rigorous test of good character from candidates for membership. Each association should be strictly local....... The reserve fund must never be divided among the members, hence they will have no temptation to practise usury. (*Dupernex*, 39-40, 172).

These societies have two aims: (1) to provide the peasant with facilities for borrowing at a low rate of interest, so that agricultural improvement on borrowed capital may be profitable, and (2) to guard against the peasant's tendency to borrow imprudently and to spend the loan unproductively. The educational influence of such banks on the character of the peasantry is even more important than their economic results. Where they have been successfully worked, the peasants have been raised to a higher level of thrift, prudence, self-restraint, business capacity, and mutual help. Such a bank "forms a centre of local progress and reform. All are admissible, even the poorest, if they are of a worthy character. In Italy the mere possibility of joining a society [of this kind] has reclaimed men from drunkenness and extravagance, and has given them an impetus to sobriety, industry and education." It is difficult to introduce such societies among a people of low intellect and character; but where the attempt succeeds, the people learn confidence, thrift, self-help, and mutual help through association.

A co-operative credit society is worked in the following manner. (1) A bank is started by some select persons in a locality subscribing the capital among themselves either entirely, or raising a portion of it on their own credit. No member is permitted to take more than a fixed number of shares. (2) The bank lends money only in its own locality, *i.e.*, the creditors and the debtors belong to the same place and know each other. Strict care is taken that the new applicants for membership are men of good character. (3) The managers of the bank work gratuitously, and the dividend on the shares cannot exceed a low fixed rate, usually the market rate of interest. The rest of the profits are added to the reserve. (4) Loans are given only to known persons and for productive purposes, such as agricultural improvements, the purchase of plough-cattle, digging wells, &c.

The general features of a co-operative credit society are the following :—

(*a*) It is strictly *local* ; the limits of the village (or group of small villages) are the limits of its membership and operation.

(*b*) The administration is equally local ; members alone can hold office, and their services are *gratuitous* ; hence, economy in the *management*.

(*c*) There is but small share capital ; all funds being borrowed on the corporate security of the members and of the reserve; hence all *profits* (after paying the interest) *go to* swell *the reserve.*

(*d*) *Only members, i.e.*, residents of the particular village (or group of small villages) *can get loans.* "The bank is at the borrower's doors."

(*e*) All funds are the result of local thrift; hence these banks create local capital and cause such capital to be locally employed in a reproductive manner. (*Nicholson*, i. 144—147.)

In short, the bank is managed gratuitously (and therefore economically) by the most substantial and trustworthy men of the community who have a perfect knowledge of the applicants for loans and can reject all unworthy men. As shareholders of the bank can themselves borrow money from it on easy terms, the peasants are induced to practise thrift and industry in order to qualify themselves for the advantages of membership. If a debtor proves false to his contract and spends the loan unproductively, he can be immediately checked, or at the worst prevented from contracting fresh debts. Moreover, the public opinion of his neighbours as represented by the managers of the bank, effectually holds him to his promise in most cases and prevents fraud. Even more important is the moral good done by such banks, *viz.*, "their steady *educative influence* in matters of thrift, association, and self-help, and their tendency to develop high forms both of individual capacity, of public life, and of national character." (*Nicholson*, i. 372.)

The Indian Government passed on 25th March, 1904, a Co-operative Credit Societies Act, to "encourage thrift, self-help, and co-operation among agriculturists, artisans and persons of limited means." In the next few paragraphs I summarise the main provisions of this law.

The Societies are divided into three classes,—central, rural, and urban. A *Central Society* is a union of the representatives of a number of small societies affiliated to it. It raises loans and accepts deposits on behalf of the latter, because it can better command the confidence of capitalists. In a *Rural Society* at least four-fifths of the members must be agriculturists, and in an *Urban Society* the same majority are non-agriculturists. Each society consists of ten or more members above the age of 18 years, residing in the same town or village (or group of villages), or belonging to the same tribe, class or caste.

The rural societies as a rule work with unlimited liability and without share capital (except in Madras); the majority of urban societies have limited liability. Rural Societies are forbidden by law to pay dividends to the members, and all their profits must go to the reserve. Every urban society must set apart each year a quarter of its profits to form a reserve, before paying dividend. Every member must hold one or more shares in the society (*i.e.*, he must have a pecuniary interest in it). A society shall make no loan except to a member or to another rural society. Money should not be lent on the security of movable property. The following privileges have been granted to such societies by Government :—

(1) The shares are not liable to attachment or sale by a civil court decree.

(2) Next to land revenue and rent, a society's claim is prior to that of other creditors, upon the crops, cattle, implements, and raw materials of a member, for the unpaid portion of the loan advanced by it to him for the purchase of the last three.

(3) Free audit of the accounts of each society by the Registrar appointed by the State.

(4) Exemption from income-tax on profit or dividends, from stamp duty on documents, and from registration fee.

(5) As soon as the Registrar of Co-operative Credit Societies registers a society (free of charge), it enjoys all the advantages of a body corporate under the laws.

The Co-operative Societies Act of 1912 has widened the application of the principle of co-operation and reconstructed the Act of 1904. Societies are now classified as those of *unlimited* and *limited liability*, instead of as rural and urban. The Act has been extended to societies other than credit societies; permission has been given to some societies with unlimited liability, but share capital, to distribute profits; and provision has been made for societies of which other societies should be members, *i.e.*, central unions or federations of societies.

The two main difficulties in the case of village societies were as regards proper supervision (most of their members being illiterate) and the provision of funds. The remedy has been found by establishing *central societies* or *central banking unions*, *i.e.*, federations of village societies within a radius of 8 miles. These central unions maintain a staff of trained inspectors for supplementing the official inspecting staff (in auditing the village societies) and also act as bankers for their affiliated societies, as the former can more easily secure loans for the latter from the open money market. In Bombay this work is done by a Central Co-operative Bank for the whole province. Such big or "apex" banks are being established in other provinces also. [In 1913 there were 329 central societies and banks in all India.]

The village societies have unlimited liability. The rate of interest charged by them varies from 9½ to 15 p. c., while they pay 6 to 9 p. c. on the deposits they receive. The urban credit societies, a small but growing number, are limited liability concerns, chiefly formed among salary-earners. They hold nearly one-fifth of the amount of working capital possessed by agricultural societies.

The progress of the movement will be seen from the following table :—

Year.	Number of Societies.	Number of members.	Working capital in Rs.
1905	283	28,600	4·8 *lakhs.*
1908	1,963	184,700	80·7 "
1911	8,177	403,300	335 "
1914	16,295	762,000	857 "

The total working capital in 1914 was thus made up :—

	Rs.
Share capital and deposits of members	246 *lakhs*
Loans and deposits of non-members or other societies	543
Reserve funds	50 "
Loans from Government ...	11 "

Of the 16,295 societies in 1914, as many as 16,016 were *agricultural*, holding about half the total working capital, while the *non-agricultural* societies hold a little over one-tenth and the *central* societies or banks a little less than four-tenths of the total.

In spite of the war, these societies have continued to progress. In Bengal, for instance, their number rose from 939 in 1912 to 2243 in 1916, the number of members from 40,600 to 1,21,000, and their working capital from 26 *lakhs* to 124 *lakhs* in these four years. By January 1917 the capital had increased to 130 *lakhs*, and the number of central banks to 40. In the Punjab the number of rural societies has increased 60 p. c. and their working capital nearly doubled (1911). Two-thirds of their capital is supplied by the members and only 1½ p. c. comes from Government loans. The members not only supply the share capital, but place considerable deposits at the disposal of the (rural) societies, which thus act as savings banks.

The movement is tending to create a revolution in rural India. The ryots have developed an extraordinary capacity for united action, and the Co-operative Credit Society is stimulating interest in education and in sanitation. A demand for night and vernacular schools has sprung up in Bengal and the U. P., to which the local societies contribute out of their profits. The villagers in certain districts are beginning to submit their disputes to the Co-operative Committees. Another most hopeful development is the discouragement by the local committees of extravagant expenditure upon marriage and funeral ceremonies. As the members of the society stand to lose if one of their number borrows more than he is able to repay, many cases have arisen where the local societies have cut down the amounts of loans for such ceremonies. In this way village opinion, which compelled the ryots to incur ruinous expenses on ceremonial occasions, is now exerting an opposite influence.

In some cases village feuds of long duration have been settled as a result of the movement, and rival factions have joined in harmonious work in one society. There is indeed here the "promise of economic regeneration and of village life invigorated and made healthier in all its relations." (*Bengal Report*, 1910). "The general atmosphere of progress engendered by the societies makes the members keen on the extension of education...In Unao and Benares, several of the Pasi and Chamar societies have forsworn the use of intoxicating liquor." (*U. P. Report*, 1910). In the Punjab, money-lenders, both professional and zamindars, are lowering their rates of interest in order to compete with the societies.

In 1911 and 1912 the success of the movement in the Punjab was most gratifying. "The small money-lender has disappeared from some hundreds of villages in Jullundur...Agricultural economy in the Central Punjab is already in process of revolution, and the Punjab peasant is rapidly becoming the financier of his own industry....The Sessions Judge of Jullundur attributes a decrease of 1,100 civil cases in that district last year (1911) mainly to the existence of village banks."

"The village societies are much utilised by the Agricultural Department for assisting demonstrations, distributing seed, &c. In some cases they have begun to interest themselves in primary education and village sanitation. Their efforts at settling disputes between members have led to an appreciable decrease in litigation......Surprisingly little is drawn [as loan] for uneconomic purposes such as expenses of ceremonial." (*Moral and Mat. Pro.* 1913-14, p. 51). In Bengal it was found (1912) that one-third of the loans taken by members of rural societies was for productive purposes and nearly one-half for the repayment of old debts, while the amount borrowed for ceremonies (such as marriage) was less than 5 p. c. of the total. But we must "remember that this is only the beginning. We have touched only the fringe of the great problem of indebtedness in India." (Lord Carmichael).

Considered as a whole, the economic effect of co-operation has been to cheapen rural credit greatly from the average 25 p. c. of the money-lenders to the 12 or 15 p. c. of these societies. The agriculturists who are members of credit societies make a total saving of 20 *lakhs* of Rupees a year in interest alone by borrowing from them instead of from the *mahajan*, (1914). The other benefits are still more important: "Business habits have been inculcated with the...result that the (Indian) agriculturist has learnt to conduct his own work more efficiently. Thrift has been encouraged, the value of savings better appreciated,...and a sense of communal life instilled." (*Indian Year-Book* for 1917, p. 487).

The co-operative movement has spread in India

with astonishing rapidity. Private Indian gentlemen are assisting at the work in very large numbers without any remuneration; unlimited liability has not scared away members; societies have not found the absence of a summary legal procedure an insuperable difficulty in collecting their debts: much capital has been attracted from the public, while loans from Government have declined from 15 p. c. at the beginning (1905) to only 1·3 p. c. in 1914. Indeed, with a view to prevent a too hasty and unsound growth, the Government policy in most provinces has been one of consolidation rather than expansion.

Three serious problems are facing our co-operative societies in this the second decade of their existence in India. The first question is the maintenance of an adequate fluid reserve. The second, which is really a part of the first, is the maintenance of a proper correlation between the period of the deposits received by a society (or union of federated societies) and the loans issued by it. The third is,—should central banks be allowed to attract capital from outside (which they cannot do under the present rules), instead of having to raise it locally? The removal of this restriction would, no doubt, increase their resources when most needed,—namely, when there is a dearth of money locally. But this course has its dangers, too; because outside depositors are much more subject to panic than local men, and several German co-operative banks have come to grief by securing capital from far and near. Indeed, special care has to be exercised to prevent certain societies (especially the urban ones) from becoming mere joint-stock companies paying a high dividend, while enjoying all the advantages of registration under the Co-operative Credit Act. To guard against this evil, the maximum rate of dividend can be fixed only by the Registrar of Co-operative Credit Societies.

In 1915 a Co-operation Committee, appointed by Government with Sir E. Maclagan as President, recommended as follows :—

(1) Great care should be taken in forming new primary societies, and the principles of *co-operation* should always be borne in mind if the societies are to last and do real good.

(2) To encourage thrift, every effort should be made to increase the amount of *local* deposits.

(3) Securities for loans should be taken in preference to mortgages on land, because "real credit on a wholesale scale is not quite compatible with the spirit of co-operation."

(4) Primary societies which accept deposits, (instead of merely borrowing from the central banks), must provide an adequate *fluid resource* for themselves. After this has been done, they may utilise their surplus assets by adding to their working capital. [The question is,—how is this reserve to be kept, in Government Paper or as floating deposits in central banks ?]

(5) Central Banks must keep fluid resources suffi-

cient to meet *half* the deposits due for repayment in the next 12 months, and the "apex co-operative bank" of each province one-third. [This amount lies idle, and has been criticised as too high and rigid a proportion; but it enables the banks to meet a crisis easily.]

(6) The share-holders of Central Banks should not be exclusively individuals, but at first individuals and other societies and ultimately societies only. *Guaranteeing unions* of the Burma type, (which do not exercise banking functions, but are federations for the purposes of inspection, control and mutual guidance), should be formed as intermediaries between the primary societies and the financing agencies (*viz.*, the Central and Provincial or "apex" Co-operative Banks).

CHAPTER III.

THE STATE.

Pax Britannica and its economic effects—The British have established the rule of one Power over India, and brought even the native states under their suzerainty. Thus, absolute internal peace has been established in the place of anarchy and the struggle of kingdom against kingdom, race against race. At the same time the strong arm of Britain has made foreign invasion impossible. Since the day when Gilbert chased the Afghan horse back into the Khyber Pass (1849), no armed foreigner has trodden the Indian soil as an enemy. The results of the peace that now reigns over the land are:—

(*a*) Security of life and property, from the suppression of *dacoits* or organised gangs of robbers. (*b*) Safety of the roads, in consequence of the extermination of the Thugs and lawless chiefs and the establishment of a regular police. Merchants can now travel far with their goods without any fear of being robbed on the roads. (*c*) Peace has fostered an immense increase of population. *i.e.*, of the labour supply. (*d*) Increase of population has made necessary, and peace has made profitable, the extension of cultivation and internal commerce. Hence the prices of land and agricultural produce have risen, to the benefit of the landlord and the cultivator. (*e*) At the same time the cost of production has been reduced in proportion to the decrease in the cost of defence and watching. Formerly skilled industries could be carried on and even tolerably rich people could reside in security, only in walled towns or in moated granges. Our old private houses were built with a view to stand a siege. In Oudh even villages had mud walls or impenetrable thorny hedges round them in the Muhammadan period. This expenditure on defensive construction is no longer necessary. (*f*) Peace has not only favoured the accumulation of capital, but also tempted it to come out of its hiding places, because no man now runs the risk of being tortured and plundered if it is known that he has wealth. Hence, British peace is destroying the "shyness of Indian capital." (*g*) This increase of available capital is steadily lowering the rate of interest. (*h*) Moreover, now that India is a part of the British empire, we can import foreign experts to be our teachers in manufacture and to run our mills, at much lower wages than in the troubled times before British rule. Under the Mughal emperors, the European artificers who cast cannon were attracted to their dominion by very large rewards, and had then to be forcibly prevented from running away.

The most striking example of the benefits to British peace is to be seen in the Bombay Presidency, which had been devastated by incessant wars for centuries before the English annexed it (1817). Population had greatly declined through war and through famine, which was then the inseparable companion of war. Large areas of arable land had lapsed into deserts or jungles, and innumerable robber bands roamed over the country. The English completed their first settlement of the province about 1825, and within fifty years of it the commercial and industrial prosperity of Bombay rivalled the agricultural wealth of Bengal, the most fertile part of India. Similarly, in the fertile districts of Noakhali and Backerganj in East Bengal, a wide belt of land along the rivers had been utterly depopulated by Burmese pirates and remained so as late as 1781 when Rennell drew his *Bengal Atlas*. These are now the richest growers of rice and betel-nut.

The Disadvantages of Pax Britannica—(1) One of the great natural checks on population, *viz.*, war, having been removed, the Indian people are increasing too fast for the food supply under the old unscientific system of cultivation, and we have an almost chronic state of scarcity which, in adverse seasons, is intensified into famine. The rapid transport of food to affected areas, which railways have rendered possible, can alleviate but not prevent famines. The increase of population without any advance in the standard of comfort and sanitary knowledge of the common people, has led to overcrowding (especially in the cities), and the death-rate has greatly risen in recent years. In some districts of Lower Bengal it has overtaken the birth-rate. Thus

Nature is sternly restoring the equilibrium. (2) British peace, by making it safe for foreign manufacturers to send their cheap machine-made goods to India, has killed our indigenous handicrafts. Every year numbers of Indian skilled workmen, such as weavers, smiths, etc., being defeated in the competition with foreign manufacturers, have to give up their hereditary trades and swell the ranks of poor landless labourers in the villages or casual wage-earners in the cities. They sink to a lower stratum of society and increase the pressure on land. (*Report of Famine Com. of 1898, Ranade* 29). The Indian workman is ignorant and untrained in modern methods, and he is sure to be exterminated in a competition with foreigners armed with all the resources of modern science and organisation. Thanks to British peace and railways, European manufactures penetrate to the humblest Indian village and the Indian artisan's occupation is gone. The growth of *modern* industries is the only possible salvation of our surplus population. (3) Foreign capital is being invested in India more and more in proportion to the increased security of the country. This is partly a gain and partly not. These foreigners have greatly extended the field of Indian labour and caused the development of many natural resources which would have remained neglected (at least for some generations) but for their enterprise. At the same time, however, they have quite naturally forestalled the native capitalists of the future by taking up the most profitable lands and concerns. The belated Indian capitalist who is now venturing into the same field, finds that only third-rate concessions are left for him. For this reason, in Japan foreigners are debarred by law from owning land and acquiring mining concessions, and the Railway Act prohibits the pledging of railway properties to aliens,—though eminent statesmen like Count Inouye and Baron Shibusawa admit that such restrictions retard the industrial growth of their country. (*Japan by the Japanese*, 315, 387, 410). But "the conservation of natural resources" for the future of the nation is of deeper importance to a people than the quick development of mines and industries. Moreover, at present we derive in the form of royalty only a small fraction of the value of our minerals exploited by foreign capitalists. "When a metalliferous ore is exported in its raw state, and the cost of its transport to market is many times more than the price paid for it in India, it is obvious that whatever changes in its value may occur in future [*i.e.*, after being manufactured in Europe], the country [of origin] is not now getting for the mineral more than a small fraction of its actual worth." Hence, caution in exploiting Indian minerals would have ultimately benefited the country (Sir T. Holland). Most of these foreign concerns (*a*) have their directing boards in England, (*b*) employ foreign labour except in the lowest and least-paid grades, and (*c*) send their annual profits outside India to be paid as sterling dividends. They, no doubt, exploit the natural resources of our country, but it is for their own gain, and the only classes of Indians whom they benefit in the process are the landowners who have granted them concessions and the coolies and clerks whom they employ. As Sir T. Holland told a body of business men in England, if the capital of the Tata Hydro-electric scheme had been provided by England, the profits of the business would have come to *England*, whereas they would now remain in India. [The good done to India by these foreign concerns will be described in Chapter V.]

What British rule has done for India economically—The economic change can be summed up by saying that British rule has *modernised India* and made her free from the mediæval spirit. The most noticeable feature of this New India is that the country is no longer isolated, but has been *connected with* the whirlpool of *the world's commerce* and speculation. Our horizon has been immensely extended. A man's opportunities are very much greater now than they were a century and a half ago. He has a larger market to take his goods to, a wider field wherein to hire out his skill, and a more numerous body of suppliers to choose from, and he may deal in transactions extending over provinces and even countries, instead of being confined within the narrow bounds of his village or city, as in the days of our ancestors. Thus, greater careers (economically) have been opened to the clever and the daring, though the weak, the dull and the lazy find it harder to live in this new world of hurry and strenuous toil than in the old days of peaceful life and rude plenty.

In the sphere of economics open competition is the rule, and advancement depends not on race or creed, but on merit alone Here, career has been opened to talent as the result of British rule. Men are raising themselves from very low beginnings to wealth and influence by their inborn capacity for managing labourers, supplying contracts, and conducting industries. In the present age their *opportunities* are much *greater* and their rewards on a vaster scale than was possible in mediæval India.

At the same time *individualism* has been *developed* in the place of the *collectivism* which held sway over our ancient society. A man can now safely be in a minority of one; he can defy social opinion by leaving his hereditary profession or creed. Apart from the strict toleration enforced by the Government, the very fact that our rulers are a casteless and individualistic people, saps the foundations of our old collectivism. Slavery has been abolished. It lingered in India as late as 1810, when, according to Dr. Buchanan Hamilton, a full grown male slave could be purchased in the Purnea district for Rs. 15 to 20. The dignity of labour is steadily asserting itself against status. This individual freedom will, in future, be the root of invention, though its work at the outset has naturally been merely destructive. Then, again, the English have placed Science at the service of man, in the departments of production, transport, sanitation and medical relief. Contact with verity is the root of Science; it does not care for custom or convention. Hence, in proportion as Science has been advanced in India, a social and economic reconstruction has been silently set on foot.

Other effects of the modernisation of India are the *substitution of money economy* for natural economy, (*i.e.*, of cash for barter), of definite contract for vague usage, of machinery for manual labour, of corporate effort for individual undertakings, (*e.g.*, of joint-stock firms in the place of family concerns). Hence, works which the richest banking houses of old could not undertake are now easily financed by our joint-stock banks. Public corporations carry out water works, land reclamation schemes, and harbour extensions, the cost of which would have staggered our kings in the past.

The influence of British rule in increasing the capital in circulation and giving us a modern system of communications and transmission of news, has already been noticed. From the latter cause our business has gained wider range and greater mobility. A factor which we are apt to forget, but which greatly contributes to the same result, is the establishment of one currency and one language for public business all over India. The confusion, loss and waste of time which result from the existence of divers currencies and variations of value among the same class of coins according to differences in the year of coinage, can be easily perceived in the course of a day's journey from British India to the Nizam's Dominions. On the other hand, not to speak of our metallic currency, even a Government currency note has one fixed value from Simla to Cape Comorin. The benefit to trade from such a fixed and portable medium of exchange is very great.

The study of a big capital like Calcutta reveals the full extent of the economic modernisation of India. The following features of it are most noticeable :—

(*a*) Higgling has given place to fixed prices not only in the bigger shops, but also among the retail traders of foreign goods in Chándni Chowk, Rádhábázár and Murgiháttá, and among the dealers in country-made brass utensils and foreign cutlery in Barabazar.

(*b*) The value of time is recognised and punctuality practised as a habit. This is observable not only in the European offices, but also among the servants of many Indian employers. The makers of tinboxes, sieves, wooden cases and furniture, and the braziers and coppersmiths, who live in the narrow lanes, ply their trades all the day with patient regularity, with very few intermissions of idle chatting. Evidently they have got the keen money-making spirit of the west, and are determined to make every day yield the utmost possible amount of work.

(*c*) Advertising has made great progress. Apart from posters, handbills, newspaper advertisements and other printed means of drawing the consumer's attention, the attractive decoration of shop-windows (which was not practised even by the European firms of Calcutta before 1860), has been developed into a fine art, and houses in the commercial quarters are now being rebuilt with a view to securing big front windows.

(*d*) The concentration of a vast population in one city offers a ready market for immense quantities of goods. Hence the rise of a class of wholesale dealers and importers and of dealers specialising in particular varieties of goods.

(*e*) The attraction of a big city alters the economic condition of the district around it over a radius of a hundred miles or more (by rail). The mechanism of the food supply of Calcutta deserves a special treatise by itself. There is a belt of market gardens around it, which has already spread beyond Dum Dum. Here everything is grown solely in view of the Calcutta demand, but the transport is usually by cart or boat. Fish comes by rail from Damukdia Ghat and Goalundo, 125 miles away, mango, potato and cauliflower from Patna, 330 miles distant, poultry from Bihar, sheep and goats from Buxar, still further off. The dairy market at Poradah (103 miles) has been known to throb in sympathy with the Calcutta market.

[Similarly, the summer capital Darjiling is supplied with fish from Sara Ghat, Katihar, and even Calcutta, more than 300 miles away.] Special crops are raised in particular spots and despatched in their entirety to Calcutta. For instance, boat-loads of edible stems (*danta*) arrive from Kálna where the people cultivate the Calcutta market in respect of this article only. Throughout a belt of a hundred miles or more, local prices are raised to the Calcutta level, after making allowances for the cost of transport and the inevitable exactions by the railway men and the police.

The chief British Indian systems of land tenure. —Three systems of land settlement are found in British India :—

(1) The *Permanent Settlement*, which occurs in nearly the whole of Bengal, Bihar, the Benares Division of the U. P., and the north-eastern part of Madras (between the Godavari and the Mahanadi).

(2) The *Mahalwari* or *Village Settlement*, which is found throughout the U. P., the Punjab, and the Central Povinces,—while in Oudh villages are placed under *taluqdars* or middlemen with whom the Government deals directly, but who have little power over their tenants.

(3) The *Ryotwari Settlement*, which prevails in Bombay, Sind and Madras. The principle of this system is also applied to Assam and Burma. A few hilly tracts in Bengal and the coast strip of Orissa have been *temporarily settled.*

One-fifth of the total surveyed area of British India thirdbeen permanently settled, (*viz.*, about $\frac{5}{6}$ of Bengal and Bihar, $\frac{1}{8}$ of Assam, $\frac{1}{10}$ of the U. P., and $\frac{1}{4}$ of Bengal), one-third is under mahalwari and 47 p. c. mahal ryotwari settlement.

I. The **Zamindars,** as a class of men standing standing between the king and the actual cultivators and serving as collectors of revenue, while possessing while sort of ownership in the land, were known in the Hindu period; the name was first given by the permanent by Government to its agents in the collec- were of revenue, who had no permanent right to the and. But the fact of Bengal being a frontier province its away from the capital of the Mughal empire and the evershifting character of its rivers and alluvial land surface (which made a new survey necessary every 2 or 3 years), enabled the zamindars in the seventeenth necessary acquire in practice a hereditary ownership of the soil with many of the powers of the feudal barons.

In 1793 Lord Cornwallis made the Permanent Permanent with the zamindars, by which (*a*) he recog- made them as *proprietors of the soil* with the rights of loss *hereditary* succession, sale and mortgage, but demand to the loss of their property on failure to pay the revenue on a fixed date. (*b*) He limited for ever the State demand to a fixed revenue and certain duties on services. Some of these services were afterwards (1870) commuted into cesses. (*c*) He stipulated that the zamindars should safeguard the rights of their tenants by granting them *pattás* or documents stating the area and rent of their respective holdings. (*d*) The zamindars were made "subject to such rules as might be enacted by the British Government for securing the rights and privileges of the tenants in their respective tenures and for protecting them against undue exaction or oppression." All *abwabs*, or cesses levied by the zamindars in addition to the rent, were abolished. The transit duties and road and ferry tolls were taken over by the Government, but the market tolls and profits from fisheries, trees and waste-lands were left entirely to the zamindars. (*e*) The *taluqdars* of Bengal were raised to the position of zamindars and allowed to pay a fixed revenue directly to the Government, instead of through a superior zamindar. (*f*) In Madras and Orissa many petty tributary chiefs have been deprived of their ruling powers and reduced to rank of zamindars, subject to the payment of a fixed revenue.

II. The Village Settlement (*Mahalwari*)—The revenue is settled for a limited period (30 years in the U. P. and 20 years in the Punjab and C. P.), with the *entire body of villagers* who are *jointly* and separately *responsible* for the revenue of the whole village. Their head, called the *Lambardar*, signs the agreement with the Government to pay the revenue, on behalf of the villagers. The total revenue is then apportioned among the villagers, some of them retaining their ancestral shares of the village-lands subject to the payment of this revenue. The assessment of the revenue by the village council (or *Lambardar*) is supervised by the Settlement Officer of the Government, and the village maps and records of right are carefully preserved and brought up to date. The Government demand is estimated by a careful calculation of the value of the land, the price of the crops, and the recorded actual produce of the fields. The rate fixed at each new settlement cannot be enhanced during the next 20 or 30 years. But the Government remits the revenue or a portion of it in years of famine.

In the Mahalwari settlement, the Government deals only with middlemen,—whether individuals or groups of villagers,—who are held responsible for the revenue. Nearly half the area thus settled is cultivated by these middlemen themselves, and the other half by inferior tenants subject to the middlemen. The Government demand was formerly 90 p. c. of the net assets, but it has now been reduced to 50 p. c. or even less, except in Bombay, where there is no limit to the maximum. The *net asset* is taken to be the economic rent which the actual cultivator pays to the superior proprietor, where there is subletting. In other places, the net asset is arrived at by deducting from the assumed price of the crop the approximate cost of production, (including the peasant's subsistence, the depreciation of his implements, and the remuneration of the village menials,) and a little extra for his luxuries. But all these calculations are made entirely at the discretion of the Settlement Officer, who is, however, directed by the rules to consider the character of the soil, the price of crops, and the rent of neighbouring fields (where there is sub-letting). From his decision there is no appeal to any rent court.

In addition to the revenue thus settled, *cesses* have been imposed for (*a*) roads, schools, and dispensaries, (*b*) the remuneration of village officers, such as the headman, the accountant and the watchman, and (*c*) "insurance against famine" [abolished in 1906]. The usual rate of the cess is one-sixteenth of the revenue.

In the province of Oudh, the Government settles the revenue of a group of villages, for the usual term of 30 years, with a *taluqdar* or chief, instead of with the community of each village separately. The revenue payable by the *taluqdar* is the total of the sums levied by him as rent from the different villages under him, after deducting the cost of collection and the sum which the Government is pleased to leave to him for the support of his life and dignity. Thus, the *taluqdars* of Oudh *differ from* the *zamindars* of Bengal in two respects: (1) the settlement with the former is temporary, and (2) they have no absolute right over their estates such as the Bengal zamindars possess. Hence the *taluqdari* is a double tenure, *i.e.*, the Government estimates and fixes the revenue of each village (which is collected by the *taluqdar* as his *rent*), as well as the total amount to be paid by him to the Government as *revenue.* In fact the *taluqdar* is merely a big revenue-farmer with some pecuniary gain, but none of the rights and influence of the Bengal zamindar.

III. The Ryotwari Settlement.—In the Ryotwari tracts the Government *deals directly with the cultivators* and recognises no middleman. Each village is carefully surveyed, and every cultivator's holding or plot of land in it is marked and separately numbered. Village maps with accurate boundary lines, classification of the soil, and the names of the occupants, are carefully compiled and preserved, and the revenue is assessed on each occupant. This right of occupancy can be inherited and transferred by the peasants; hence there is some amount of sub-letting even in the Ryotwari provinces. In other respects the method of assessment is the same as in the Mahalwari settlement.

The rights of tenants.—Under the Permanent Settlement the zamindars were required to give to each tenant a *pattá* or document specifying the area and conditions of his holding, and they were to take from the latter a *qabuliyat* or written acceptance of the terms. But this was not done in practice, and the zamindars enhanced rents and evicted tenants as they liked. In 1859 a Rent Act was passed which granted to the ryots "occupancy rights," and limited the zamindar's power of enhancement. Every tenant who has held the *same* field continuously for 12 years, gains the right to be regarded as an "occupancy tenant," and as such he cannot be evicted at will, nor can his rent be enhanced beyond the rate of other occupancy tenants in the neighbourhood or beyond the limit indicated by a rise in the value of crops.

The Bengal Tenancy Act of 1885 provides (1) that a ryot shall enjoy the "occupancy right" if he has held *any* field in the same village for twelve years in succession. It was enacted to prevent the zamindars from evading the Act of 1859 by shifting tenants from one field to another before they had completed 12 years' occupation of any particular field.

(2) The same law gave legal recognition to the position of some classes of privileged tenants, midway between the zamindars and the actual cultivators, *viz.*, (*a*) 'tenure-holders', (called *taluqdars* or *jotdars*, generally holding 100 *bighas* or more), who have full sub-proprietory rights; (*b*) 'ryots at fixed rates', who cannot be ejected nor their rent enhanced; (*c*) 'occupancy tenants' (formed under the Act of 1859), and (*d*) 'settled ryots' (who have held different fields in the same village for 12 years). The last two also are protected from unjust eviction, and their rent can be increased only in certain circumstances, which may have to be proved in a law court.

(3) The Act also empowered the Local Government to make a cadastral survey and a record of rights by means of its Settlement Officers, one-fourth of the cost being borne by the Government and the remainder being equally shared by the zamindar and the tenant.

In 1891 a cadastral survey of North Bihar was begun, and later on that of Eastern Bengal.

(4) The Act enables a tenant to appeal to the law courts against any enhancement of rent by the zamindar, and the court is empowered to fix what it considers a fair rent on the basis of the rates prevailing in the neighbourhood.

(5) It provides safeguards against the oppression of tenants at eviction and distraint by landlords. The distraint has to be made through a law-court (and not by the zamindar's servants), and only the crop can be attached. In short, the Act of 1885 has greatly reduced the zamindar's summary powers, and protected the tenants against oppression, unfair enhancement of rent, and unjust eviction.

In 1907 the law was further amended with the following objects:

(1) To discourage landlords in evading the provision of the Act of 1885 with regard to the enhancement of rent, by entering into unfair inequitable and collusive compromises with their tenants. "No court shall give effect to an agreement or compromise between landlord and tenant the terms of which, if they were embodied in a contract, could not be enforced under the Act. The revenue officers and courts have been given a wider discretion in dealing with such agreements and compromises."

(2) To give greater authority to the record-of-rights when such record has been duly prepared and

published. In fact, the preparation of the record-of-rights has now greatly modified agrarian conditions. In rent suits, the law was most often evaded by the zamindar not producing the record, and getting an unfair decree in the absence of the ryot. The law of 1907 provides for the production of the entry regarding rent in the record-of-rights in *all* rent suits, and lays down that every entry in a record-of-rights shall be *presumed to be correct* until it is proved by evidence to be incorrect and that a court passing a decree at variance with any such entry must record its reasons for so doing.

(3) To give power to Government to distinguish between good and bad landlords and to take steps in the case of the latter for the reduction of rent, when they appear to have been so unduly enhanced as to be oppressive. In areas where a record-of-rights has been prepared and is maintained, zamindars favoured by the Local Government may recover arrears of rent by a shorter and more summary process than a rent-suit in a civil court; they can get a certificate issued by a specially appointed officer, without the ryot being first heard in his defence, and have the certificate executed on the defaulting tenant by a revenue officer instead of a civil court peon.' (*Rampini*, 4th. ed., xiv—xvi).

The Permanent Settlement; its disadvantages:—(1) An enormous loss to the State of at least 4½ *crores* of Rupees annually, being the unearned increment since 1793 which the zamindars take. (2) This loss of revenue has compelled the Government to increase the general taxation, so that the rest of British India has to pay heavier taxes as the result of the Bengal and Madras landlords enjoying a purely unearned increment. (3) The unproductive use of rent by the majority of zamindars. Cornwallis had hoped that the Indian zamindars would imitate the English landlords by superintending and financing the improvement of agriculture; but this hope has been falsified: the zamindars as a class spend their wealth in luxury and many of them are absentees. (*Ind. Emp.*, iv. 231, *Seton-Karr*, 47-48, 65, *Jones*, 143.)

Its advantages:—(1) It has saved the land-revenue of the State from annual fluctuations and uncertainty of collection. (2) It avoids the expense and harassment to tenants which attend every periodical renewal of settlement in the other parts of India. (3) The zamindars have greatly extended cultivation by bringing large areas of waste-land under tillage, planting colonies of peasants by means of concessions and pecuniary help, draining marshes, clearing jungles, and digging tanks, (*Seton-Karr*, 45-49. The actual work of reclamation of soil was done by the ryots, but under the indispensable help and protection of the zamindar.) "The proprietorship conferred on the zamindars has also much to do with the introduction into Lower Bengal, nearly alone among Indian provinces, of new and vast agricultural industries."

(Maine's *Vill. Com.*, 163). The zamindar is on the spot, he is not changeable like the rapidly shifted Government *tahsildar*, and he enjoys the entire benefit of the increased production; hence, he has every inducement to increase the cultivation. But he has not yet attended to *intensive* cultivation or agricultural "improvement" as understood by English landlords. The new Agricultural Colleges may, however, equip our future zamindars with the knowledge necessary for the latter purpose. (4) The zamindar alone can introduce costly agricultural improvements and machinery, which are beyond the means of the petty individual cultivators. Hence agriculture on a large scale is possible only in the permanently settled parts of India. (5) At present the zamindar is the only channel through which new knowledge and the comforts of civilisation can reach the cultivators. His manor is an oasis of culture amidst a dead level of ignorance and poverty. In Bengal, it has generally a school, a dispensary and a post office, which benefit all the neighbouring villages. To his temple at Puja time flock all the peasants, male and female, Hindu and Muslim; it plays the part of a club to them, and affords the only source of collective amusement they have. By the agency of the zamindar a new sanitary measure, a new method of cultivation, or a new kind of crop can be quickly introduced among the peasants. "Scarcity is met, relief works are set on foot, and supplies are transported (in a famine) with greater facility, where there are large zamindars, than in provinces where the settlement has been made with the heads of village communities, or with each ryot direct." (*Seton-Karr*, 70). In short, the zamindar holds all the threads of village life in his hands, and his power for good (as well as for evil) is great. Where there is a great resident zamindar, crimes are hardly known. But where the peasants are independent (as in Backerganj), many murders are committed in the villages and go unpunished. [But unless the zamindar is resident, he cannot police the rural parts, and there is nothing in the Permanent Settlement to compel him to be in residence.*]

(6) It has created a rich and loyal body between the Government and the people. The zamindars were conspicuous for their loyalty during the Mutiny. (*Seton-Karr*, 69). Their aid to education, sanitation, famine-relief, literature and art, all over the country, has been most liberal.

(7) The Permanent Settlement, co-operating with the law of equal inheritance of all the sons, has *created a* large *middle class* with a secure income, which is the cause of the social, literary and educational advancement of Bengal. The political importance of such a middle class cannot be exaggerated; without it,

* Town-life was the aversion and terror of our old-fashioned zamindars, and they preferred to live in inaccessible villages. But the new race of zamindars, with hardly any exception, are absentees and have a craze for living in Calcutta.

representative Government cannot be successfully conducted. The very absence of the law of primogeniture, though it has split up many estates into small bits (and thus rendered cultivation on a large scale impossible), has tended to swell the number of the middle class. Every Bengal "squireen" has just enough to educate his sons with, but not enough to induce them to lead an idle life. They, therefore, display something of the proverbial keenness and enterprise of "the younger sons" of the English aristocracy. (See also *Dutt*, 461.)

Disadvantages of temporary settlement.—(1) The expense and harassment of the present assessment work, which have to be repeated every 20 or 30 years. (2) Neglect of cultivation on the approach of a revision of settlement, in order to remove the ostensible assets. "As the period for revision draws nigh, a certain amount of distrust and disquietude arises in the minds of the population. Wealth is concealed; lands are purposely thrown out of cultivation; and many unfair means are resorted to in order to avoid an increase of rental." (*Seton-Karr* 68). (3) The investment of capital in land is discouraged, as there is no certainty that the improvements made at the tenant's expense will not be appropriated by the Government in the form of enhanced revenue. (4) The people cannot lead a full and contented life, as they are not the proprietors of the lands they cultivate. (*Ind. Emp.*, iv. 231). "The peasant must have land to till or must starve. The body of the nation is therefore in every case dependent upon the great sovereign proprietor for the means of obtaining food. ...Intermediate and independent classes there are none; and great and small are...the slaves of that master on whose pleasure the means of their subsistence wholly depend....The tendency of such a state of things is to perpetuate the despotism it creates." (*Jones*, 100-101, 123. See also *Dutt*, 486, 502.)

Recent reforms in the revenue policy of the Indian Government.—For a long time a strong party of reformers and philanthropists advocated the extension of the Permanent Settlement to all India. But the vast majority of officers objected to it, and at last in 1883 the Secretary of State definitely negatived the proposal. Mr. R. C. Dutt, in an open letter to Lord Curzon, ably urged the improvement of the ryot's position by the statutory limitation of the State demand to a definite share of the produce, extension of the term of settlement, enhancement of revenue on certain definite conditions only, such as increase in the price of crops, resort to civil courts to settle the ryot's objections to a new assessment,—in short an approach towards the conditions of the Permanent Settlement. The Viceroy fully reviewed the whole question and after negativing all the suggestions of Mr. Dutt, authorised certain reforms, among which were the following:—

(1) Assessments are not to be made, as formerly,

upon the basis of the *prospective* yield of the land during the coming period of settlement, but upon the *actual* yield at the time of assessment.

(2) The principle of exempting or allowing for improvements by the ryots should be further extended.

(3) Where the enhancements are large, they should be imposed on a progressive scale and spread over a number of years, in order to mitigate the hardship of a sudden rise. In Madras, the Settlement Code limits to 25 p. c. the enhancement which may be imposed at once, the balance being imposed by annual instalments, each not exceeding 12½ p. c. on the original assessment. In Bombay the maximum enhancement may not exceed double the former amount. [But in rapidly developing provinces like the C. P. and the Punjab, there is no such limit.]

(4) There should be *automatic remission* or reduction of the land revenue in years of failure of crop. The revenue *collection* should be more *elastic* in future, and promptly adjusted to the variations of the seasons and the circumstances of the people. This is necessary as the ryots are not provident enough to save in good years for bad years, and it is also difficult to forecast how many years of the coming lease will turn out bad.

(5) There should be a more general and prompt resort to reduction of assessments even during the course of the lease in cases of local deterioration, due to famines, epidemics and other causes which decrease the population.

By previous legislation and the general improvement of the administrative machinery, some other reforms had already been made, *viz.*—

(6) Where a tract was properly surveyed at the last settlement, and the old maps and village records have been punctually corrected and kept up to date, the measurements and records are usually accepted as valid at the new settlement, and local investigations and detailed surveys are not repeated, so that the ryots escape harassment and extortion.

(7) The methods of assessment have been simplified, and it now takes four years to re-settle an entire district, (as against eight years formerly).

(8) In Bombay a classification of soil made for the second time is accepted as final by law, and in many parts of Madras by custom.

The economic consequences of the chief Indian systems of land tenure.—

(A). *Permanent Settlement.*—The protection of the rights of the cultivators for which Government had stipulated with the zamindars in 1793, was long neglected, and has been secured by later legislation. The occupancy tenants of Bengal (who form 85 p. c. of the total number of cultivators) and the cultivating village owners of Bihar, now practically occupy the position of the peasant-proprietors of Europe, and are subject to the 'magic of property.' The first-named class enjoy the entire fruits of their labour and capital and always a certain portion at least, in practice the whole, of the unearned increment. They have every interest in improving their lands, and agriculture flourishes under them. Where illegal cesses are still levied by the zamindars, it is due to the corruption or weakness of the police, but cannot be called a necessary consequence of the Permanent Settlement. The vigilant care of magistrates is rendering such unauthorised extortion less frequent, in the same way as it is putting down dacoity and 'bad-livelihood.' Where a ryot is non-occupancy he cannot spend his capital on improvements, and industry is discouraged. But the zamindari system is theoretically favourable to agricultural improvement at the cost of the zamindar, because he is the permanent owner and can recover his outlay from the land. Moreover, zamindari estates being large in area, if a zamindar betakes himself to farming, he can derive all the advantages of production on a large scale, which is impossible in the small plots of the mahalwari and ryotwari areas. The Permanent Settlement by creating a rich and leisured class, has fostered the accumulation of capital, and large industries may be rendered possible in eastern India by the financial backing of zamindars. (See Gokhale's *Speeches*, 493.)

(B). & (C). *Mahalwari* and *Ryotwari Settlement.**—

* It is, I think, essentially wrong to class the *mahalwari* system with the *zamindari*. True, there are some bodies of villagers called by courtesy *zamindars*, with whom the land is settled by Government, and the actual cultivators are sometimes

Under this system, the State is a landowner with all the advantages of a monopolist. The competition among landlords for tenants which Ricardo's theory of rent presupposes, is wanting here, because there is only one landlord, *viz.*, the Government. (1) The ryot is at the mercy of the State-proprietor, and the rent here being a monopoly-rent must theoretically be an element in the price of agricultural produce. (2) Government lets the land only in very small plots, averaging 5 acres each, so that agriculture on a large scale is impossible, even when a capitalist is ready to undertake it. (3) The chance of enhancement of the revenue at every periodical settlement discourages industry and the investment of the ryot's capital in land. The ryot, having no right of property in his holding, has no inducement to become a devoted agriculturist. (4) Capital cannot accumulate from the pursuit of agriculture, because the bare subsistence is left to the ryots, and the surplus produce of the land is "swept

their tenants. But these so-called zamindars have not the power and rights of the Bengal zamindars; they have no permanent ownership, no guarantee against unfair enhancement of revenue at the end of 20 years, and their earthly providence, the Settlement Officer, is less in fear of the police and the District Magistrate than the Bengal zamindar is in dealing with *his* ryots. Moreover, the small size of their holdings weakens their defensive power. As Burke says, "The great masses of property......form a natural rampart about the lesser properties in all their gradations......Its defensive power is weakened as it is diffused." (*Reflections.*)

into the coffers of the State." (5) A revenue system administered by petty Government servants according to fixed rules, is sure to be inelastic, and the ryots are likely to be ruined by the strict enforcement of the State dues in years of famine, unless remission of revenue is promptly ordered by the head of the Government. On the whole, all Indian writers on the subject before the recent rise in the price of food-stuffs regard the ryot in these tracts as "a helpless and daily impoverished class, incapable of education, or effort to raise himself and without resisting power in distress." (Gokhale *Speeches*, 103, *Dutt* 492-495, *Ranade*, 276, 309). The official apologists deny it, and assert that the State takes less than half the economic rent or 'net assets,' leaving the other half to the cultivator in addition to the bare expenses of subsistence.—*Ind. Emp.*, iv. 234.) The subject will be further discussed in Chapter IX.

Foreign Capital.—The introduction of foreign capital during British rule has made India the home of many industries and conveniences which would have been utterly impossible without it; and the present economic development of the country and the wonderful growth of its foreign trade are almost entirely due to European capital and enterprise. The British capital alone invested in India has been roughly estimated at 700 *crores* of rupees (1909.) (1) The capital of the Indian railways could not have been raised in India. The guaranteed railways were financed by joint-stock companies formed in England, and much of the money sunk by the Government on the State Railways has been also raised there in the form of sterling loans. Without railways the coal of Raniganj could not have reached Calcutta and Cawnpur, and large steam factories would have been impossible. (2 & 3) Coal-mining and tea-farming originated entirely in European enterprise, though Indians have of late been largely taking to both of these. *Modern machinery* was originally introduced into India by European capitalists, and the organisation and *transport* of large numbers *of labourers* from their villages to factories or plantations is entirely a European creation in India. Steamers are almost exclusively owned by Europeans. In short, the modernisation of India described before has been due, after the action of the State, mainly to European capital and initiative. Indian capitalists are now joining in the work in increasing numbers. Examples of industries due to European capital will be given in Chapter V.

The political relations of India and England and their effect on the balance of trade.—

India is a dependency of Great Britain. In consequence of her dependent political position, she has to employ a large number of high English officers,—('the *corps d'elite* must be European', as Lord Curzon said,) —and a strong garrison of British troops, (which numbered 80,581 in 1911). The pension of all these and their savings while in service in India are sent to England. The English cannot breed and multiply in India. They have to send their children above four years of age to Home for education; a large part of the father's income (sometimes amounting to three-fourths) is remitted to England for maintaining the young ones there. In one year (1910) above 13,800 European soldiers came to India from abroad and 12,000 were sent back to England or British Africa. Very often these numbers have been exceeded. India has to pay their transport expenses. She also pays the recruiting and depot charges in England for the annual reliefs of white troops sent to India, the number of which has increased under the modern short service system.

Then, again, certain classes of Indians have to pay England a large amount of what may be called 'boarding charges' and also the price of status. Under Government rules, offices of the highest position and salary in our land are filled in England only. A candidate has to be "recruited in England" if he is to draw full pay. But if with the very same qualifications he is "recruited in India," his salary undergoes a depreciation of 33 to 50 p. c. The distinction applies even to men trained in England: an Oxford graduate selected in England for an Indian college starts with Rs. 500 a month; but if he is appointed to the same chair *in India* he gets Rs. 333 as. 5 pies 4 only. [In Bengal the amount is lower still, Rs. 250.]

Even for certain private professions, an English status is exacted in the highest rank. By the Charter Act of 1774 nobody can plead in the Original Side of our High Courts unless he is a barrister. It is not contended that a newly-called barrister knows even half as much law as a newly-passed vakil. There is no *guarantee* that an Indian barrister will at least acquire a superior knowledge of the English language as the result of his sojourn in England.* A call to the English bar is, therefore, no indication of merit; it merely represents a status which is necessitated by the Charter Act of 1774, passed in the infancy of British rule in India. Since then nearly a century and a half have passed, and India has now thousands of sons who have received the highest modern education at home; but their disability continues. A Rash Bihari Ghosh or a Muthuswamy Aiyar cannot appear before the Original Side, and even in other courts he must subside into a junior as soon as a barrister joins him. Every Indian who wishes to practise law consistently with self-respect and profit is, therefore, driven by the Charter Act to go to England, live there for three years, and pay an

* I know an Indian barrister who pleads in Urdu because he cannot express himself in English. Another Indian barrister, innocent of humour, puzzled the Judge of Patna by invariably speaking of "*the he-cock*" when he meant *Mr.* Heycock, I. C. S. A third Indian barrister (B. A. Oxon!) uses the preposition *about* after the transitive verb *concern*.

English Inn £170. Each barrister represents at least Rs. 10,000 sent out of India, for which we do not get our money's worth in the shape of a legal knowledge unattainable in India. As the professional education of a Vakil does not cost more than Rs. 600, there is relatively a great waste of money in turning out a barrister instead of a vakil, even if we grant that the former does not know less law than the latter. The total amount which India has paid to England on the barristers practising in our country is enormous. In a single year (1908) more than sixty Indians were called to the bar in England. Early in 1910, three hundred Indians are said to have left a single province (the Punjab) to "eat their terms" in London.

Nearly all the capital of the Indian railways and the sterling loan of the Government came from England, and the interest on them has be to sent there. Many European companies working and earning money in India have their head offices in England, and their profits have to be sent there for the payment of dividend.

The English law of copyright is in force in India, and we have to pay the European prices of many books which we might otherwise have cheaply reprinted here. A self-governing country like the United States did not allow copyright to foreigners till 20 years ago, and volumes of Ruskin selling in England for a guinea or more, were reprinted in America for half a dollar each. The continental nations can buy English books very cheaply in Tauchnitz's pirated edition. But India has to pay nearly half a *crore* annually as the price of books imported from Europe.

The result of these political and economic causes is that India is in the position of *a debtor country i.e.*, her payments or exports must exceed her receipts or imports. The net excess of our exports now reaches about 24 *crores* of rupees a year. This is a permanent state of affairs, and its economic effects are the following:—

(*a*) India, in the present undeveloped state of her industries, parts with raw materials to pay her debt abroad. The profit on agricultural produce is smaller and relatively less certain than that generally made in manufacture, which is more dependent on human skill and less on Nature. Thus India would have been a loser even if her exports had balanced her imports. (*b*) Manufactured articles being much smaller in bulk than raw materials of the same price, Indian exporters have to pay far more in freight than European importers into India. Thus the cost price of an Indian export is increased when it reaches the consumer in a greater degree than is the case with the manufactured foreign goods which we import. This causes a heavy financial loss to our producers whose market is thus comparatively restricted. (*c*) As more goods go out of India than come to it, the ships carrying Indian exports abroad cannot get full cargoes on their return voyage, the so the exports from India have to pay very high rates, amounting to nearly 1½ times the freight paid by our imports bulk for bulk. India as a debtor country has to bear this burden. (*d*) From the national point of view, the raw materials, especially grain, constitute the very means of nourishing the people, and these we have to part with, whereas if we could have exported manufactures (which are mostly luxuries) the nation's loss would have been less. (*e*) The money represented by the excess of our exports over our imports goes out of the country altogether, instead of remaining here to increase our capital and nourish our industries. There is, therefore, an annual drain from India to this amount. Relatively to the past, India is no poorer, because the European capital and the labour of European officers, which are paid for by this excess of exports, have increased our production by many times the amount of the drain. But from the point of view of abstract theory, there would have been no drain and this money would have remained here, if all our capitalists had been Indians and all our officers had made India their home, as was the case during Mughal rule.

CHAPTER IV.

CONSUMPTION.

The nature and progress of consumption.— Consumption is the ultimate aim of all economic activity; men produce only in the hope of consuming either immediately or in future, (which latter is called saving). Consumption is of two kinds, *viz.*, productive and unproductive. Unproductive consumption ends only in the destruction of the thing consumed, while productive consumption cannot strictly be called consumption at all, but it is only a means of the production of new wealth; for example, sowing seed is productive activity and not really consumption. Consumption by man, or the satisfying of human wants, is the last stage of the economic process; at all previous stages the wealth was still being produced, *i. e.*, it was being merely consumed in a lower form and then reproduced in a higher. Spending is benefical only when it causes a transfer of wealth from relatively unproductive channels to more productive ones. The rich man exerts a great influence on productive activity because he can, by regulating his expenditure, decide which industries should flourish and which not.

As the result of the well-known laws of consumption, the articles which we use may be classified thus :—

(1) Our primitive *animal wants*, namely food, drink and clothing, are the first in point of time. (But our capacity for food is limited in amount). (2) Articles which satisfy our craving for *distinction* are next in importance. We wish to have things other than the barely necessary ones or the most ordinary kinds of food and clothing, *i.e.*, we desire lavish hospitality, extravagance in dress, etc. (3) We desire *variety* even in satisfying our animal cravings; the same kind of food palls upon our taste after a time owing to monotony, and we like to eat different dishes in different seasons or holidays. (4) With the growth of civilisation and mental culture each individual desires greater *house-room* and privacy for carrying on intellectual work without disturbance, as distinct from mere protection from sun and rain, which is a primitive need. (5) We have an ever increasing number of *wants resulting from our activities*, physical and mental. For example, athletic games are pursued, and novels, dramas and art-works are studied for their own sake, as the result of man's over-flowing activity; and these very soon come to be regarded as necessary things, *i.e.*, they are felt as wants. Such is the progressive nature of man that in a healthy state new activities prepare the way for new wants, instead of our activities resulting from our wants as a means of gratifying the latter. In short, though the wants of the uncivilised man are nearly the same as those of animals, every step in our progress increases the variety of our

wants, and also the variety of our methods of satisfying those wants, *i.e.*, we desire not only larger quantities, but better qualities or a greater choice of things. (*Marshall*, i. 161-164).

The Indian standard of comfort as determining Indian consumption.—Nearly three-fourths of the Indian people are directly or indirectly dependent on agriculture. The Indian peasant is "the most frugal in the world." He lives in a thatched or tiled hut with walls of mud or plaited straw. His wants are very few, and they are supplied by the local artisans and menials whom he sometimes pays with a share of the harvest. Religious prejudices also stand in the way of many classes of the Indians using several foreign commodities, such as soap, prepared food, leather goods other than shoes, &c. Thanks to our warm climate, our need of clothing is reduced by Nature to the minimum consistent with decency. The Indian standard of comfort is very low, and the consumption of imported articles is extremely limited. As a European observer has remarked, "Why the Indians live is the question ever forcing itself for answer. It is not that they may enjoy food: all that they eat is some coarse grain.........It is not for pleasure: all their enjoyment is a pilgrimage." In rural India, nine-tenths of the population live by tillage or cattle-keeping, and nearly the whole of their income is spent on the necessaries of life (the demand for which is naturally inelastic). It is impossible for them to buy any luxury, home-made or foreign, except the cheapest,—and that too they can buy only when brought to their doors. Even in our cities one-twelfth of the people are dependent on agriculture and two-fifths on the preparation and supply of material substances. Taking India as a whole, only one person in 26 is engaged in commerce, (or, including dependants, one in 17). This clearly shows to what a large extent our wants are supplied locally, and how few articles made in distant places are needed by us. The Indian consumption can increase only with a rise in the standard of comfort, that is, if the people spend their earnings on better dwellings, and on food and clothing of larger quantity and higher quality. Among many classes of people, the few who save anything continue to live in the same style as their ancestors and caste-brethren, and merely hoard their wealth, instead of spending it to rise to a higher standard of life, because such a rise would mean social isolation, as in India, unlike Europe, the rich do not form a caste by themselves. The life of the average Indian corresponds to the standard of abject poverty in a rich European country like England. (*Ind. Emp.*, iii. 269).

Classification of Indian consumption.—An attempt is made below to arrange the articles of Indian consumption in the order of decreasing demand, beginning with the lowest rank of the people and the most widely used things:

I. *Grain*, *salt*, cotton-*cloth*, and earthen pots and dishes,—the barest necessaries of life, which all consume. Also the inevitable jug for every family. It is called a *lotah* among the Hindus and a *badhna* or *áftábáh* (the latter having a spout) among the Muslims, and is usually made of brass, the Muhammadans preferring copper.

II. Intoxicants and stimulants, especially *tobacco* which may almost be placed in class I, as nearly every one smokes, even the poorest, both male and female. The common *huqqa* or pipe is the symbol of caste-brotherhood, and a man's exclusion from the communal pipe is a sign of his being outcasted (*huqqa pani band*). The next intoxicant in popularity is *toddy* or palm-juice. *Bhang* and opium may be bracketed together as a bad third. (In Bombay and Bengal *tea* is rapidly advancing to a place in this class). Oil, sugar, sweets, kitchen-vegetables, and, in Bengal and Madras, fish. Advancing still higher we have a few metal utensils, (*viz.*, cooking pots, dishes and cups), the Hindus using brass and the Muhammadans tinned copper. *Lac* bangles for women.

III. Next come extra articles of apparel such as coats, umbrellas, wrappers or "German shawls" (really made of jute), shoes; canvas bags (a great favourite), furniture (only bedsteads), boxes, a more extensive service of metal untensils; *tea* (in towns); *ghee*, meat and other richer food stuffs; silver ornaments for women and chidren; cheap priestly ministration.

IV. Better houses; steel trunks; a few gold ornaments; luxuries like soap and scents; cheap gramophones; pilgrimages; *pujahs* on a more showy scale.

V. The luxuries of the upper classes, which need no description.

The above list requires some explanation and qualification. Among the poorer classes in the plains woollen clothing is not worn even in severe winter. But in most parts of India outside Bengal, the bodice is as essential a part of the female dress as the *sari*. In Upper India, again, shoes are put on by all classes above the lowest, but they are treasured by the poor as a luxury, and on long journeys carried slung from a pole, the owner going bare-footed, because Nature will repair any damage done to our feet but will not give us the price of a new pair of shoes! Socks are not worn in the plains even in winter, except by youngmen who have degenerated by receiving an English education. Outside Bengal even the upper middle classes do not put on socks, except on ceremonial occasions. Silver ornaments are not entirely a sacrifice to feminine vanity; they are the safest means of investment known to villagers and town-labourers. "The poor man's wife is his bank; on her person he hangs his savings." In all famines before the closing of our mints to the free coinage of silver, women's ornaments largely came to the mints for conversion into rupees. Our country being tropical, the ostentation dear to the feminine heart takes the form of ornaments and not that of new fashions in dress.

Rising standard of life.—As the result of British rule and contact with Western civilisation, a rise in the standard of comfort is steadily taking place in India, though the change is most striking in Burma. Everywhere Indians are building better houses, and even the peasants of Bengal have begun to wear coats and use cloth umbrellas. (But outside Bengal, Burma, and the Punjab, the peasants and rural labourers do not seem to have been affected by the improvement in any great degree.) Many servants, petty traders and artisans of the towns now take ærated waters and ice on occasions. The habit of drinking tea is very rapidly spreading, the number of its consumers among our people probably doubled twice during the last 10 years. Within our own observation the use of gold ornaments has extended to classes which formerly wore silver. Our ladies certainly encumber themselves with fewer ornaments than their grandmothers, but what they do wear is mainly of gold. We imported, in 1913, two millions of umbrellas, besides 32 *lakhs* of rupees worth of umbrella fittings from which 8½ millions more of umbrellas were manufactured here. The increase in the number and circulation of our newspapers, the deluge of monthly magazines in every province, the large annual output of vernacular books and their enhanced price as compared with similar works of a decade ago, all illustrate the rise in our standard.

Another noticeable feature is the rapidly increasing consumption of tailor-made suits. In most towns the tailors have their hands full of work, especially in winter. The costly shawls of old—which however, only a few men could buy,—have gone out of fashion. Hindu friendly dinners, especially in Bengal, are now usually conducted in a style which formerly marked the richest classes only. (Our import of shoes and boots more than quadrupled from 1900 to 1914, the figures being 7 and 33 *lakhs* of pairs respectively. The import of tobacco, mainly cigarettes, leaped up from $3\frac{3}{4}$ to $7\frac{1}{3}$ million lbs. between 1900 and 1909.

The circulation of newspapers in Northern India probably doubled between 1906 and 1915 on account of the introduction of cash sale in the mufassil towns (where previously they used to be subscribed for a year and brought by post individually) and the reduction of price to half an anna by the *Indian Daily News* and the *Bengalee* and to one anna by all the other dailies except one. This low price and the hawking of the papers at one's doors have created a taste for newspapers throughout our middle class and much of the lower middle class.

The Indian villager is not immovably conservative or abstemious. He is quite ready to adopt a new thing, when he has seen its usefulness with his own eyes. In rural Bengal, owing to the frequency of fires and the difficulty of supporting tiled roofs on bamboo structures (—timber being very scarce), the use of corrugated iron sheets for roofing has very rapidly extended during the last ten years. During the same period, too, Dietz Junior Lanterns, on account of the superior white light they yield, have sold by the million every year ; in the towns all over India almost every man, and in the Bengal villages half the families have bought one of these. Cloth umbrellas have become universal in rural Bengal, replacing the old ones made of leaves.

The standard of living is being raised in our society mainly through the children. People clothe their sons and daughters in a more costly style (particularly in garments of a European cut and patent leather boots), feed them on more varied things, and indulge them in far more luxuries than they themselves had been accustomed to in *their* own childhood. Many parents of the lower middle class stint themselves in order to please or even pamper their young ones. I know of a poor priest who goes about in slippers, buying boots and a tricycle for his little boy ! But the luxuries of one generation become the necessaries of the next. The children thus petted, when they grow up refuse to return to the simple style of their forefathers,—which passes away for ever, and the general standard for the *whole* society is thus raised one step. This process is going on in almost every home, and spreading rapidly from town to country.

It has been found by a careful study of figures in Europe and America, that, as the income of a family increases, a smaller percentage of it is spent on food, while the proportional expenditures for clothing and rent remain the same. But the percentage spent on education, health and amusement rises constantly with the income. The new tendency is most observable among our middle class, professional men, town artisans and tradesmen, and along the railways; though among the common people the increase of consumption is, naturally, slight and slow owing to the low state of poverty from which they are gradually emerging.

Luxury means the gratification of a superfluous want. But it need not be condemned in every case, as our orthodox people and conservative writers seem inclined to do. Even the poorest might have a little of the superfluous, otherwise his life would be no better than that of a beast of burden. Every new want was in its origin superfluous, and, if it had been then suppressed as a luxury, society would have remained in its primitive barbarism. Luxury is condemnable only when it degenerates into wastefulness, *i.e.*, a disproportion between the amount of social labour consumed and the degree of individual satisfaction obtained, or in other words, when the consumer of the article of luxury does not contribute to social progress. (*Gide*, 673).

The rise in our standard of comfort must produce far-reaching consequences in society. (1) Thanks to the caste system and the altruistic religions of India, our poor had so long lived on voluntary alms. The census of 1911 returned 33 *lakhs* of professional beggars, or a little over one p. c. of the population. Now that every man is called upon to spend more on himself, he will have less to spend on charity, and in the no very distant future we must have a department of poor relief maintained by the State on the proceeds of compulsory taxation. (2) The people must be prepared to work harder than their forefathers, as they cannot live on the same low income which sufficed for the latter. Every man must now make himself a more efficient wage-earner or he will starve. Those who are not willing to do either of these two things. will naturally swell the ranks of criminals. (3) The joint family will be broken up, as it is becoming increasingly difficult for the head of a household to maintain the drones. (4) The age of marriage must rise with us, and we must gradually approach the European standard in which a man marries only when he has the income necessary for bringing up a family. As a natural consequence of this, a certain portion of the population must live and die in celibacy. (5) A readjustment of our wants and a modification of our social manners and mode of private life, are bound to take place. Such changes imperceptibly go on in every age; but the impact of European civilisation on our society will make these changes in our midst revolutionary in character. The relative importance of our different luxuries (and even of some necessaries) will be altered, and many things valued by our forefathers will be rejected by us altogether. (6) Our home producers must change the nature of their old business altogether in order to supply these new needs, as, in many cases, their time-honoured manufactures will cease to have any demand whatever in modern India.

A rise in the standard of comfort is a blessing only when it teaches the people to live in more sanitary houses, eat and dress in a more nourishing style, and elevate their daily life by the introduction of refinement and intellectual delights,—in short, when they are impelled to put forth greater exertions and raise themselves to a higher grade of workers than before. We must, however, take care to remember that in the case of many of our people, both rich and poor, what looks like an improvement in the standard of living is not really the adoption of a more expensive style, but only a *rearrangement* of life's enjoyments, their *total expenditure remaining the same* as before but being distributed in a different manner among the various articles of consumption. For example, everywhere around us we see tea-drinking increasing and the consumption of *ghee* disappearing; ærated waters are displacing more primitive but certainly more substantial luncheons.

Average consumption in India and England.— In the case of India the statistics are often mere rough estimates, and for several commodities the necessary information is altogether wanting. The annual consumption in the United Kingdom for 1906 is the average for 1905-7 given in Webb's *New Dictionary of Statistics*, 1911, occasionally supplemented by the *Statesman's Year Book*, 1908 and the *Review of the Trade of India*, 1911.

Average annual consumption per head of the population :

United Kingdom.			India, 1911.
Meat (1906)	117	lbs.	
Wheat, barley, oats and maize	15·7	bushels	
Coffee	0·67	lbs.	
Cocoa	1·02	,,	
Tobacco	1·97	,,	cigarettes imported 2·3 ,, manufactured 9·5
Sugar (import) ...	88	,,	24.26 lbs.
Salt (for all purposes)...	72	,,	12·5 lbs.
Clothing	67·8	,,	10¾ yds.
Alcoholic liquors ...	29	gallons	one-fifteenth gallon (including non-potable spirits)
Expenditure on liquor (1911)	£ 3-10-9		
Tea (1911)	6·47	lbs.	one-nineteenth lb.
Imports of merchandise (1911)	£ 14	16s.	5s. 10½d.
Total volume of foreign trade (1911)	£ 24	13	15s. 6d.

Statistics of Indian consumption.

(*a*) *Food articles:*

(1) *Salt*—The consumption has steadily risen year by year with the lowering of the tax on salt. In 1902 each person in India used 10 lbs. only, but the amount was 12·5 lbs. in 1911 and 13·4 lbs. in 1914. In the United Kingdom the consumption of salt per head, including what is used in manufacture, was 72 lbs. in 1906. In 1911 our estimated total consumption was 1,759,606 tons (out of which 563,984 tons or *nearly one-third was imported*). This amount, distributed over a population of 315 millions, gives 12·5 lbs. per head. With some negligible exceptions all the Feudatory States get their salt from British India.

(2) *Sugar*—To a vegetarian people like the majority of the Hindus, sugar is the only luxury among articles of food. It enters largely into the composition of confectionery, huge quantities of which are eaten by Hindus, Muhammadans, Indian Christians and even Eurasians at birth, marriage, funeral and other ceremonies and at social dinners, besides forming the daily luncheon of the professional classes and students in towns. That its consumption has greatly increased we can infer from the increased importation of foreign sugar, which has more than doubled in the last 10 years, rising from $5\frac{1}{4}$ million cwt. in 1900 to $12\frac{1}{4}$ million cwt. in 1911 and 18 mil. in 1913, while the export of Indian sugar is very small. Though no reliable statistics are available,

"there is reason to believe that [all] India now produces about 3 million tons of [raw] cane-sugar." (Noel Paton.) Adding to this the 412,400 tons of foreign sugar imported and retained in 1911, we get an average consumption of 24·26 lbs. per head (including both refined sugar and molasses). We also manufacture a fair amount of unrefined sugar from the juice of the date-palm, but it may be set off against the export of sugar from India by land, which I have not taken into my calculation.

(b) Drink:

(1) *Tea*—The habit of drinking tea has very rapidly spread among our upper and middle classes, and even among the labourers in the cities (particularly in Bombay and the Punjab), and also along the railways. It is almost universal among the hillmen of the Himalayas. In 1911 we consumed about one-nineteenth lb. per head according to the following calculation:

Tea produced		268,854,000 lbs.
„ imported by sea		6,611,000 „
„ „ „ land worth Rs. 18 *lakhs* = say		2,428,000 „
		277,893,000
Deduct		
Exported by sea	260,778,000	
Re-exported by sea and land ...	758,000	
		261,536,000
Total consumption in India ...		16,357,000, or ·052 lb. per head.

(2) *Liquor*—In India there is one liquor-shop to every 2,400 persons, while in England the proportion of public-houses to the population is ten times as great. The average annual consumption of *country* distilled intoxicating liquors in 1902 was (*Ind. Emp.*, iv. 257)—

Punjab	...	14 gallons *per 1000 persons*
Burma	...	10 ,, ,,
Bombay	...	127 ,, ,,

1911.

Import of foreign liquors		...	6,144,417 gallons
Produced by Indian breweries (malt liquors)	...	...	4,083,806 ,,
Spirits issued from Indian distilleries	...	...	10,092,139 ,,
Total	...	...	20,320,362 ,,

or an annual consumption of about $\frac{1}{15}$ of a gallon (exactly 0·065 gallon) per head, *i.e.*, 65 gallons per thousand of the population. In the above computation, the spirits, both foreign and home-distilled, include not only liquors but also methylated and perfumed spirits which are not drunk.

The habit of drinking is rapidly increasing among the labourers in the Bombay Presidency and the peasants and workmen of the Punjab. Among the upper classes of our society those who have adopted a European style of life have (with some exceptions) lost our old aversion to drinking. But among the middle class people education has roused social opinion against the consumption of intoxicants even by classes and castes which have been long using them.

(3) *Hemp-drugs* and *opium*—Certain numerous classes of Indians (especially of a lower rank) consume these intoxicants, though their use is rare in England. In 1902 our average annual consumption *per 1000 of the population* was (*Ind. Emp.*, iv. 244 & 261)—

		Hemp-drugs.	*Opium.*
Bombay	... ...	7·5 *seers*	2·4 *seers*
U. P.	... ...	9 „	1·3 „
Madras	... ...	1·2 „	1·1 „
Assam	... ...	—	8·8 „

The import of *cigarettes* in 1911 has been estimated from the weight as 2·3 (numbers) per head of the population. The local manufacture of cigarettes in Bengal and Bihar (1910) was considered to have been about 3000 millions, or 9·5 per head.

(*c*) **Clothing**—In 1911 we used 10¾ yds. of cloth per head.

Imported woollen piecegoods	...	24·00 mill. yds.
Imported cotton piecegoods	...	2,437·89 „ „
Indian mill piecegoods retained for home consumption	... ...	1,020·28 „ „
		3,482·17 „ „
Deduct re-export of imported piecegoods, worth 169 *lakhs* of Rs. or 4 p. c. of the total import=say,	... ...	97·51 „ „
Total consumption by 315 mill. persons	...	3,384·66 „ „

The above list does not take into account the silk cloths, cotton handkerchiefs and shawls (imported and home-made) and the woollen goods woven in the country for local consumption. (The woollen fabrics that we export are rugs and carpets and not clothing.) If we include the production of our hand-looms, which is roughly guessed at 1650 mil. yds. for cotton goods, our *average* consumption per head will rise to about 16 yds.

(*d*) **Gold and Silver.**—In 1911 India absorbed 1*s.* 9*d.* 3½ farthing worth of gold and silver per head, without taking into account the importation of treasure on behalf of Government; if we take the average of the three years 1909—11, our consumption of treasure was 1*s.* 6*d.*, whereas in England in 1908 it was 2*s.* 5½*d.* per head of the population.

India, 1911.

Gold (private) imported ...		£27·66 mil.
Silver " " ...		7·95 "
		35·61
Deduct Gold exported	£2·48	
Silver "	4·42	
		6·90
Net absorption by 315 million persons		28·71

(*e*) **Other things.**—The use of *umbrellas* is extending, and though the importation of foreign umbrellas has greatly declined during the last decade, a busy local manufacture from imported umbrella-fittings has sprung up. In 1913 we imported 19·6 *lakhs* of separate umbrellas; the 32 *lakhs* of Rupees worth of umbrella-fittings imported that year produced something like 85 *lakhs* of umbrellas; so that our total was 105 *lakhs* or *one umbrella for every 30 persons.* In 1913 *books* were imported to the value of 49½ *lakhs* of Rupees, *paper* and *paste-board* 150 *lakhs*, and *stationery* 70 *lakhs*,—making a total of 270 *lakhs* of Rupees. In addition to this we used 81·37 *lakhs* worth of paper produced by our own mills (1910). Our annual *cousumption of paper* is 75,000 tons, or half a lb. *per head.* We printed 12,189 *books* in 1913 (against 8,036 in 1900), while the total copies of *newspapers* sent through the Indian post-offices increased from 32 millions in 1900 to 56·4 millions in 1913. Besides these a large but unknown number of copies is delivered by messengers or sent by book packet or railway parcel. The Indian demand for paper is very rapidly growing, and our mills are utterly unable to meet it. *Boots* and *shoes* are being worn, especially by the young, in increasing numbers: in 1914 we imported 33 *lakhs* of pairs, against only 7 *lakhs* in 1900, besides keeping an army of shoe-makers busy at work in the different towns of India. The importation of *hardware* and *cutlery* doubled in value from 1899 to 1907, that of *machinery* from 1903 to 1908, and that of *tobacco* from 1900 to 1907. Our import of *cigarettes* rose from 23½ *lakhs* of Rupees worth in 1902 to 51 *lakhs* in 1911.

CHAPTER V.

PRODUCTION.

The economics of a mainly agricultural country as opposed to those of a mainly manufacturing country.

1. An agricultural country, if it is old, suffers from the *Law of Diminishing Return*, *i.e.*, every additional dose of labour and capital produces a less proportion of goods. In India, especially, owing to the ignorance and indebtedness of the ryots, "the exhaustion of the soil is fast proceeding, the cropping is becoming more and more inferior, and the crop-yield per acre, already the lowest in the world, is declining still further." (Gokhale's *Speeches*, p. 178). But recent investigations by the Agricultural Department have shown that many of the old fields have reached a low stationary degree of fertility and cannot possibly deteriorate, while the newly cultivated soils alone are declining in productivity. A manufacturing country, on the other hand, has the advantage of the *Law of Increasing Return*. The price of the raw material forms only a part of the cost of manufactured articles. Manufactures are far more susceptible of mechanical improvements, labour-saving contrivances, and division of labour, than agriculture is. Hence, in a manufacturing country an increase of demand often lowers

the proportional cost of production and secures to the country the advantages of production on a large scale. On the contrary, in an old agricultural country an increase of demand raises the cost of production, *i.e.*, it raises the price of food. The people, therefore, must work harder, or eat less, or obtain their usual food by sacrificing a part of their other customary comforts. (*Mill*, p. 118). But where the people have an unlimited supply of virgin soil, as in Canada, an increase in the demand may actually cheapen agricultural produce by causing the replacement of hand labour by machinery.

2. In agriculture there is much greater dependence on Nature, *e.g.*, fertility of soil, sufficient rainfall, absence of hail-storms and floods, &c., than is the case in manufacture, or in other words, agriculture is far more precarious than industry.

3. In a manufacturing country an increase of the labouring population lowers wages and cheapens production in the same proportion. But in an old agricultural country an increase of the population means that more mouths have to be fed and resort must be had to worse soil. Agriculture, therefore, becomes less efficient and more costly in proportion to the extension of the margin of cultivation.

4. Manufacture requires higher skill and greater brain-power than agriculture, *i.e.*, the former calls forth general ability and tends to raise the workmen to a higher standard of comfort than agriculture,

which keeps the people dull, conservative and without any means of improving their lot by taking up a higher grade of work. Manufacturing hands are mostly artisans, and therefore form a higher and richer class than the peasants who are hardly better than common labourers. The various branches of agriculture differ from one another in general character less than the branches of manufacture do. But agriculture has made little progress because "the most enterprising agriculturists drift towards the town; those who stay behind live more or less isolated lives. The minds of villagers have always been more staid than those of townsmen and less ready to follow new paths....The chief agricultural improvements have been made by landlords who have associated a good deal with townsmen and by manufacturers in trades subsidiary to agriculture." (*Marshall*, 737-738). But in manufacture most of the inventions and new contrivances have been the work of men actually engaged in it. We must, therefore, discard the belief common in India that factory labourers are a brutalised set of drudges while the peasants lead an idyllic life of purity, freedom and comfort. The densest ignorance and the most unrelieved toil often go with agriculture, and certain kinds of vice prevail as much in the country as in towns.

5. Agricultural capital and labour are immobile, while manufacture, by compelling the congregation of labour in one place, makes it easy for workmen to

escape the loss from a decaying industry by going over to a more profitable one. In manufacture, general ability and even several kinds of mechanical skill (except the purely technical) are transferable from one industry to another. But the capital locked up in the plant is often entirely lost, when that particular industry is abandoned.

6. Agriculture cannot be a localised industry, *i.e.*, increase of business in agriculture means *increase of area*, or the addition of more fields. Not so in manufacture, where an increase of business only means that more raw materials are to be brought to the *same place* for being worked up and that the same machines are to run for more hours than before.

7. High specialisation is possible in manufacture but not in agriculture, because workers on land are compelled by differences of season to raise *different* crops instead of confining themselves to one branch of their trade throughout the year as manufacturers can do.

From 6 and 7 it follows that the economics of production on a large scale are not quite similar in the case of agriculture and manufacture. (*Marshall*, p. 738).

8. In agriculture, co-operation is very difficult, but the opposite is the case in manufacture. Hence, even supposing the intelligence and industry of the workmen to be the same in both cases, labour must be less efficient in agriculture than in manufacture. (*Marshall*, p. 743).

9. It is commonly asserted that in an agricultural country the people are benefited by an increase in the price of grain. Such a general statement requires much correction and modification. First, if the appreciation of food-grain has been attended by a corresponding diminution of the yield, the peasants are no better off than before. Secondly, all labourers (including those employed in tillage and pasture) who do not receive their wages in kind, suffer a loss if their money wages are not raised in exact proportion to the increase in the price of food. Thirdly, the benefit of high price with an undiminished crop-yield is ultimately enjoyed by the landowner, and the vast majority of actual cultivators derive no profit from it unless they are proprietors of the land and have to pay fixed rents,—which is not always the case in India. Lastly, if the other necessaries and comforts of life appreciate in proportion to the dear bread,—as most of them are bound to do in the long run, though not in the same proportion,—even the landowner's *real* wealth is not increased to the extent of the enhanced price of grain. But where an old *money contract* (such as a debt) of a *fixed* amount has to be discharged, the repayment under the new conditions involves the rural debtor in a smaller sacrifice, because he has to part with a smaller store of grain to get the same number of Rupees as before. Also, in proportion as the appreciated grain is sold in *foreign* countries, the wealth of the producing land is increased, provided

that its imports do not also rise in price. In practice it is often found that the high price of food grains merely causes an increase in the *money* currency and not a proportionate increase in the *real* wealth of the producing country. The benefit of dear bread to an agricultural country is, therefore, mostly illusive *in the long run*. The appreciation of manufactures which are not among the prime necessaries of life, does not inflict the same wide-spread hardship on the producing country as dear bread does on an agricultural land, and in the former case the main portion of the increase of the national wealth resulting from the higher price may possibly be contributed by foreign consumers. But dear bread is sure to afflict some—possibly even a majority,—of the home population, because *every* man is a consumer of it. Over-production is possible in most manufactures but not in agriculture, because there is an almost infinite power of expansion in the demand for food-stuffs over all the world collectively.

Correlation between agriculture and Industry.—No agriculture can be really productive which is divorced from a neighbouring non-agricultural market, represented by thriving towns and cities. In the absence of such *near* markets, the next available substitute is a large export trade to foreign countries; but the latter is not very desirable, as it cannot fully take the place of the former. (*List*, 127). If an old country like India exports food, it proves that her industry is in a backward condition, because her capital, and consequently population also, have not increased sufficiently to make food rise to a higher price. (*Mill*, 120). "The productive power of the cultivator and of the labourer in agriculture will always be greater or smaller according to the degree in which the exchange of agricultural produce for manufactures...can proceed more or less readily...... ...A nation which has already made considerable advances in civilisation, in possession of capital and in population, will find the *development of a manufacturing power* of its own, *infinitely* more *beneficial to its agriculture*, than the most flourishing foreign trade can be without such manufactures, because it thereby secures itself against all fluctuations to which it may be exposed by war, by foreign restrictions on trade, and by commercial crises, because it thereby saves the greatest part of the costs of transport, because [at home] improvements in transport are called into existence by its own manufacturing industry, while from the same cause a mass of personal and natural powers hitherto unemployed will be developed, and especially because the reciprocal exchange between manufacturing power and agricultural power is so much greater, the closer the agriculturist and manufacturer are to one another and the less they are liable to be interrupted in the exchange of their various products by accidents of all kinds". (*List*, 127). "A nation which possesses merely agriculture and merely the most indispensable industries, is in want of the first and most necessary division of commercial operations among its inhabitants, and of the most important half of its productive powers". (*List*, 124 ; see *Jones*, 51 and 145).

Special conditions of land, labour, and capital as affecting Indian production.

Land.—In India agriculture is the main industry of the people, but even in this branch production is greatly limited by (*a*) the ignorance of the peasant, (*b*) the lack of agricultural capital, and (*c*) the small size of the holdings. Indeed, many of the evil effects of the Irish cottier tenancy are to be met with in India. Owing to the indebtedness and helplessness of the ryots and the absence of modern manuring and scientific agriculture the production per acre has greatly decreased and the soil in many places has reached its lowest limit of productivity. The food supply cannot be quickly increased to meet a new demand. Moreover, in large tracts of the country agriculture depends for the necessary water on rainfall which is uncertain and often insufficient.

In the first chapter we have considered the physical conditions and climate of India and their bearings on production.

Labour.—Indian labourers vary so greatly according to differences of race and province that every general remark about them is subject to many qualifications and exceptions, though a common Indian stamp is unmistakably evident on their character.

Our *artisans* are capable of acquiring the greatest skill and can quickly learn almost any art, however new, delicate or foreign to their habits. The *peasants* are most industrious and patient, especially in Bihar, whose ryots have hardly any equal elsewhere in steadiness, diligence and self-reliance. But in the pestiferous climate of Bengal and Assam they have grown rather languid and fond .of repose. The labourers of Bombay and Upper India are stong and hard-working. Though dishonest to strangers in the matter of cheating at purchases and pilfering stores, our workmen are remarkably honest as regards *money*: among our many thousand postmen and mail runners, who are only one or two grades above the commonest labourers, very few cases of misappropriation occur in any year. All except a small minority of Indian workmen are free from the drunkenness and gambling habit which disgrace and incapacitate labourers in Europe. (Here drinking is often the effect of caste traditions and not of occupation.) Except in tasks requiring prolonged muscular exertion and concentration of attention, they are very patient and persevering at their accustomed slow rate. But Indian labourers in general have two great defects: they are not reliable, and they do not habitually follow any standard of good workmanship. They are constitutionally negligent and prone to idleness and slackness, and cannot, in the absence of supervision, be trusted to work hard, to take care of their tools and materials, and to display the best standard of workmanship of which they are capable. They may be called *dishonest* in the sense of lacking steadiness and reliability and of not being fit to be left to themselves. Hence, Indian labour, in spite of its seeming abundance and cheapness, is inefficient and dear in the long run, as the cost of supervision is very high. (See *Morison*, 182). Speaking of our *common labourers* we may say that they have no desire of accumulation, no ambition to rise to a higher scale of life by superior exertion, no pride in their work or generous ambition to beat other nations by the excellent quality of their production, (such as characterise English labourers). This adverse remark does not, however, apply to all of our artisans. The Indian villagers are good at agriculture of the primitive kind, but they cannot be easily turned into factory-hands or miners. Already the Indian mines have absorbed the entire available mining labour of the country. Our most easily available class of labourers are landless villagers who form the lowest rank of unskilled workmen. They are unsuited to the needs of manufacture without a long practical training. Even the Indian artisans are singularly wanting in originality. In the sculptures of our old caves and temples and in our wood carving and metal decoration we see the same figure or design repeated *ad nauseum*.

Our climate (except in the uplands in winter) makes strenuous toil impossible and fosters a love of ease. But factory-work of the modern type requires exertion on a stretch for hours and hours together without any slackness or cessation. Only a few races of India are capable of this sort of work. Hence the Indian mills have great difficulty in getting suitable workmen and are compelled to recruit only among certain select tribes (such as the peasantry of the Ratnagiri District). The hot and damp climate of the most fertile and populous regions of India, namely Bengal and Madras, makes a colony of sturdy labourers lose their strength in a few years, and the labour supply has to be constantly renewed from the colder and drier parts. Thus in Bengal and Madras we cannot have the factory type of workmen breeding and multiplying locally. The weaving mills of Bengal have been greatly hampered by this lack of a suitable class of labourers from among the local population. Similarly, the Assam tea-planters have to run to immense expenditure in the recruitment and transport of indentured labourers from a distance and from the waste of coölie-life through uncongeniality of climate.

In short, the great obstacle to the improvement of Indian production is the fact of our labourers being ignorant, unenterprising, immobile, resigned to their lot, bound by custom, and fond of repose. *Skilled labour* is very limited in number, in comparison with the strength of the population and the industrial needs of the country. What little of it we get usually shows a lack of reliability and of conscientious workmanship which is the despair of the managers of industries.

Even more scarce is educated labour of the type required in modern business. We have great difficulty in getting young assistants who will be methodical, hard-working and reliable. Such a class has to be created, as no Indian home or school (excepting a few under the Brahmo and Christian missionaries) teaches a child method and discipline. We take things too easy. Order or methodical arrangement has been well called the beginning of all good things; but Indian children do not learn the principle, "Everything in its own place, and a separate place for everything." The long discipline of feudalism, drill in the militia, and above all the orderliness of life on board men-of-war, have given to Englishmen the best training of character for industrial success; but all of these have been unknown to us. The youngmen sent forth by our colleges have neither the training nor the habits of business assistants, and so the head of a firm here has to waste much time and money before he can discover the gifted few among them and give them the requisite practical training.

Still more harmful is the scarcity of business capacity of the highest kind. Indian firms, even with large capitals, are too personal in their management; the absence or illness of the one head paralyses work and his death often ruins the whole concern,—just as the fall of the general leads to the flight of an Oriental army even at the moment of victory. In an English business, on the other hand, there is a chain of able officers, and a vacant place is quickly filled by promotion. In England a lad enters a business as an assistant, or even lower, as an apprentice. He then rises step by step till he becomes the senior partner of the business to whose success he has so long contributed. Hence an English firm is carried on from generation to generation in unimpaired efficiency by an unbroken succession of fresh chiefs of tried ability and ripe experience. But business owners in India seem to have a genius for driving away their ablest managers, who usually set up a rival shop over the way with a colourable imitation of their late master's title and trade mark. Senior assistant after senior assistant leaves the business with his heart full of resentment at his further promotion being hopeless, and at his being ever treated like a servant and never made a partner. Thus, in India *experience and skill are divorced from capital*, and the efficiency of both is greatly diminished. After the rupture the old business continues under a new and raw manager, and its affairs quickly get into confusion or decline; at the same time the new shop set up by the rebellious expert after a brilliant start withers away for want of the necessary capital. In time, no doubt, matters will right themselves. A new and more modernised generation of our capitalists will discover how to come to terms with their managers and experts.

Our recent industrial awakening has created a sudden demand for business managers. Experienced men of this class are not available in sufficient number, and so our new ventures are run by amateur managers (such as lawyers, retired public servants and others), who with the best intentions are unfit to take the place of trained business men. For this reason many of our new joint-stock companies have already failed. It is only by conducting a small concern with success that a man acquires the capacity to run a big business. But, unfortunately for us, in the keen competition of the industrial world in the modern age a concern must be large and fully equipped if it is to gain success. So we have been driven to launch forth big companies with large capitals, though we can get hardly any manager qualified by his experience to run even a small firm! Sixty-one per cent. of the joint-stock companies registered in India have failed.

Capital.—In India the principle of accumulation is weak. Centuries of misrule and disorder and tropical languor have left the population careless about the future and unwilling to put forth any extraordinary exertion for gaining additional wealth. Indian religions also teach quietism and disregard for the world and its joys. Hence, there is a great lack of capital in India, and its vast natural resources have been left comparatively undeveloped for this want. What little capital is possessed by a few Indians is not invested in productive works. Usury and to a small extent the support of the distributing agency are the only business of Indian capitalists; they do not like to finance production. People here will not invest their money except for very high profits. Capital well-directed and well-employed is the chief economic need of India. In proportion as foreign capital has flowed into India our industries have been developed and the country's production increased. Happily a change for the better has set in during the last ten years: Indian capital is being attracted to industries in daily increasing proportions. Many joint-stock companies have been floated, and their capital,—forming many *crores* in the aggregate,—has been raised entirely in India. Notably, the Tata Iron and Steel Co., which could not be floated in London, has been fully financed here. It is a very hopeful sign that the great middle class now prefer to invest their earnings in industries and banks, instead of buying the Public Debt. But most of our newly started small factories and steamer companies are foredoomed to failure by reason of the insufficiency of their capital.

General prospects of Indian production.—"India needs an increase of industry and of the effective desire of accumulation; the means of the change are:—(1) A better government, security of property, moderate taxes, and permanent tenure of land. (The first three of these have been gained since Mill wrote about 80 years ago). (2) Improvement of the public intelligence,—the decay of superstitions, kindling new desires in the people. (3) The introduction of foreign arts which raise the returns derivable from additional capital, and (4) the importation of foreign capital which places before the people a stimulating example and tends to create in them new wants, increased ambition, and greater thought for the future." (*Mill*, p. 117).

In our agriculture, the production remains scanty and the drudgery great, because the capital necessary for adopting labour-saving contrivances is wanting. But there is little scope for such machinery here, because India is a country of small holdings, poor cultivators, and very cheap rural labour. The main hope of Indian agricultural improvement lies in (*a*) irrigation, (*b*) selection of seed, and (*c*) opening new lands in scantily peopled tracts by means of railways. Manure, though greatly needed, is only a question of money; the peasants already know its use, but are too poor to apply it. Even scientific manure may be introduced among them. The Indian peasant is not hopelessly dull or lazy, but eager to grow better crops and to accept any agricultural improvement of which he has seen an actual demonstration in his neighbourhood. He looks askance only at theories and paper-knowledge.

Turning to our indigenous industries, in the case of articles of a purely *utilitarian* nature our handicraftsmen are rapidly losing their occupation as the articles manufactured in factories on modern lines (either in India or abroad) are stronger, more durable and in every way better than those made by the hand by native methods. European metal manufactures, in particular, are driving our blacksmiths out of the market. As for the articles of *artistic* interest made by the hand in India, they cover only a small field and the demand for them is only kept alive by tourists and curio-collectors. (*Worsley*). But an industry with such an artificial life cannot be expected to last much longer. The produce of handicrafts suffers from two great defects, *viz.*, (1) the out-turn cannot be suddenly increased to meet a new demand, (2) the articles lack finish, neatness, and uniformity of quality. Speaking generally, the greatest weakness of Indian manufacturers is their inability to keep to the same standard of excellence in production. Increased out-turn is almost always followed by deterioration of quality. This result is sometimes due to dishonesty but more often to inability to increase the trained labour supply. Its effect is most irritating to the purchaser and fatal to the good name of Indian manufacturers.*

Manufacturing industries in India labour under certain disadvantages: (1) The immense cost of setting

* The British Consul at Constantinople writes, "The sale of Indian cotton yarns would be very much larger [in the Levant and S. E. Europe] if the Indian manufacturers were reliable, but the spinning is irregular and the goods sent are usually below sample."

up, repairing, and replacing machinery in India. (2) The inefficiency of Indian labour in spite of its apparent cheapness, and the cost of concentrating it. Hence, even machinery is less productive in India than in Europe. (3) Indian manufacturers cultivate only the Indian market, which is comparatively small. The manufacturers of Europe, on the other hand, study the world-market, and India is only one of the many countries which they supply. Hence, the loss of the Indian market would do them only a slight harm, while it would ruin a modern industry established in India. Manufacturers in Europe live in daily competition with one another and improve their instruments and methods by sleepless vigilance in order to cheapen the cost of production. Indian manufacturers have not this spirit, and so their production is less efficient than if the same business had been started in Europe. (*Hunter*, 715, *Ind. Emp.*, iii. 280.)

Then, again, the difficulty of reaching the masses acts as a strong deterrent upon manufacturers in India. Very few of them employ travelling agents; there is an absence of a distributing agency at all adequate to the vastness of the population. Hence a manufacturer in India producing commodities which would have a ready sale among the village population, would encounter the greatest difficulty in getting into touch with his customers. But the growth of cheap communication is partly removing this disadvantage. (*Morison*, 183.)

Comparative efficiency of labour and cost of production in the chief industries of India and other countries.

Cotton manufacture.—One Lancashire "weaver" can look after six looms at a time, against only one loom by an Indian mill-hand. The wages of the former are almost thrice as high as those of the latter, hence weaving in India is only half as efficient as in England. Other classes of our factory labourers are similarly costly relatively to their work. The Indian cotton manufacturer has several advantages over his English rivals: (*a*) The raw material and the market for manufactured goods are both very close to the Indian producer whose goods escape the double freight with which Lancashire manufactures selling in India are saddled. (*b*) Indian unskilled labour is cheap, abundant, docile, and not (until very recently) liable to strike like English labour. But he has many disadvantages too: (*a*) The cost of erecting a mill here is three times as great as in England. (*b*) In India capital has to be raised at a higher rate of interest than in England, (usually 50 per cent. higher.) (*c*) The Indian cotton, being mostly short-stapled, is not suitable for the finer kinds of cloth worn in Bengal and Madras. Hence the Indian cotton mills can produce successfully only the coarser kinds of cloth, which sell in China. Fine *dhotis* for home consumption are being woven now as the result of the Swadeshi movement, but with less efficiency and greater cost than in Lancashire, and in many of our mills the yarn (thread) used is imported from England, as it cannot be so cheaply spun in India. (*d*) Indian labour is not really cheap. "Although the hours of labour are longer in Indian mills than in England, the strain upon the workers is nothing like so great. There is a laxity and freedom about the working arrangements (in the Indian mills) which would ensure the dismissal of half the mill-hands of Lancashire if they were to practise it." (*Keir Hardie*, Apr., 1908). Moreover, owing to the ignorance of the Indian labourers, when they do strike, the time is so ill-chosen as to cause great loss to both the parties and a decline of the industry, whereas in England strikes are declared and ended by the intelligent leaders of highly organised trade-unions, in such a way as to benefit the labourers with a minimum loss to the business.

The following figures illustrate the comparative efficiency of labour in the mills of Lancashire and India. (*Indian Magazine and Review*, Jan. 1911, p. 11).

	Lancashire.	India.
Operatives per 1000 spindles	4·2	30
" " 100 looms	4·4	90
Annual out-turn of yarn, average per operative, *lbs.*	7,736	3,700
Annual out-turn of cloth per operative, *yds.*	37,740	14,000
Average monthly wages per operative, *Rs.*	81	13

Mining.—The average daily output of coal per miner employed is ½ ton in India, 2½ tons in England and 5 tons in America (where mechanical coal-cutting plant aids human labour). Thus the Indian miner is only one-fifth as efficient as his fellow in England. However, a steady improvement is taking place in India, the average annual production per head having risen from 89 tons in 1904 to 116 tons in 1913; in Japan it is 158 tons.

Agriculture.—Agricultural labour in India is very efficient so far as the ryot himself is concerned. But the out-turn per acre is very low in comparison with other countries: the out-turn of wheat is 13 bushels per acre, as compared with 16 bushels in U. S. A., 22 in Canada, and 32 in Great Britain. In cotton our average yield is 61 lbs. per acre or only one-third of that obtained in America.

Sugar.—The out-turn of raw sugar per acre under cane is about 1·2 tons in India, 2 tons in Cuba, and 4 tons in Java. The remarkable abundance of the Java sugar crop is due to "systematic and scientific cultivation, the rational and frequent application of fertilisers, a careful selection of the cane based on the experience of past years, coupled with the best possible attention to the prevention of cane disease". A sugar estate in Java has generally an area of 1200 to 1500 acres, and the cane is planted every year in new fields. The chief defect of the Indian sugar industry is the sporadic cultivation of cane in small plots of land; hence the difficulty of transporting the ripe cane to the factory. Only huge central factories equipped with the latest and most improved machinery can turn out sugar most cheaply. Small factories with cheap and simple machinery, like those established in India, have no chance of profit in competition with the former. Every other quarter of the globe where sugar is grown, is establishing central factories as most economical. To run such a big factory there should be a plentiful supply of canes near at hand, and to secure this supply in India, for the present at least, the plantations should be owned and controlled by the factories, *i.e.*, a sugar manufacturer here must be a cane-grower also. Unless such an arrangement is made, great difficulty will be felt in concentrating a large quantity of cane at the factories and passing the whole quantity through the mills within the cane-season of three or four months. (Cane cannot be stored up to be worked leisurely; it must be crushed within 24 hours of being cut, if there is to be no loss of available sugar). Attempts to cultivate sugar-cane in large blocks, of about 4000 acres each, are now being made in only three places of India, *viz.*, C. P. Assam and Burma.

The inefficiency and high cost of Indian sugar-refining is due to (1) the employment of primitive wooden presses, which extract only 50 p. c. of the juice, while the best steel machines of America can extract 96 p. c. The cheap hand or bullock-worked steel presses which we are now using, bring out about 70 p. c. of the juice. (2) The cumbrous and costly process of boiling the juice into molasses and then refining the latter into white sugar. The direct manufacture of sugar from juice is the most economical process, and it also prevents any waste or chemical change of the sugar ingredients. But this process is unknown in India, and beyond the means of small factories. (Noel Paton's *Notes on Sugar*, 32—50).

National Wealth of India.—"H. D. Macleod said, in his book on Indian Currency, that persons of the highest authority estimated the ***hoarded wealth*** of India at £300,000,000. And a prominent financial organ says that the hoarding averages 11 millions sterling yearly." (Sir Ernest Cable, in the *Times*, 17 Aug. 1908). The *Times*, in commenting on the above letter, remarks that Macleod's estimate related to the hoards of gold alone, and did not take into consideration the enormous sums also hoarded up in silver rupees and silver ornaments by the Indians. The annual absorption of about 23 million pounds' worth of *gold* and *silver* by India gives some indication of the annual increase of our national wealth. Ibbetson calculated the total value of the annual *agricultural* produce of India to be 349 millions sterling, from which we must deduct the food of our population of 294 million souls, before we can estimate the net annual surplus or increase of national wealth. On the basis of the crop estimates and official price records, Noel Paton estimated the aggregate value of India's production of cotton, jute, rice, wheat, tea, linseed, rape, mustard, sesamum and ground-nut at 336 millions sterling (1911).

Average production and income per head.—Accepting Ibbetson's calculation our agricultural production per head is Rs. 18 a year. Mulhall estimated Rs. 40 as the average farm product per head of the agricultural population only, in 1891. (*Dictionary of Statistics*, 4th ed., p. 631).

1901	Pop. in millions	National income in millions	Income per head
United Kingdom ...	42	£ 1710	£ 40·7
British India ...	231	584	2·5

The figures for the U. K. are on the authority of Mr. C. Money and those for India on the authority of Mr. F. J. Atkinson. (*Morison*, 7.) Lord Curzon estimated the average income of an Indian at £2, but all such figures are mostly conjectural. A later and more elaborate estimate made by Atkinson gives the average income in India as Rs. 39 in 1895, compared with Rs. 30 in 1875. In Japan the average income has been estimated at between £2 8s. and £3.

The development of manufacturing industries in India: The work of foreign capital.—The transition of India from an agricultural, to an industrial country and the replacement of handicrafts by steam or electric power manufactures, are due entirely to European initiative. Foreign capital and enterprise have *introduced* into our country *many industries* and civilised appliances, which would have been unknown, at least for some generations, but for them. Production has been greatly increased. The new undertakings begun by the Government and Europeans give employment to more than three millions of people. Our industrial development and the working of our natural resources, begun by Europeans, are even now mainly financed by foreign capital. In 1911, the foreign companies registered abroad and working exclusively in India, had a capital and debenture of 185 *crores* of Rs. against the paid-up capital and debenture of only 78·3 *crores* of all the joint-stock companies registered in India, (1912) many of which are also built on European capital. (*Cf. Howard*, ch. v.) But the paid-up capital of joint-stock companies registered in India doubled between 1900 and 1913.

Though Indian capital is now engaging in the work in increasing proportions, we cannot too highly praise the service rendered to our industrialism by foreigners. Their enterprise opened every branch of modern production and transport in India, bore all the trouble and loss of pioneer work, and practically demonstrated to our richmen how capital can be profitably invested in modern industries. The *educative influence of foreign capital* and enterprise on a home-staying and conservative people like the Indians has been invaluable. The success of the Europeans held an example before our eyes which we are now hastening to copy. If they had not come, we, unlike the Japanese, could not have visited foreign countries and learnt modern industries for introduction into India. Our capitalists would have continued to distrust the idea of success being possible in the case of machines and large factories, just as they at first refused to subscribe to the railway as an incredible fairy tale.

Even more beneficial to India has been *foreign industrial skill*, without which native capital, however large, could have found no profitable investment. In many of our large factories, such as cotton-mills, paper-mills, and even modern banks, though the capital is mainly Indian, the direction is mostly in the hands of trained European agents, and in almost every case the machines are looked after by expert European mechanics. It is difficult to over-estimate the advantage which Indian capitalists have in being able to hire trained skill from Europe, where centuries of industrial work, mental activity, and constant competition have perfected mechanical knowledge, business capacity, and methodical and orderly habits. Very often European experts brought over to India by foreign firms are induced to join Indian firms after a time. The latter, therefore, get such experts much cheaper than if they had to import them directly. In this respect our Indian capitalists enjoy an advantage similar to that of our feudatory princes, who can hire the best educated Indian officers from British India without having to pay for educating this class of men in their own dominions. (The disadvantages of employing foreign capital and skill in India have been described in Chapter III, pages 112 and 113).

We owe railways, post and telegraph offices, and cinchona plantations to Government (backed by foreign capital). Jute mills, woollen mills, paper mills, gold-mining on scientific lines, breweries, modern tanneries and leather works, rice mills, saw mills and rubber plantations (in Burma), silk filatures, tile factories, indigo factories with modern equipment, and dockyards are almost entirely owned by Europeans. But tea and coffee plantations, coal-mining, flour-mills, ice-factories, sugar factories, and iron and brass foundries are shared between Indians and Europeans in varying proportions,—while many minor factories, though originally introduced by Europeans, are now owned and conducted entirely by Indians,—among them being the following: cotton presses and gins, jute presses, ærated-water factories, oil mills, &c. In fact, a variety of small industries conducted by machinery and requiring small capitals, have spread over the country, and are now owned and managed by Indians. In 1914 we had 2936 factories, great and small, employing 9½ *lakhs* of men, in British India.

N.B.—No factory employing less than 50 persons, no indigo factory or tea or coffee plantation, and no factory worked without mechanical power is included in the above number. But if we count the factories of all classes in all India, their labourers totalled 10½ *lakhs* in 1912.

The distribution of our factories:—cotton gins and presses mostly in C. P. and Bombay; cotton mills in Bombay, Madras and C. P.; jute mills and presses as well as silk filatures in Bengal; flour mills, in U. P. and Punjab; sugar factories in U. P.; rice mills, saw mills and petroleum refineries in Burma; iron and brass foundries in Bengal and Bombay.

In 1913 there were 2588 *joint-stock companies* with a total paid-up capital of 74⅓ *crores* of Rupees in operation in India. To this must be added debentures of about 10 *crores*. Two-fifths of the share capital are invested in cotton, jute, and other mills and presses, and eight per cent. in private railways and tramways. The capital invested in coal companies quadrupled in the ten years from 1901 to 1910. "While the railway and tea concerns are mainly financed from abroad, the great bulk of the mill and press companies are registered in India,"—but their shares are not necessarily owned exclusively by Indians. (*Cd. 147*, p. 68.)

The following tables show the different classes of capital invested in *all India*, (1913), as far as information is available.

A.—*Exclusively under Europeans*:—

Industries, etc. 1913	Capital employed. Rs.	No. of persons employed.	Annual production, etc.
Railways ...	495 *crores*	6⅓ *lakhs*	34,656 miles open, 45 *crores* of passengers carried.
Tramways and light railways (reg. in Ind.).	7 "	...	...
Jute mills ...	11·6 "	2·16 *lakhs*	28¼ *crores* Rs.
Gold mines ...	4·15 "		3·4 *crores* Rs.
Woollen mills ...	*lakhs* 53+	4053	5·1 mil. lbs. =61 *lakhs* Rs.
Paper mills ...	71·3 "	4600	60 mil. lbs. =80 *lakhs* Rs.
Breweries ...	21×3 "	1328	3·6 mil. gallons

B.—*Mainly under Europeans.*

1913	Capital with debenture, Rs.	No. of persons employed.	Annual production, etc.
Coal mines ...	7·6 *crores*	1·45 *lakhs*	16·2 mil. tons =5·7 *crores* Rs.
Petroleum refineries ...		9,189	277 mil. gallons =1½ *crores* Rs.
Tea plantations ...	28 *crores*+	6·6 *lakhs*	307 mil. lbs.
Banks:—			
12 Exchange banks with offices outside India.	56·7 *crores* (including reserve.)	...	...
3 Presidency and 15 joint-stock banks located in India.	16·68 *crores.*	...	...
Rice-husking mills ...	4¾ „	22,199	...
Saw and timber mills..	55 *lakhs.*	11,121	...
Flour mills ...	72 *lakhs.*		...
Sugar factories ...	1·4 *crores.*	7,870	...
Iron and brass foundries		? 17,622	...
Indigo factories (1915)	...	...	38,500 cwt.

C.—*Mainly under Indians.*

1913	Capital with debenture.	No. of persons employed.	Annual production, etc.
Cotton mills ...	21 *crores.*	244,002	...
Ice factories ...	29 *lakhs.*	...	...
Cotton gins & presses.	3 *crores*	1 *lakh.*	...
Jute presses ...		34,034	...
Printing presses ...	...	27,886	...

Though we have about 3,000 factories of all kinds worked by mechanical power, their total output supplies only a small fraction of India's needs. In almost every manufactured article of ordinary consumption, the foreign imports far exceed the home production. Nor have we made uniform progress in all the industries started among us. Our industrial position at the end of 1907 was thus summed up by Prof. Kale, "While we have been making during the past twenty years, very gratifying progress in the manufacture of cotton and jute, in the working of coal and gold mines, in tea plantation and in the kerosene industry, we have been marking time as regards sugar refining, oil pressing, iron mining, paper making, wool and silk manufacturing; and in the matter of glass, leather, umbrellas, metal manufactures, stationery, carriages, etc , we are almost nowhere." In 1914 manufactured goods formed 26 p. c. of our total exports, while the proportion of manufactured articles to our total *imports* was 77 p. c. The import of machinery rose from $3\frac{1}{4}$ *crores* worth in 1901 to 7 *crores* in 1908, and this fact proves the growing industrial activity of the country. Since 1909 there had been a steady decline in the import of machinery, but the arrivals in 1913 rose to $7\frac{3}{4}$ *crores* worth. We shall now examine the **condition of the chief industries** of India and ascertain the progress made since the beginning of the **Twentieth Century:**

A.—*Cotton Mills, (in all India)*

	1901	1911	1915
No. of cotton mills ...	197	253	261
No. of spindles, in *millions* ...	5	6·5	6·6
No. of looms	41,800	86,200	108,000
Yarn produced, in *million lbs.* ...	560	625	722
Woven goods, in *million lbs.* ...	116	266	352
Capital (as far as known), in *crores of Rs.*	16	...	21
Excise duty levied, in *lakhs of Rs.*	$18\frac{1}{3}$	48	49

In 1912, out of the 266 cotton-mills in all India as many as 85 were situated in Bombay City and 59 in Ahmadabad. The Bombay Presidency contains three-fourths of our spindles and looms. The year 1905 was one of phenomenal activity in our cotton manufacture. Since then there has been a steady decline in the production of yarn (with a slight recovery in 1911). But the *production of cloth* has gone on increasing;. it has *more than trebled* in the first fifteen years of the 20th century. We consume at home ninety per cent. of the cloth our mills produce, only 10 p. c. being exported. We import only 6 p. c. of the total mill-made yarn used in India. In 1915 the Indian mill production of woven cotton goods was to our imports as 69 to 100; but in 1911 it was as 47 to 100 (in length.)

The production of our hand-looms was roughly estimated in 1906 at 1650 million yards, but such figures are very unreliable. The chief defects of hand-woven cloth are want of bleaching and of finishing; the sun-bleaching process followed by our weavers neither gives a fine feel to the cloth nor preserves its strength; hence our large foreign import of white cloth. "Industries conducted in a small way and by hand are of little use today, and it is not wise to encourage their multiplication. Such industries inevitably succumb as soon as they are brought into competition with the products of factory labour, and each mile of railway extension increases the vigour of such competition." (*O'Conor.*) A few pseudo-Ruskins and many old-fashioned leaders in India are trying to revive our hand-loom industry for the supply of *ordinary* clothing; but their attempt is bound to have the same success as an army equipped with bows and arrows when opposed to troops armed with magazine rifles and Maxim guns. This artificial encouragement of an obsolete and doomed industry will only cause a great loss of national capital and retard our industrial growth. On the other hand, our mills have made a phenomenal progress: in the thirty years from 1879 to 1908, the *number of mills increased* $3\frac{1}{2}$ times, that of persons employed $4\frac{1}{4}$ times, and the number of looms and spindles 4 and $3\frac{1}{2}$ times respectively, while the *percentage of our home production* of grey and bleached goods *to our imports, doubled in the eight years*, 1901—1908. But from 1907 to 1914 there was a depression.

B.—*Jute Mills*, (British India only).

	1901	1911	1915
No. of jute mills ...	36	61	70
No. of spindles, in *thousands* ...	331	696	812
No. of looms, in *thousands* ...	16	35	39
Capital (as far as known), in *crores of Rs.*	6·96	14·75	...

C.—*Woollen Mills.*

	1901	1911	1915
No. of mills	4	4	6
No. of spindles	22,900	...	40,700
No. of looms	594	...	1151
Production, in *million lbs.* ...	3·9	4·7	10
Capital, in *lakhs of Rs.* ...	44·5	...	271

In the pre-war days these mills supplied *less than one-eighth of the Indian demand;* their production in

1911 fetched 51 *lakhs* of Rupees, while we imported 340 *lakhs* worth from foreign countries! Much hand-loom weaving is done in several parts of India, but the production consists mostly of coarse blankets, carpets, and rugs, and some amount of shawls or sheets. The Indian mills chiefly produce warm clothing for the army and the police.

D.—*Paper Mills.*

	1901	1911	1915
No. of mills	9	8	11
Production, in *million lbs.* ...	46·7	59·4	68
Capital (as far as known), in *lakhs of Rs.*	73	50	49·5

In 1904 the values of paper manufactured in India and of that imported were alike 61 *lakhs*; but in 1910 the imports mounted to 113 *lakhs*, while the home manufacture rose to 81 *lakhs* only. The public demand for paper is steadily on the increase, and the Government requirements have been increasing as rapidly. The existing paper mills in India are old-fashioned and inefficient. They make paper from rags, supplemented by *sabai* grass, and have utterly failed to keep pace with the public demand; so they are being every year beaten by Europe, where paper is made from cheap wood-pulp. In this commodity especially, "our industrial and economic prostration is due not to a lack of demand but to a lack of supply." (*Kale.*) In India the paper-maker is forced to be a rag-dealer, with his own collecting agents in the principal towns, whereas in Europe rag-collecting is a separate industry, and the rags are carefully sorted by skilled labour before they are delivered to the mill. Out of 100 tons of dirty-white rags received in an Indian mill only 32 tons were finally left as available for manufacture. In the case of wood-pulp there is no such loss and the quality of the paper is more uniform.

E.—*Coal-mining.*

		1901	1911	1915
No. of labourers employed	...	95,000	116,000	151,000
Production, in *million tons*	...	6·6	12·71	17
Imported, in mil. tons	...	0·23	0·29	0·132
Exported, in mil. tons	...	0·52	0·87	0·8

"For the very hard work of driving mining headings in the coal, one English miner would be equal to at least five Bengalis, but in some of the lighter coal cutting, two Bengalis would do as much work as one Englishman. One Pathan does more work in a given time than two Bengalis (1905). In 1908 each Indian labourer employed below the ground extracted 153 tons of coal per annum, whereas the average for the United Kingdom (1907) was 362 tons, and for Germany 344 tons." Since then there has been some improvement in our production. Our output per person employed underground in 1911 was 172 tons.

F.—*Petroleum.*

	1901	1911	1915
Production, in *million gallons* ...	50	214	282
Percentage of foreign kerosene to the total consumed in India ...	84.8	47	27

India's consumption of Kerosene oil nearly doubled in the ten years ending 1908. On the average of the years 1910 and 1911, our annual consumption of mineral oils was 147 million gallons out of which 68 million gallons were imported. But in 1915, our consumption (both home produce and import) totalled 355 mil. gallons. Oil refineries have been erected in Rangoon and the various constituents of the crude oil are put on the market in the form of kerosene, petrol, lubricating oil, fuel oil, candles, and paraffin wax. There is a rapidly increasing export trade in benzine and petrol from Burma, the figures for 1915 being 25 mil. gallons worth 23 *lakhs.*

G.—*Gold mining.*

	1901	1911	1915
Output, in *oz.*	532,303	583,567	616,728
Value, in *mil.* £ ...	1·93	2·23	2·37

On the average of the 3 years ending in 1911 we imported eight times as much gold as we produced.

H.—*Tea-plantation.*

	1901	1911	1915
Area under tea in *acres* ...	495,000	574,000	636,200
Quantity produced, in *million lbs.*	191·3	268·6	372
Quantity exported, in *mil. lbs.*	179·6	260·7	340

In 1915 India supplied 71 p. c. of the tea consumed by Great Britain.

The labour employed in the Indian tea-gardens was 698,300 and the joint-stock capital was 31 *crores* of Rupees, besides a vast but unknown amount invested in the gardens under private owners (1915.)

Technical education: its effects.—Technical education concerns itself with the details of particular trades. The old and *humbler ideal* of technical education was to impart *manual dexterity* and an elementary knowledge of machinery. But an intelligent lad can quickly learn these things by actual work (as in our railway workshops), without having to attend schools. Technical education in its *higher sense* should develop the faculties; it should (*a*) give the pupil a general command over the use of the eyes and fingers, and (*b*) impart to him artistic skill and knowledge and methods of investigation, which are useful in particular occupations, but which mere practical work cannot teach. Practical instincts are acquired by spending the youth in a good workshop, but in the higher branches of production such instincts should be fortified and improved by scientific training. In this higher branch the Germans have made wonderful progress, especially in Applied Chemistry, by reason of the diffusion of scientific knowledge among their middle and working classes and the close association of the highest students of science with practical manufacturers.

No doubt many lower grades of industry can be very efficiently carried on by uneducated workmen, and in their case the benefit of high education will not be direct. But even here the indirect increase of efficiency is great, as the labourer when educated becomes more intelligent, trustworthy, and inquisitive. Much of the best natural ability in the nation is born among the working classes; but the whole of it is now left undeveloped and so lost to the nation, for want of proper education. With us a low-born genius spends his life in lowly work, and thus there is a waste of latent ability. (*Marshall*, 288—292.)

The indigenous apprentice system of India.— The Indian child learns his hereditary craft from his father, or is appenticed to a master craftsman who is always a fellow casteman and often a relative of the pupil. The child picks up his knowledge by watching the workmen at their tasks, and soon learns to handle the tools well; next he begins to earn a low wage from his master, and this is increased with his growth in age and skill, till his training is complete. This system of apprenticeship was an excellent means of technical education in old days and still prevails among the Indian carpenters, shoe-makers, &c. It is very cheap, as the master's workshop is in the same quarter of the town as the boy's home, and he can quickly come to his own house for his daily meals. But the indigenous master's teaching merely reproduces his old-fashioned knowledge and does not tend towards progress. Hence, foreign imports are rapidly supplanting the products of Indian hand industries, and the quality of the impoverished Indian craftsman is quickly deteriorating. (*Ind. Emp.*, iv. 436, Major Atkinson in *Modern Review*, May 1907, Supplement, 30.)

Caste no doubt secures the transmission of hereditary skill, but it also (*a*) hinders the natural grouping of pupils in technical schools and (*b*) the free choice of professions according to a boy's natural aptitude, and (*c*) the caste-elders look askance at new knowledge and new tools, as they refuse to be wiser than their ancestors. But the difficulty of introducing modern European methods of production into India is not unconquerable. The Indian mechanic is ready to adopt a new tool *if it is fairly cheap* and proof of its superior efficiency has been given before his eyes. Witness the universal extension of sewing machines among our tailors, and the adoption of leather sewing machines by an increasing number of our shoe-makers, (especially by capitalist employers of hired *muchis*).

Technical Education in India: its failure.— The chief obstacle to India's industrial development is the *divorce between brain and muscle.* The intellectual castes dislike work with the hand and hanker for a literary education. The artisan classes are content to move in the old grooves, and they dislike even that bare minimum of literary education without which artistic skill cannot be developed. Hence, the artistic or mechanical genius born among them runs to waste. Sir T. Holland speaks of "the wide gap between industry and education in this country, where practical men are uneducated and educated men are unpractical." The beginnings of technical education in India have been marked by uniform failure for the following reasons: (*a*) Lack of qualified instructors. The teachers are either young-men fresh from some technical (usually engineering) institution, who have a very superficial knowledge of handicraft and no experience of trade methods and workshops, and who therefore attach more importance to scientific than to technical knowledge; or pure workmen masters who simply continue the habits of their craft without any thought of improvement. The Cassanova system was tried at Lucknow. "The idea was to induce master artisans to open their workshops in the Government technical school, work there with their own men and take in boys as apprentices...The only master workmen who could be induced to come, came on a monthly salary which they were quite content to draw and do nothing else." (*Atkinson.*) (*b*) Lack of genuine students. We have home-staying instincts, and hence pupils really wishing to learn a trade prefer the caste workshop near their homes to the modern school situated some miles from their houses and amidst unfamiliar surroundings. Through an ambitious educational ideal, these technical schools, instead of attempting only the practicable and improving the mechanical skill of the common artisans, adopted a too literary or theoretical teaching, which repelled the children of the artisan classes. The few pupils of the gentleman class who joined these schools merely came there to receive the literary education without learning mechanics at all. They were not prepared to lead a life of manual toil. Hence, in this country technical education "has in nineteen cases out of twenty come to mean the teaching of carpentry and smithy work to boys who have no intention either to become carpenters or blacksmiths or to engage in any manual occupation whatever." (*Buck.*) (*c*) The absence of a basis of universal primary education, so that our technical schools are at first compelled to offer lessons in the mere rudiments of education to their pupils, instead of devoting themselves chiefly to instruction in science and art as applied to industry. Before the course in the technical schools can be shortened and made more fruitful, we must have a foundation of universal popular education in primary schools accompanied by hand and eye training and the development of habits of attention, method and mental alertness. (*Atkinson*). The result hitherto has been that almost all the lower technical schools started in India have merely taught surveying and turned out *amins* instead of mechanics. They are technical in name only, and have not even attempted to teach *technique*; hence they have had no effect on the industrial development of the country.

The fact is that in Europe factories were opened

first, and technical schools long afterwards. Such schools arose to supply a real need for trained workmen felt by the existing factories. In India the converse process has been attempted. Many public leaders demand the starting of techinical schools, as if the turning out of trained mechanics will call industries into existence. Now, it is clear that people will not learn an art for which there is no demand in the labour market, and our artisans cannot be induced to go through the cost and trouble of learning the improved form of their crafts in technical schools with modern European tools, while the consumers are contented with the old-fashioned style of work done with primitive tools, and are not ready to pay the higher price which alone can make better turned work paying. For instance, "if you show the workman how to turn a *degchi* (cooking pot) out of one piece (of metal), instead of the ordinary bazar method of joining up copper straps, he probably could do it. He does not do it because it could not be sold say under Rs. 2-8 a *seer*, whereas the ordinary *degchi* sells at Rs. 1-10 a *seer*, and so no one would buy it". (*Atkinson*). Hence, there was for a long time a lack of earnest students in our technical schools ; they were joined only by the failures of ordinary schools, and artisan pupils had to be attracted by stipends. But now that many modern industries have been started in the land, there is a ready market for the services of trained mechanics, and our technical schools are getting genuine students in larger numbers.

Again, the keen spirit of self-improvement which animates European workmen is wanting in our society. In the Manchester School of Technology there are "five thousand night students who represent *actually* trade *workmen*, willing after a long day's toils to attend night classes of their own free will, and *at their own expense*, with the idea of bettering their knowledge of the technicalities of their trades, and thereby *making themselves more efficient wage-earners*," while the day students, or youths learning an industry from the beginning, number 400 only. (*Atkinson*). But in India, there has hitherto been no careers for the pupils of small primary technical schools, and they have usually been of the nature of a sham, as shown above.

The future policy of technical education.—The most successful plan is to have three classes of technical schools, *viz.*, (1) Lower or caste-schools for improving artisans in their hereditary crafts and teaching them the use of improved European tools; (2) Technological Institutes of a middle standard, for training apprentices, mechanical engineers, mechanical draftsmen, electrical engineers, skilled mechanics of a higher order, and permanent way inspectors, and (3) Polytechnic Colleges for the education of highly gifted and advanced pupils in art and invention.

A.—*Lower Technical Schools.*—A few youngmen should be chosen and taught the special craft of their caste, but according to modern methods. They should then be sent forth as teachers to spread their new knowledge among their caste fellows. In large towns, technical schools restricted to one caste or guild and teaching its distinctive industry may flourish, provided that the teacher is a local man and a member of the caste, because a stranger will fail to attract pupils. Such a teacher's knowledge may not be perfectly modern, but he should be helped by special instructors trained abroad, who should not however throw him into a subordinate position. In these lower schools literary education should be almost entirely discarded, otherwise the sons of mechanics will not stay. The pupils should learn only to read figures and names, work ordinary sums in arithmetic, and the simplest principles of geometry. The *use and care of tools* and *work with the hand* should be made the *all important* subjects of instruction. "A sound training in handicrafts may be given to a man who cannot read and write," (*e.g.*, Indian mechanics trained in railway workshops are illiterate but highly efficient). "It is well to remember that Indian workmen can take in a limited amount of new knowledge in one generation". Hence the reading and writing taught in such industrial schools is quickly forgotten by the pupils, as they find no use for it in their daily work. Such useless knowledge should be avoided and the time utilised in teaching more necessary things. It is a waste of energy to attempt the development of higher æsthetic genius or inventiveness among the pupils at such schools. They should be taught to give up their primitive tools and mediæval habits, and to learn modern methods, orderly habits, and the use of improved tools,—which would double their efficiency without making them literate. (See Wallace's paper in *The Industrial Conference held at Surat*, pp. 166—180, Major Atkinson, in *Modern Review*, May 1907, Supplement and *Ind. Emp.*, iv. 435—439).

Central Jails and Reformatories in India are excellent seats of modern technical education of this humbler type. But unfortunately very few of their inmates on regaining their liberty practise the trades they learn there. Is it due to their inability to buy modern tools or to the lack of demand for superior workmanship? Mere mechanical *skill* is being successfully taught in these institutions and also in railway workshops under European supervision. But here the men learn no science and are incapable of adding to what they have been taught. They are good animated tools and nothing else, and no *invention* can be expected from them.

B.—Of *Secondary* or middle standard *Technical Schools* we have some already, *viz.*, the Victoria Jubilee Technical Institute of Bombay and the apprentice and artisan sections of the Rurki and Sibpur Engineering Colleges. They have been very successful in turning out exactly the grade of mechanics, draftsmen and overseers for whom there is a great demand now. These schools have a useful, if modest, aim. They do not undertake to produce high grade engineers, men with the highest scientific education, and heads of departments or foremen for large industrial concerns, as there is no opening at present for *Indians* with such advanced technical training.

The Schools of Art which are flourishing at Lahore, Jaipur, Poona and Bombay, teach the fine arts rather than mechanics, and they have no influence on the *industrial* development of India, so far as the manufacture of articles of everyday use is concerned. The *Kala-bhavan* or Temple of Arts in Baroda is one of the biggest and most popular technological institutions, and has special departments for teaching dyeing, applied chemistry, weaving, and mechanical technology.

C.—*Polytechnic Colleges.*—The highest stage is a polytechnic to which the most promising youths of the country are sent up. It is only the most advanced and fully equipped polytechnics that can qualify our youths for the highest industrial work and invention. Here the scholars must come with a high general education and must be distinguished by intellectual keenness, if they are to profit by the advanced teaching imparted. "Manufactures and industries [of the modern type] require a good deal of education, brain development and intelligence, combined with manipulative skill. Here the industrial school [of the lower standard] is of no use...Successful industrial and commercial competition, and a high standard of manufacturing production, depend much more upon the adequate training of the *leaders* and managers of our industries and commerce, than upon that of the *workmen*" (*Atkinson*). One common delusion must be corrected. Many of our writers believe that a technical college can turn out ready-made *entrepreneurs* and persons capable of managing or taking up a position of authority in an industrial concern. No study of theoretical science can impart the requisite qualities of such leaders of industries. The strength of *character*, methodical habits, energy, alertness of mind and adaptability which a business manager must have, can be acquired only in the school of *actual* work in a factory or business. Even technical instruction of the highest grade would be premature at present, as there is no opening for Indians of the high grade or "University" type of technical education, employers preferring Europeans for the higher posts on the ground of their being more practical and reliable. "The higher engineering courses at the Indian universities will produce a man who has less chance of success than his technically educated and more practical but less scientific brother.

In 1912 Lt. Col. Atkinson and Mr. T. S. Dawson collected the views of a large number of employers of labour about the employment of technically trained Indians. "The general opinion seems to be that, in prompt and regular attendance, steady application to work, constant care and supervision when in charge of delicate machinery, the average Indian is unreliable...[Employers] state that in most cases students from technical institutions will not work with their hands, will not observe factory hours, ask too high wages for learning their practical work and generally think they know everything."

Again, it was found "that certain races in India are not, on the average, naturally fitted for technical work...Though willing to work with their hands in technical institutions, they are mostly unwilling to do so when they enter the stern reality of the workshop and consider that they need only supervise." The Parsis, however, form an exception; graduates of this race are willing to take up the humblest work in order to gain their practical experience. "It is a fact well known to the practical world at large that a man, however carefully prepared in a technical institution, is utterly useless to an employer of labour till he has had practical experience. He must in all cases begin at the lowest stage and work up gradually in time...Students are totally unfit for any *position of authority* on leaving their [technical] institute, and must first of all be subjected to discipline and learn under practical conditions the *details* of the work which they eventually hope to supervise...[In western India there are] many students from technical institutes in highly paid and responsible positions, but these have been in every case men who on leaving their institutions have recognised the necessity for working hard with their hands and gaining their experience in a subordinate position with a low salary at starting."

Leaving the production of high grade technical men to a future "when Indian capital comes forward on a large scale to finance industry,...when by education and heredity the character of Indian engineers becomes more reliable, full of energy, push and adaptability,..." the above two officers recommend that engineering education of every grade should be concentrated when possible in large colleges where the lower classes can obtain the supervision of a high-grade competent staff. Preferably more than one professional subject should be undertaken at each of these institutions; "as much of the elementary theoretical work is common, the saving in staff will be obvious, and the efficiency greater. In a large institution it is possible to have a specialist in each important subject". Further, no certificate or diploma should be given unless the student has gone through at least two years' practical apprenticeship in some works, after leaving school.

As for mining, a mine manager is trained in the same way as a ship's captain, *i.e.*, by actual work in a subordinate position; theoretical knowledge *alone* is of no use. "Unless Indians of the better class begin as English boys do, as workers underground, they can never be mine managers. Such officers are obtained almost wholly by promotion of subordinates who have had practical apprenticeship *in the mines.* The more ambitious and intelligent mine labourers acquire the necessary *theoretical* knowledge in the evening technical classes on the coal-fields, after their day's work. Thus mere practical skill is supplemented by science, in order to form an ideal manager. The converse process rarely succeeds: students of mining colleges who have not gone through the rigid discipline of living and working in a mine, cannot gain an efficient practical training afterwards, unless they are prepared to work underground like uneducated miners and acquire that vigilant care, strict method and punctuality which are indispensable in a mine manager." (*Holland*).

Factory legislation.—India being a semi-tropical country, much work is done out of doors or in sheds without walls. There has, therefore, never been in Indian factories any such over-crowding, bad ventilation, and undesirable mixing together of the sexes as marked the factory system in England before Peel's reforms. Nor has there been, except occasionally, any severe over-working of our adult labourers, as they are physically incapable of working strenuously for more than a certain period daily, even when tempted by overtime payment. Even when they are present at the mill for 15 or 16 hours, they render less than twelve hours' effective labour, as they spend the rest of their time in loitering about, taking their food, smoking, and even bathing in the mill compound. Children have, no doubt, often been kept at work *longer* than they should, but such work has not been *severe* enough to break down their health. Our coal-mines are not deep enough, and our miners are averse to remaining underground long. India has, therefore, been spared the horrible abuses which were revealed in the English mines by the Parliamentary Commission of 1842. (*Cunningham*, ii. ch. 21).

In fact, factory legislation in this country can properly move on the following lines: (*a*) Restricting female labour in order to enable mothers to attend to their babies. (*b*) Limiting child labour to prevent the arrest of their healthy growth. (*c*) Providing sanitary conveniences and pure drinking water for the mill-hands, ensuring the drainage and cleanliness of the mill premises, fencing revolving wheels and other dangerous machinery, maintaining safeguards against fires, &c. (*d*) Subjecting all factories to inspection by duly authorised persons.

The Indian Factories Act of 1881, as amended in 1891, defined a factory as "a premises where not less than 50 persons ordinarily work for at least 4 months during the year, and where steam, water, or other mechanical power is used." Indigo factories and tea and coffee plantations are excluded from the operations of the law. (*a*) The period of employment for women was limited to 11 hours, with intervals of rest amounting to 1½ hours. (*b*) Children were defined as persons between 9 and 14 years of age, and their labour was limited to 7 hours a day, it being declared illegal to employ any person below 9 years, or any 'child' in night-work. (*c*) Sunday labour was forbidden (except in a few cases), and intervals of rest prescribed for men also, but adult male labour was not otherwise restricted. (*d*) Machinery was ordered to be properly fenced. (*e*) The Local Governments were empowered to make rules to regulate water supply, ventilation, cleanliness, and other sanitary matters in mills.

In 1911 a fresh Factories Act was passed with the following new provisions among others :

(i) *In textile factories* no person shall be actually employed for more than *12* hours and no "child" (*i.e.*, person between 9 and 14 years of age) for more than *six* hours in any one day. [In other than textile factories the hours of children's labour remain 7 a day.]

(ii) *In textile factories* no person shall be employed before 5-30 A.M. or after 7 P.M.

(iii) *In textile factories* mechanical or electrical power shall not be used for more than 12 hours in any day. [But rules (ii) and (iii) will not apply to any factory in which a system of shifts approved by the inspector is in force.]

In all factories generally, (iv) no woman or child is to be employed before 5-30 A.M. or after 7 P.M. [Women's working hours remain *eleven* as before.]

(v) No child shall be employed unless he has a

certificate of age and physical fitness from a surgeon appointed by Government, and while at work carries either the certificate itself or a token giving reference to such certificate.

(vi) Managers as well as occupiers of factories shall be liable for breaches of the provisions of the Act.

(vii) Women and children shall not be employed in certain dangerous works specified in section 19, or in rooms where cotton-openers are at work.

Provisions have also been made for better ventilation, lighting, purity of the atmosphere in working rooms, supply of pure drinking water, and conservancy. (Chap. III. of the Act.)

CHAPTER VI.

DISTRIBUTION.

Rent as affected by custom.—The influence of custom is stronger in agriculture than in any other industry. "The conditions of agriculture even in England, [the most competitive country in the world] offer a strong resistance to the full action of free competition." (*Marshall*, 743.) The same has been the case to a much greater extent in India and with beneficial results. "Custom is the most powerful protector of the weak against the strong. Custom is a barrier which tyranny is forced in some degree to respect." Among a weak and timid population, the strongest lays down the law, but he often finds it expedient to relax it in practice; and every such relaxation has a tendency to become a custom, and every custom to become a right in the course of time. The payments made by the cultivator to the landowner are, in all societies except the most modern and advanced ones, determined by the usage of the country. It is only in modern times and in very advanced countries, that the conditions of the occupancy of land have been an affair of competition. In India the *occupier* for the time has very commonly been considered to have a *right to retain his holding while he fulfils the customary requirements.* The ryot was not, until about two generations ago, usually regarded as a tenant-at-will or even as a tenant by virtue of a lease; he was thought to be entitled to retain his land as long as he paid the customary rent. Even under arbitrary rulers the rent itself was not openly enhanced, but the landlord's exactions were increased by adding to the rent certain dues called *abwabs* under distinct names and separate pretexts. (In one district the *abwabs* consisted of thirty-three different items!) The fact that the landlord had to make his exactions in this indirect manner, proves that he could not, for very shame, change the customary rent itself. There was, therefore, once in India an effective limitation, a *real customary rent*, and the right of the ryot to till the land was recognised. The British Government, wishing to simplify the process of collection and save the ryots from harassment, has consolidated the various assessments into one sum, thus making the rent an arbitrary thing or at least a matter of specific agreement. And thus the sway of custom has been broken. (*Mill*, 148-149.)

In most backward countries all rights to property depend on general understandings rather than on precise laws and documents. Practically the ownership of land is vested not in an individual but in a firm, of which one member (*viz.*, the State or the zamindar) is the sleeping partner, and another member (namely the ryot) is the working partner.

"The payment made by the working partner is not economic rent at all, but is that part of the gross proceeds which the (unwritten) constitution of the firm binds him to pay." In so far as unalterable custom or law regulates these payments, Ricardo's theory of rent is not applicable to them. (*Marshall*, 724, also *Jones*.)

Custom alone influenced ancient Indian land-tenure, and its sway is still undisputed in the most stationary and sparsely peopled parts of the country. Before the relations between landlord and tenant were rigidly defined by Anglo-Indian law-makers, the conditions of partnership betwen the two were expressed in terms which were seldom capable of exact definition and measurement. The landlord's share included, besides rent, certain labour services, dues, tolls, and presents, and the amount which he obtained under each of these heads varied from time to time, from place to place, and from one landlord to another. The nominal rent remained the same, these minor imposts were increased or decreased; still "custom rounded off the edges of change" and protected the ryot. The moral sense of all around the landlord usually protested against any attempt on his part to make a sudden or violent increase in these extra customary dues. In Mughal history we sometimes read of *jagirdars* and revenue collectors—both temporary men—being harsh and exacting to the ryots, and of the Emperor dismissing or censuring them. *Abwabs* abolished by one Mughal Emperor were often collected by the provincial governors against his knowledge and had to be forbidden again by a later Emperor. Indeed, such cesses had a persistent tendency to recur, and *custom tended to perpetuate them.* The consolidation of the peasant's payments into one money sum is a blessing to him. Often the money-rent remained fixed for very long periods together; custom and public opinion gave the tenant a kind of partnership in the soil. In those parts of Bengal where there has been no great change of population and the police are strong and honest, the ryot pays only the customary share of the producer's surplus from the land, *i.e.*, his payment to the zamindar is not really *rent* in Ricardo's sense of the term, but simply *profits* shared between the two partners of a firm. (*Marshall*, 727-730).

How custom is broken.—Custom is more plastic in its working than appears at first sight. Customs imperceptibly grow and dwindle again, to meet the changing needs of successive generations. Even in modern England money-rents do not invariably follow the changes in the real letting-value of land, and, whenever they do follow, the change is tacitly and unconsciously effected. For example, an English landlord who has a steady tenant will do many things that are not stipulated for in the lease in order to retain him; in this case while his *money rent* remains stationary, his *real rent* decreases. In India war, famine and pestilence have depopulated even rich tracts, and have been followed by a competition for tenants among the landlords who had to offer very favourable terms to induce cultivators to come from a distance and re-people the land. (In this way Santal peasant colonies are being settled in many parts of North Bengal). At every such epoch the continuity of the former custom, as regards rent, was deliberately broken for the ryot's benefit. (*Marshall*, 730).

From an opposite cause the customary rent is being now-a-days deliberately set aside for the landlord's benefit. With the increase of population and extension of markets for food grains, the demand for land has rapidly increased, and since 1860 rent has generally become a matter of contract, except so far as customary rates are respected in the case of privileged tenants under Rent Laws, and in the case of Government ryots by the settlement rules limiting enhancement. The landlord, when not thus restrained by law, can safely defy custom. Thirdly, Anglo-Indian legislation has broken the force of custom, as described in the first paragraph of this chapter.

In short, the incidence of rent depends on the interaction of three forces, *viz.*, custom, competition, and legislation. In the early days of British rule custom was everywhere paramount, and even now the influence of competition is slight as between one district and another, and a rise of prices is not immediately followed by a general rise in rent. But as among the ryots of the *same* village, competition is often very keen, especially in the teeming plains of Northern India. The rent legislation of India, as. Mr. Maclagan points out, (*Ind. Emp.*, iii. 454), "starts from a basis of custom and seeks to confine the influence of competition within reasonable limits" by maintaining the customary rights of tenants against landlords. "*Custom is* therefore *still*, to a large extent *the foundation of Indian rents*." Competition, however, strongly operates in determining the rent of building-sites and of vegetable farms near big towns.

Rent in India as affected by State-landlordism.—Over four-fifths of the area of British India the State is the sole landlord, and the actual cultivators are liable to enhancement of rent (called land-revenue) every twenty or thirty years. Here the State has a monopoly of land, and competition among landlords (the basis of Ricardo's theory) is impossible, as there is only one landlord. A monopolist landlord can exact rent even from the worst land under cultivation. The rent is assessed on the whole tract included in a grant, and for the full period of the settlement (*viz.*, 20 or 30 years), and does not vary, like economic rent, with the actual produce of the field and the net profit of the cultivator from year to year. The State-demand is, therefore, (1) of the nature of monopoly rent; which is an element in the price of agricultural produce. Moreover, like monopoly rent elsewhere, (2) it may not always be a tax on rents proper (*i.e.*, on the superior tenant's net gain) but may encroach (and according to Ranade does frequently encroach) upon the profits and wages of the peasants. The disadvantages of State-landlordism in India are the following in addition to the above two:—

3. It often neglects local custom, because a settlement by subordinate officials carrying out general rules and obeying a central authority, is apt to be too systematic and too machine-like.

4. Absence of elasticity in the demand and of personal relations with the tenants, which are very important factors in a backward and mainly agricultural country.

5. The State being impersonal and its officers being an ever fluctuating body, there is no safeguard against undue enhancement of rent and no provision for bettering the peasants' lot, except an extraneous force, *viz.*, public opinion in a far-off island. Mr. Machonochie's inquiry showed how the Guzrat peasantry were put to great suffering and loss through the local officers' stupid literalness and zeal in collection, in spite of the benevolent general orders of the head of the Government.

At first the English Government used to take as land-revenue 90 p. c. of the economic rent. But gradually its share has been reduced *in practice* to about 50 p. c. of the net assets. [There is however, no *statutory* limitation of the State demand, and the 'Saharanpur rule' of halving the net assets has been expressly repudiated in Bombay and was conceded to the C. P. as lately as 1912.] According to the theory laid down for revenue settlement, the remaining 50 p. c. of the net assets of a field (or a little more or a little less) should be left as a substantial net rent to be enjoyed by the middleman or farmer. In such cases "the net rent is, historically speaking, a relinquishment of part of the profits of land by the Government to the land-owners, whereas in most countries the land-revenue is an assignment from the rent made by the land-owners to the Government." (*Indian Empire*, iii. 448.)

In the temporarily settled parts of India, the immediate cultivators have not gained perpetuity of tenure at a fixed rent. The Government manages the land like a good Irish landlord, not putting it up to competition, nor asking the cultivators what they will promise to pay, but *determining for itself* what they can afford to pay. (*Mill*, 199). The revenue is adjusted to the probable surplus produce of the land, after deducting the cultivator's necessaries and his little luxuries, according to the customary standard of the place. "Thus as between man and man in the same place, the land revenue is of the nature of *economic rent*. But since unequal charges will be levied in two districts of equal fertility...its method of adjustment as between different districts is rather that of a *tax*, than a rent. For, taxes are apportioned to the net income which actually is earned, and rents to that which would be earned by an individual of normal ability." (*Marshall*, 730.)

The Famine Commission of 1900 calculated that the proportion of land revenue to the *average* value of the gross produce then was—

in the C. P. 4 p. c.
Punjab 7 p. c.
Deccan 7 p. c.
Guzrat 20 p. c.
Madras 10 p. c. (including water-rates.)

(See *Hunter*, 520, *Ind. Emp.*, iv. 216. For the other side see *Dutt*, 462, 499, *Gokhale*, 370). But such estimates are somewhat conjectural, and are based upon the supposition that the crop will be a normal one, which is seldom the case. The Muhammadan government theoretically claimed as land-revenue one-third of the *actual* gross produce in a particular year, but often levied extra cesses or *abwabs*. As for the Punjab in 1908, Sir James Wilson calculates that the true incidence of the land revenue in wheat land, measured in wheat, is 4 p. c. of the gross produce, and that in the case of all the lands of the province, after adding to the crops the income from the livestock, firewood, timber and other products of the uncultivated areas belonging to villages, "the present land-revenue assessment is well below one-sixteenth of the annual value of the present gross produce of the land."

Rent in India as affected by Permanent Zamindary Settlement.—In the permanently settled laws, of India the zamindar has theoretically the power of extracting the full economic rent, except in the case of certain classes of privileged tenants. But his power of enhancing rent has been greatly diminished by various laws, *e.g.*, the Acts of 1859, 1885, and 1907. Even before the passing of these laws zamindars did not rack-rent their tenants as a general rule, and rent was not always determined by a heartless competition among starving peasants, as is the case with the Irish cottiers. Custom and personal relations softened the zamindar's tyranny. As Mill wrote in 1848, the ryots are in a condition somewhat like that of the cottiers, but different in many respects. "The payments of the ryots have seldom been regulated by competition. The rule common to a neighbourhood" was usually followed. (*Mill*, 197.) But rack-renting has greatly increased since that time, as we have explained before.

The income of the zamindars increased about 27 times in the course of the century following the Permanent Settlement. When that settlement was made (1793) the Government left to them only 10 p. c. of the economic rent at the time. But now, owing to the increase of the population, extension of cultivation, and rise in the value of crops, the zamindars' share amounts to 75 p. c. of the rent collected from the peasants. (*Ind. Emp.*, iii. 448). And as the total amount now paid by the ryots is 3·6 times the amount of 1793, the income of the zamindars as a body has increased 7·5×3·6 or 27 times. But the ryots have not been squeezed to the same extent; the incidence of rent per cultivated *bigha* has not increased 27 times or even 3·6 times in every field during the period; a large portion of the increase in the *total* amount of rent is accounted for by the reclamation of waste land. The money rents have no doubt been enhanced but not probably out of proportion to the rise in the price of crops. Hence, the ryot under the zamindars is not more severely taxed now than he was in 1793; only his holding is more strictly surveyed and he has lost the chance of making extra gains from the groves and fish ponds in his neighbourhood which were formerly neglected and unassessed.

On the other hand, all classes of ryots except the tenants-at-will are distinctly richer, because the Rent Laws practically prevent the zamindars from appropriating any new unearned increment and exacting the full economic rent, as it is extremely difficult and costly for the latter to make out a case for enhancement in the law courts. What the zamindar thus loses is enjoyed by the ryot, who therefore pays under the name of rent only "a share of the profit of the firm." Where the zamindar cannot exact the full economic rent by litigation or force and the soil is fertile, there is every inducement to sublet the tenancy, and there are various grades of intermediary proprietors between the supreme landlord who pays revenue to the Government and the peasant who actually cultivates the field.

Rent in India as affected by land-tenure legislation and rent laws.—Most of the old families with whom the Permanent Settlement was made, soon afterwards lost their estates as they could not pay the revenue on the fixed date. Under the Revenue Sale Law ("Sunset law") their estates were sold by auction, and a new race of zamindars was introduced who were bound to their tenants by no hereditary relations or old family traditions of sympathy and generosity, and who often wished to make the utmost profit out of their newly purchased property. Many of them rack-rented their peasants as the population increased and with it the demand for land. In many estates large numbers of ryots were hopelessly in default to their landlords, so that even in prosperous years they could not enjoy the benefit of the full harvest. The zamindar left to them just enough to maintain their lives, but took every thing else away in payment of arrears which could never be cleared. Still he did not sell them up for default as was formerly the inexorable rule of Government in the mahalwari and ryotwari tracts.

How the laws of 1859, 1885 and 1907 have safeguarded the ryot's rights and protected him from arbitrary enhancement of rent, has been described on pages 123-126.

Rent as affected by the pressure of population

on the soil.—In the most thickly peopled parts of India, the pressure of population has (*a*) enhanced rents to the maximum point, (*b*) led to the division of fields into very small holdings, and (*c*) fostered intensive cultivation and the consequent decreasing return to fresh doses of capital and labour.

In a country where agriculture is the sole occupation of the people, increasing numbers produce an increasing tendency towards the partition of the cultivating units. North Bihar is "the country of the petty proprietor," in Muzaffarpur the density of population is 937 per square mile and in Saran 853: the effect of this overcrowding is that in these and similar districts of Bihar, the average size of a peasant's holding is less than half an acre, whereas in the Punjab it is 3 acres and in the ryotwari parts of Madras 8 acres.

In Europe increase of population has been accompanied by a lowering of price and rents, owing to (*a*) agricultural improvements which have cheapened the cost of production, (*b*) increased yield per acre through scientific manuring and selection of seeds, and (*c*) improvement of the means of transport, by which foreign grain can be cheaply imported. In India the first two of these counteracting agencies do not operate, and the third has been ruinous to the home consumer. Hence the increase of our population in the 19th century has been followed by a tremendous rise in the price of food and a great increase of money-rents, though theoretically "the extent to which higher prices are by themselves capable of increasing rents is relatively slight." (*Pierson*, i. 126).

An increase of population is not necessarily followed by a proportionate increase of rent. In the ryotwari parts of Madras the population increased by 61 p. c. between 1853 and 1890, but the cultivated area increased by 75 p. c. and the total Government land revenue by 31 p. c. only. The new lands brought under cultivation are less productive and have been assessed at a much lower rate, and hence the *average* revenue for the *total* cultivated area fell from Rs. 2-8 an acre in 1853 to Re. 1-14 in 1890. (*Hunter*.)

The average incidence per cultivated acre :—

(1912)	of land revenue.		of cash rents.	
Permanently settled parts—	Rs.	As.	Rs.	As.
Bengal	1	1	3	8
Bihar & Orissa ...	0	9		
Benares Divn. ...				
Temporarily settled parts—				
U. P. (Agra) ...	1	13	4	3
Oudh	1	15	5	3
Punjab	1	8	3	11
Madras (incl. irrig.) ...	2	1		
Sind „ ...	3	0		
Bombay	1	9		
C. P.	0	10	0	11
Berar	1	5		
Assam	2	0		
Lower Burma	2	13		
Upper Burma	1	13	(*Ind. Emp.*, iii. 453)	

In the permanently settled area of Bengal the land revenue represents less than 25 p. c. of the rental.

The incidence of land revenue per head of the population in British India was Re. 1-4 in 1913,

(*Moral & Mat. Progr.*, 50th No., p. 27.) The Bengal Government in a letter of June 1901 estimated the proportion of the *rent charged by the zamindars* to the gross produce thus :

Nadia and Midnapur districts ...	7 & 8 p. c.
Backarganj, Noakhali and Tippera ...	9 "
24 Perganas	10 "
Rajshahi	13 "
Hughli, Gaya, Cuttack	14 "
Birbhum	15 "
Muzaffarpur	16 " (*Dutt*, 462)

Characteristics of Indian wages.—In India the labourer usually works on his own account; in Europe he is usually a hired man working for an employer. But there are some labourers in India, especially in the towns, who occupy the same position as wage-earners in Europe. (*Morison*, 4.) Payment of wages in kind widely prevails among agricultural labourers in India. Usually a farm-labourer gets from his master free meals and lodgings and a certain fixed portion of grain. He occasionally gets a piece of cloth or a small gift too. In some cases (increasing in Bengal) a cash wage is paid in addition to the free meals. Village artisans and domestic servants are paid in kind. Cash wages are paid only in industrial villages, in and near towns, and by large employers of labour in industries. (*Ind. Emp.*, iii. 467). "By far the most important class of labour [in India] is agricultural......Payment in kind is commonly practised, either for the entire wages, or as a supplement to cash wages, and the supplements vary according to the season and the nature of the employment. The regularity of employment also varies greatly, and employment is practically nowhere continuous throughout the year." Hence the statistics of Indian agricultural labour and domestic service are not reliable. (*Prices and Wages in India*, Ed. 1912, p. 177.) But in rapidly developing provinces like the Punjab, and along important railway lines, the old order is disappearing, and cash and competition wages are rapidly displacing other kinds of payment for labour. An interesting wages survey carried out in the Punjab villages at the end of 1909 showed that purely *cash rates* obtain in 49 p. c. of these villages, cash rates with supplementary allowances in kind in 48 p. c., and *purely grain rates in 3 p. c. only.*

The rate of wages varies greatly in different parts of the same province, according to the relative importance of agriculture and manufacture and the density of population. In all parts of India where agriculture is the chief occupation and the population is dense (as in Bihar), the wages are low and remain so for generations. But where the peasantry are prosperous (as in fertile East Bengal) or where the population has been lowered by malaria and plague (as in Central Bengal and Bombay respectively), high wages prevail. (*Ind. Emp.*, iii. 464). In the British period (especially after 1860) large public works, canals and railways, mills, factories and mines have raised the demand for labour and with it the wages of certain classes.

In Bihar wages are rising through extensive inland emigration to Bengal and Assam, and through heavy plague mortality in recent years. All over India the rise of wages has been accelerated and the shortage of the labour supply relatively to the demand has become very acute since the beginning of the 20th century. The chief causes of the shortage are—(*a*) extensions of railways and canals on a larger scale than before, (*b*) our new industrial outburst, leading to a rapid increase of factories, mills, plantations and mines, and (*c*) the depopulation caused all over Upper India and Bombay by bubonic plague, which carried off nearly 8 millions of persons in the 14 years ending with 1911. "In some parts of the Punjab and the United Provinces the mortality has been so severe as to disorganise the labour market and to affect the level of prices." (*Moral and Mat. Progr.*, 47th No., p. 112.) Malaria caused a million deaths in the U. P. in 1908, and the same disease so severely affected the Punjab also, that ripe grain had to waste in the fields for want of reapers.

Recent rise in real wages.—Mr. Krishna Lal Datta, a very able and experienced officer of the Finance Department, conducted an inquiry (1910-13) into the rise of prices in India and submitted a valuable report full of useful information on a variety of connected subjects. He points out how the statistics of wages published in the annual blue-book *Prices and Wages in India* do not give reliable information. "A *syce* or horse-keeper is taken as representative of a domestic servant, but the class represented is very unimportant. A common mason, carpenter and blacksmith are taken as types of 'skilled labourers' and one rate of wages is published for all of them, though their remuneration is actually far from equal. The group, 'unskilled labour', is represented by only an able-bodied agricultural labourer, which expression itself is but too vague. No discrimination has also been made between the rates of wages prevailing in rural and urban areas...The statistics are in many cases wholly unreliable." (*Datta*, p. 18.)

For the purpose of securing wage and price statistics that would serve as a reliable index of the fluctuations, he has divided India (excluding Burma) into 20 "homogeneous circles", with the 4 great ports forming four additional circles. Each of these circles is studied apart, as it has practically the same economic conditions throughout its parts and may be regarded as a self-contained unit of economic inquiry. (Pp. 3-8). He has also very properly studied the wages of each trade separately instead of grouping together a variety of them under such general names as "skilled artisans," "unskilled labour" &c. For the purposes of a fair comparison the annual average of the five years 1890-94 has been taken as the "basic period". "This is a typical or normal period, unaffected by such exceptional circumstances as famine or unseasonal rainfall. (P. 14).

As the result of his very detailed and accurate inquiries, he comes to the following conclusions :—

A.—Wage-earners of all classes and in all parts of India have secured an increase in wages (during the period 1890-1912), commensurate with the rise in the cost of living. The only exceptions are domestic servants in cities and other urban areas in a few 'circles" and wage-earners employed in certain employed *viz.*, the jute mills of Bengal, the cotton mills of Bombay, Madras and Gujrat, and railway works in Southern India and Eastern Punjab. Taking India as a whole, the classes that have secured a that in their real wages are arranged below in the descending order of the rates of increase : (1) *General abourers* employed in *urban* areas other than large Bihar; highest rise in E. Punjab, U. P. and Bundel-Chota, moderate in Bihar and N. and E. Bengal, only slight in N. Madras.

(ii) *Village artisans*, esp. in the Punjab, U. P., Bundelkhand and Bihar; only 6 p. c. in W. Madras.

(iii) *Agricultural labourers*; a rise of above 50 p. c. in E. Punjab, E. U. P., and Chota Nagpur; only 13 p. c. in W. Madras.

(iv) *Artisans* employed in *urban* areas other than large cities, esp. in the Punjab, U. P. and Chota Nagpur; very slightly in Gujrat.

(v) *General labourers* employed in *cities*, esp. in the Punjab, Bihar and C. P.; very little in Madras and Assam.

(vi) *City artisans*, esp. in the Punjab, U. P. and C. P.: very little in Gujrat, Madras and Calcutta.

B. The real wages of *domestic servants* have remained stationary or very slightly risen, the very rise being in the cities of N. Madras, U. P., C. P. Berar and Bihar, and none in Calcutta, Bengal or Assam.

C. On the whole there has been very little rise in the real wages of *industrial workers*. While places classes of labourers (both skilled and unskilled) hard been more than compensated for the rise of prices few a rise in their wages,—the men employed in industries and on railways have only in a few places secured and increase in wages commensurate with the rise in prices, but have everywhere else been hard hit by the higher prices. Among the jute-mill hands while the nominal wages have risen by 43 p. c. during these 22 years, the real wages have risen only 6 p. c. and were lower in 1912 than what they were in 1900-1910. In the cotton mills, the rise in real wages has been 48 p. c. in Calcutta, 30 p. c. in C. P., with a fall in Bombay, Madras and Gujrat, the average for all India being only 6 p. c. (as in the case of the jute industry.) In railway works the rate of real wages for India generally has been stationary,—W. Punjab U. P., C. P., Bihar and Calcutta showing an increase and E. Punjab, Sind, Gujrat, the Deccan and Madras showing an actual decline. (Pp. 180-182, 186.)

The war has not improved the condition of the Indian labourer, because he has to pay much higher prices for several commodities, while his nominal wages have remained practically stationary: the average wages of 1914 were only 2 p. c. higher than those of 1913, (the only rise being in *woollen* mills) and there being no rise in 1915 (except in *tea*), though there was a boom in the jute, wool and paper manufactures and in coal-mining in 1915.

Comparative movements of wages, 1890-1912, the average of 1890-94 being taken as 100, and the figures for *real wages* being printed *in italics*.

	1895	1900	1905	1910	1912
General average of all labour for India, nom.	105	119	135	155	166
,, real.	*102*	*113*	*112*	*123*	*121*
Rural labour, nom.	106	126	148	171	190
,, real.	*104*	*121*	*123*	*135*	*138*
Urban labour, 3 classes, nom.	106	123	142	165	181
,, ,, real.	*103*	*118*	*119*	*131*	*133*
Large cities ,, nom.	104	122	139	163	174
,, ,, real.	*105*	*117*	*118*	*129*	*128*
Industries, 11 classes, nom.	105	115	126	141	146
,, ,, real.	*100*	*107*	*103*	*111*	*107*
Railways, nom.	102	108	117	136	138
,, real.	*97*	*99*	*97*	*108*	*101*
Rur. wages, E. Beng., nom.	102	124	143	157	177
,, real.	*107*	*116*	*113*	*127*	*126*
,, Bihar nom.	102	119	128	149	167
,, real.	*98*	*112*	*104*	*124*	*135*
,, E. Punjab nom.	107	132	171	222	250
,, real.	*107*	*133*	*147*	*169*	*167*
General average, Cal. nom.	103	116	128	140	146
,, ,, real.	*102*	*110*	*105*	*110*	*110*
Calcutta Jute mills, real.	*106*	*116*	*106*	*109*	*107*
Bombay cotton mills, ,,	*108*	*100*	*102*	*105*	*98*
Bengal mines, ,,	*101*	*112*	*111*	*130*	*121*
Chota Nagpur mines ,,	*123*	*204*	*202*	*224*	*207*

Movements of nominal wages.—In Northern India the money wages of masons, blacksmiths and carpenters doubled in the generation following the Mutiny. In the *thirty years from 1873 to 1903*, in Bengal the monthly wages of an *agricultural labourer* rose by *39 p. c.*, of a *syce* by *32 p. c.*, of an *artisan* (*i.e.*, mason carpenter or blacksmith) by *47 p. c.*, (against a rise of 39 p. c. in the average price of food-grains). The artisan classes secured an increase of 47 p. c. in Bengal, 65 p. c. in Assam, 50 p. c. in the Punjab, 15 p. c. in Madras, 7 p. c. in Burma, and a decline of 2 to 3 p. c. in Oudh and Bombay (*Ind. Emp.*, iii. 469-470.) Since 1903 there has been a rise of wages in most places.

In the Punjab the wages of unskilled agricultural labourers generally doubled in the 20 years ending with 1909, "the advance being specially rapid in the last five years." The wages of village artisans and ploughmen also practically doubled in the same twenty years. (*Moral and Mat. Progr.*, 47th No., p. 118.)

As regards **labour in the textile factories**, the Royal Commission on Labour, 1892, found that wages had remained almost *stationary during* the preceding *30 years*, owing to the labourers having started with "monopoly wages" at the commencement of the period. The Collector of Customs, Bombay, wrote in 1892: The mill hands are recruited from labourers, small cultivators, handloom weavers, and petty craftsmen, all of whom may safely be said to have increased their earnings from 30 to 200 p. c. by taking to mill work: the shoals of handloom weavers brought down by rail from Lucknow, Cawnpur and Delhi have found occupation in Bombay mills at rates three times their previous handloom earnings. Wages in the factories of the U. P., after remaining stationary for a long period, had begun to rise slowly but steadily by the year 1892. Since then in many branches there has been little or no rise, and in others increase of wages ranging from 20 to 40 p. c. and in the engineering department even higher.

Condition of wage-earners.—The chief obstacle to a greater rise of wages is the fact that Indian labourers generally are satisfied with a low standard of comfort and are unwilling to accept much higher salaries on condition of doing labour of a new or uncongenial nature or serving in a distant province. Hence the difficulty of getting a sufficient supply of labour in our tea-gardens, collieries, and factories, in spite of their offering high wages and regularity of employment. During recent years there has been a marked rise in wages in many occupations; prices have also ruled high. The former is not a consequence of the latter, but rather of the increased demand for labour which our recent industrial and commercial expansion has created. High prices do not always mean high money wages. Indeed, in times of scarcity wages are reduced, as the failure of rain stops agricultural operations and throws rural labourers out of work, while the scarcity increases the number of the people compelled to labour for their food. "In times of scarcity and famine in India the rise in the price of food is not accompanied by a rise in the wages of labour; on the contrary...the rate of wages offered and accepted is frequently below the ordinary or customary rate and...is not subsistence wages for a labourer with dependants to support." (*Famine Com. of 1898*, p. 363.) But where a rise of prices is accompanied by agricultural prosperity, the labour supply decreases and wages also rise, because, owing to the high prices secured by their produce, many small cultivators who in ordinary years had to supplement their income by acting as day-labourers, find it no longer necessary to do so; their land alone yields them a sufficient living now. This latter fact has become very noticeable since 1906. (*Ind. Emp.*, iii. 469.)

The Famine Commission of 1898 reported that (1) in *Bengal* the powers of the people to resist the effects of calamity of season had largely increased. (2) In *Bihar* the class of agricultural labourers (including petty agriculturists who supplement the profits of their small holdings by working for wages) had in no way benefited by the rise in the price of agricultural produce. Their wage is barely sufficient to supply food to the labourer and his family when food grains sell at ordinary prices. Hence they have no more resisting power in a famine now than formerly. [But the Bihar agricultural labourers have improved their lot in recent times, their real wages in 1912 being 27 p. c. higher than in 1890.] (3) The resources of the peasantry in the Madras *Deccan*, the Bombay Deccan, and the Southern Maratha country, had not improved during the preceding 20 years. The same is the case, with many exceptions, in the *C. P.* (4) In the *U. P.* the *cultivating* classes showed greater command of resources and power of resistance during famines, but this improvement was not materially shared by the *labouring* classes. There was no improvement among the small proprietors and cultivators of the country south of the Jumna (esp. Bundelkhand, South Allahabad, and Hardoi). (5) In the *Punjab* the labouring classes were generally well off, as agriculture was largely protected by irrigation. The *general conclusion* for all India was: "Of late years, owing to high prices, there has been a considerable increase in the incomes of the land-holding and cultivating classes, and their standard of comfort and expenditure has also risen. During the recent famine these classes, as a rule, have shown greater power of resisting famine. The skilled artisans, excepting the weavers [who number 96 *lakhs*], have also greatly improved their incomes and their style of living." (*Report*, pp. 361-363). Since 1905 even unskilled labourers have been earning higher wages.

There are only three blemishes in Bombay factory

labour, *viz.*, (1) several mills keep the wages in arrears for over two months, (2) the evil housing of the workers, and (3) the floating residuum of mill-hands, usually 25,000 persons, who get irregular or no employment and wander from factory to factory or haunt the taverns. (*Royal Commission on Labour*, Foreign Reports, Vol. II., 1893.)

The condition of labourers in 1908, after the sharp rise of prices since 1905, is thus described in the *Moral and Mat. Progr.* 45th No. :—High wages tending upwards with the demand for labour still in excess of the supply in W. Bengal, Darjiling tea-gardens, the Punjab, the C. P., Madras, Sind and Bombay, (with a decline in wages in E. Bengal); shortage of agricultural labour in Ahmadabad, the U. P., Bombay, and Madras, of coolies in Madras and Sind, and of skilled labour in W. Bengal industries. Even in 1910, in spite of lower food prices, the high wage-level of 1907-8 was generally maintained and the demand for labour continued to exceed the supply all over India. "Wages show no sign of returning to the level customary a few years ago, but are still tending to rise" (U. P.). "Customary rates have given place to competition wages, and the [Punjab] labourers move freely in search of more remunerative employment." (*Moral & Mat. Progr.*, 47th No. p. 118). The increase in the real wages of the agricultural population, especially the small cultivators, is proved by the fact that they are clearing themselves of debt very markedly in the

Punjab and to a lesser extent in Bengal and Madras. "Food, clothing, houses, and utensils all show an improvement." (Punjab, 1909).

Prices.—Before the extension of railways, many provinces were isolated from the outside world, and hence prices varied greatly from province to province and even from district to district in the same province. The annual fluctuations even in the same place were very wide. But railways are tending to level prices all over India, while the action of big speculators (who have now begun to influence the Indian market) tends to limit the range of the annual oscillations of price.

About 1860 there began a great rise in prices on account of (1) the large influx of silver into the country for the railways and public works undertaken after the Mutiny, (2) the rapid growth of India's export trade and new industrial activity, and (3) the high price fetched by Indian cotton during the war in America. If we start from the year 1875 and take the prices ruling between 1871 and 1875 as our standard and consider the average of every 5 years, we find that the general average of the prices of seven kinds of grain, *viz.*, rice, wheat, *jawar*, *bajra*, *ragi*, gram and barley,—

rose by 25 p. c. in 1876-80,
fell to the old level in 1881-85,
rose by 21 p. c. in 1886-90,
rose by 35 p. c. in 1891-95,
rose by 64 p. c. in 1896-1900,

rose by 37 p. c. in 1901-1905,
rose by 91 p. c. in 1906-10,
rose by 93 p. c. in 1911-14.

Thus the rise of 1876-1880 has been more than retained since. During most of these periods there have been famines in some province or other, which raised the prices of food grains to a very high level throughout India. But between 1881 and 1890 all the crops except rice were good, and hence the average price of grain was low during the first half of the decade. But from 1886 onwards, prices rose rapidly, though the export of grain was not larger than before and only a few provinces were visited by scarcity. The reason of the rise was probably the heavy import of silver and the increase of the currency. From 1891 to 1900 we had prolonged drought and famine in different parts of India. A strong Indian demand for rice was accompanied by large exports, while there was an unprecedented exportation of wheat owing to the failure of crops in Europe. These circumstances raised Indian prices to the highest known point, (the famine-level of previous generations,) and all parts of India have been affected by the increase of price. Prices (especially of rice and wheat) declined steadily for four years after 1900. But in 1905 began a sharp and rapid rise, which was accentuated in 1906-1908 by the wide-spread failure of crops in N. India, and the famine-level of 1897 was exceeded. Successive good harvests lowered prices generally in 1909 and still further in 1910; but a strong demand from China arrested the fall in the price of rice. In 1911 the autumn crops in northern and western India suffered from defective rainfall, and the price of rice began to mount, this movement being accelerated by a strong export demand. (*Prices and Wages*, ed. 1912.) In 1912 the monsoons partly failed in Bihar and Gujrat, and prices sharply rose in both provinces, especially after September. After 1911 the prices of grain mounted again, and reached a maximum in 1914, with a sharp fall in 1916.

RICE remains extremely dear, because (1) its export has greatly increased, while its production has not extended in the same proportion; (2) the high price of jute has led to rice-fields being devoted to its cultivation in Eastern Bengal and the area under rice being contracted; (3) Bengal and Bihar, the chief producers of rice, have passed during the present century through several seasons of flood and drought; (4) the habit of eating rice is spreading to many races of India which formerly consumed other kinds of grain. It is now eaten by five times as many persons in India as wheat. In normal years, Burma can spare for export 80 p. c. and India proper only 2 p. c. of the rice which they grow, the remainder being required for internal consumption. "It seems that India proper is gradually ceasing to be an exporter of rice and approaching the stage when it will have to obtain supplies of it regularly from Burma and other countries. It should be no wonder, then, that the prices of rice in India should be rising higher and higher."

"The demand for Indian rice in foreign countries is always fairly large and the prices in India depend more on the Indian supply than upon fluctuations in the foreign demand." (*Datta*, 36, 112-114.)

The cultivation of WHEAT has greatly increased to meet a strong demand in Europe. In normal seasons India is able to spare about 15 p. c. of its yield of wheat for export. During a wheat famine in India, the consumers of this grain eat rice or some other grain, but hardly any foreign wheat is imported, because (unlike rice which can be imported from Burma close at hand), the only countries which can send wheat to us,—*viz.*, Russia, U. S. A., &c.—are very distant. "In famine years, therefore, the rise in the price of wheat is proportionately higher than the rise in the price of rice."

Indian wheat does not compete with foreign wheat in Europe as a normal food supply, but is required there only when the foreign supplies to Europe are insufficient. Hence the export of wheat from India to Europe is subject to violent fluctuations resulting from variations in the out-turn of those foreign countries which normally supply Europe, and not from the condition of the Indian crop. "The European demand therefore, exercises a very important influence on the price of Indian wheat."

"The price of wheat in India has been rising in

recent years, in spite of an increased production. The internal demand for wheat is increasing and, with the growing prosperity of the country, wheat is replacing the cheaper grains in the dietary of certain classes" in India. (*Datta*, 36, 114-116.)

The price of Indian *cotton* is governed now more by the world's crop than that of India itself, as India is the second largest grower of this fibre in the world. *Jute* is a monopoly of India, and its price in the world-markets ought to depend mainly on the out-turn in India. But the area under this fibre varies greatly in different years according to the prices realised, because when jute prices are low and rice is dear, the Indian cultivator will place more land under rice than under jute, and *vice versa*. Hence, since 1903, the price of jute has, on the whole, depended more on the world's demand for it than on the Indian supply. (*Datta*, 121-123.)

The price of *hides* and *skins* in India is solely governed by the prices ruling in the world-markets, as India is supplying them at an increasing rate, the value of our exports of this commodity having risen from 100 in 1890-4 to 164 in 1906 and 159 in 1911. There is a greatly increased supply of hides and skins in famine years (with a lowering of prices in India), followed by a decrease in supply in subsequent years as a reaction from the exceptional loss of cattle-life before.

British India	Area under rice	Area under jute	Export of rice	Area under wheat	Area under cotton	Export of wheat
	mil. acres	*mil. acres*	*mil. cwt.*	*mil. acres*	*mil. acres*	*mil. cwt.*
1901	70	2·2	34	18·6	10·3	7·3
1902	71.6	2·1	47·4	19·6	11·1	10·3
1903	69·6	2·5	45	23·6	11·9	25·9
1904	73·5	2·9	49·4	23·5	13	43
1905	73·4	3·1	43	22·4	13	18·7
1906	73·5	3·5	38·7	25·1	13·7	16
1907	75·9	3·9	38·2	18·4	13·9	17·6
1908	72·8	2·85	30·2	21·2	12·9	2·1
1909	78·7	2·75	39·2	22·7	13·1	21
1910	78·5	2·93	48	24·4	14·4	25·3
1911	76·6	3·1	52·4	25	14·5	27·2
1912	78·7	2·97	55·2	23·8	14·1	33·2
1913	75·4	2·9	49	22·6	15·8	24
				all India	all India	
1914	76·1	3·35	31·2	32	24·5	14
1915	...	2·37	27·3	„ 30	„ 17·9	13

Average retail price of grain per *maund* in Rupees and decimals :—

		Highest price before 1901	Price in 1901	1904	1905	1906	1908	1910	1911	1912
RICE.		*(1897)*								
E. Bengal,	Rs.	4·5	3·7	2·7	3·1	4·9	5·1	3·6	3·7	4
W. Bengal ...	...	4·1	3·3	2·8	3	4·1	5·6	3·4	3·5	4·3
Madras	...	4·2	4·2	3·2	4	4·6	5·5	4·5	4·5	5·5
U. P. (excluding Oudh)	...	4·8	3·9	3·5	3·8	4·5	5·8	4·4	4·6	5
L. Burma ...	...	*(1892)* 3·7	3	3·2	3·4	3·8	4·3	3·8	4·4	5
WHEAT		*(1897)*								
U. P. (Agra) ...	...	4·1	3·1	2·4	3·1	3·3	4·8	3·4	3	3·3
Punjab and N. W. F. P.	...	3·8	2·6	2·2	2·6	2·7	4·1	3·1	2·8	3·2
C. P.	...	4·7	3·6	2·5	2·8	3·2	5·1	3·4	3	3·5
JAWAR		*(1900)*								
Bombay ...	...	4·2	2·7	1·9	2·5	3	3·5	2·8	3	3·7
Madras	...	3	2·7	1·6	2·4	2·8	3·2	2·8	2·8	3·3
		(1897)								
U. P. (Agra) ...	...	3·4	1·9	1·6	2·1	2·8	3·5	2·3	2·2	2·5
C. P.	...	3·5	2·3	1·7	2·1	2·6	3·8	2·1	2·1	2·5

Index numbers of prices during the 20th century, the *prices of 1873* being taken *as 100.*—

Year.	Index No. for 11 articles imported.	Index No. for 28 articles consumed in India or exported.	Index No. for 7 food-grains (retail prices.)
1901	96	116	157
1902	86	113	141
1903	88	103	126
1904	93	104	117
1905	96	116	147
1906	105	139	179
1907	116	145	180
1908	106	151	231
1909	99	133	195
1910	109	127	168
1911	113	136	161
1912	117	145	189
1913	117	154	199
1914	114	160	222
1915	...	...	...

Fluctuations of prices in India.—Taking the average of 1890-94 as 100, the movements in the

Indian prices of different groups of articles have been in the following proportion :—

	Cereal food grains.	Sugar.	Cotton manu-factures.	Metals	Building materials	Hides and skins.	General average of 13 groups.
1891	99	100	96	98	99	95	98
1892	110	98	95	100	99	96	103
1894	95	101	102	104	102	109	100
1897	148	101	98	105	109	109	121
1900	134	104	108	137	116	115	122
1904	97	96	121	113	125	141	106
1908	168	106	121	121	136	150	143
1911	126	109	145	119	146	159	134
1912	143	111	137	128	149	172	141

"The general pice-level has gone on increasing steadily throughout the whole period, 1890-1912. The largest increase has occurred in the last eight years" (*viz.*, 1905-12). Taking "smoothed" averages (*i.e.*, for five years, preceded by four and followed by one), the increase in the prices of all commodities taken together (above the basic period, 1890-94) has been as follows:—

1895-99	...	8 p. c.
1900-04	...	12 „
1905-09	...	31 „
1910-12	...	36 „

The five years 1905-1909 were an "era of famine prices without famine" except for a crop failure in N. India during 1908. But in more recent times prices have shown no tendency to return to the old levels. Taking the average of 1910-12, the increase in prices above those of the basic period was,—hides 65 p. c., raw cotton and raw jute 58 p. c. each, oil-seeds 49 p. c., building materials 45 p. c., food-grains 30 p. c., cotton cloth 31 p. c., and metals 22 p. c.

The increase in prices has ranged from 40 p. c. upwards in Karachi, Bundelkhand, Berar, Sind, S. Madras, N & W. Agra Provinces, Punjab, and Deccan;—and between 35 and 39 p. c. in Bihar, C. P., N & E. Madras, Bengal, Choṭa Nagpur, Gujrat and E. Agra Provinces. The average increase for all India since 1890 is 38 p. c. (*Datta*, 29-47).

Causes of the Rise of Prices in India.—Mr. Krishna Lal Datta in his interesting Report on this subject (Calcutta, 1914) attributes the rise to two sets of causes, *viz.*, world-factors and causes peculiar to

India. The *world-factors* are,—(*i*) increased supply of gold, (*ii*) development of credit, (*iii*) destruction of wealth due to recent wars, and (*iv*) increase in armaments in European countries and consequent devotion of more money and labour to non-productive work and military training.

The *causes peculiar to India* are the following, (Burma excluded):

(1) Shortage in the production of food-stuffs compared with the increased demand. (*a*) "Production has not kept pace with the growth of population in recent years." (*b*) Substitution of non-food for food crops, *e.g.*, during 1894-1911, while the population increased by 4·2 p.c., the production of food-grains increased by 1·9 p.c., that of cotton and jute together by 34 p. c., and the export of food-grains from India increased by 21 p. c. during 1900-1911. (*c*) Deficient or unseasonable rainfall, wide-spread famines in 1891, 1896, 1899 and 1908, with local failures in other years the cumulative effect of which must have been very great. [Mr. Datta rejects the theory that the Indian soil has been steadily declining in fertility owing to uninterrupted tillage, and shows how virgin soil attains to its maximum productivity in 5 years, but in 5 more years declines to a level at which it maintains steady for centuries. *Datta*, 68-73.] (*d*) Inferiority of the new lands taken up for cultivation.

(2) A greatly increased demand in India and the outside world. The purchasing powers of certain

classes (such as jute, cotton and wheat growers) have increased in the 20th century to an extraordinary extent. The town-population, with its more liberal habits of spending, has rapidly expanded. Owing to the growth of the general prosperity of the country, the standard of living has markedly improved, and with it the demand for internal consumption.

(3) Extensive export, due to (*a*) increase in communication between India and foreign countries and within India itself, (*b*) decrease in the cost of transport (*i.e.*, railway fares and maritime freights), bringing India closer to the world-markets.

(4) Increased monetary and banking facilities and credit in India, and an increase in the volume of the circulating medium. (The effect of new coinage is *cumulative.*) In the 18 years before the closing of the mints to the free coinage of silver the yearly average net coinage of Rupees was 7·51 *crores* and the hoarding, exportation, melting or waste otherwise was 5 *crores*, leaving an actual addition of 2·51 *crores* to the currency. In the 18 years following the closure of the mints, 5·66 *crores* of Rupees have been annually coined on an average, but only 2·37 *crores* have been wasted, leaving a net addition of 3·29 *crores*. The total circulating medium (Rupees and currency notes) increased by 64 p.c. between 1890 and 1912, but this increase has not been more than the increase in business. (*Datta*, 51-96, 127-129, 188.)

Mr. Datta concludes that the rise of prices is likely

to be permanent in India. In the world-markets, "prices are almost sure to continue to rise in the next decade or two, probably on the average of 2 p.c. per annum." (P. 135). This rate will be greatly exceeded in consequence of the present war.

The above local causes of high prices were assigned by Mr. K. L. Datta in his Report published in 1914; but it is interesting to observe that all of them were given on pp. 213-219 of the 2nd edition of this book, published in March, 1911. It is, therefore, unnecessary to reproduce my own words in this edition, except the following paragraphs which give new illustrations.

1. "On all sides we see that cultivation is extending, and in the older provinces resort is being had to worse lands, *i.e.*, lands naturally less fertile or more affected by bad seasons. In rural Bengal and Bihar this land-hunger of the increasing population has taken an acute form; hollows are being filled up and even the beds and banks of old and dried-up tanks are being ploughed. This resort to worse soils has diminished the proportion of return from land, and the additional food supply is being raised at a greater cost. At the same time many people (especially in Bihar and Chota Nagpur) have begun to eat rice in the place of millets and wheat. This increase in the home consumption, coupled with an undiminished export must raise prices.

2. The closing of the mints to the free coining of silver in 1893 artificially raised the value of rupees

above uncoined silver. Hence, after that date the rupees hoarded in India have been tempted to come into circulation, thereby counteracting the restriction of the coinage. This is evidenced by the fact that, though the Government has been long withdrawing from circulation the rupees of William IV. and those of the year 1840, we still get in the bazar many of these rupees in a fresh condition, showing that they were hoarded for a long time and have been so recently brought into use as not to be worn at all. This fact went to counteract the effect of the closing of the mints in restricting our silver currency.

3. Before 1893 rupees were freely melted back into silver for making ornaments, especially in the villages and smaller towns, and thus about 3 *crores* of rupees were annually withdrawn from the currency. But now that the rupee is a token coin containing only two-thirds the silver bullion that can be bought for it, this melting has ceased. Our currency is now unautomatic. Every new rupee coined after 1893 is an addition to our actual currency and has its effect in raising prices.

To these causes assigned by Mr. Gokhale, I am inclined to add the following three :—

1. Owing to the development of industries, much money has been thrown into the Indian market during the last decade. Both the combination and movement of indigenous capital in the country have greatly increased of late. Competition among the new firms has greatly enhanced wages; wage-earners (and some

professional men too) now have a greater *quantity* of money in their hands. At the same time hoarding has markedly declined. Our upper and middle classes now make it a point to invest their savings, or deposit them in banks which has the same effect. We constantly see instances of this change in our society. It is surprising how little cash even well-to-do people keep in their hands. At the same time that investment is replacing hoarding, owing to the spread of industrialism, capital is in quicker circulation than ever before, which has the effect of multiplying its volume. Financially India has become one country instead of being a group of mutually distrustful and isolated provinces. An immense amount of Indian capital has been subscribed to the joint-stock companies started during the last ten years.

2. There is a greater readiness on the part of the people to *spend* their money. The standard of comfort has immensely risen (especially in the vast middle class), and even the peasants and town labourers are not untouched by the change. The old instinct of hoarding, born of centuries of public disorder and lack of careers, the old abstemiousness taught by an ascetic religion,—have recently given place to a love of the good things of life. Indeed, certain classes are displaying a reckless and improvident fondness for enjoyment, preferring temporary stimulation or exhilaration to the nourishment of the body or the sanitation of the home. Thus, while the productive investment of

savings has greatly increased, that part of the invested capital which is spent in wages quickly gets into circulation by leaving the hands of the wage-earners. I think that in Calcutta, Bombay and other big centres and at large public works, wages were raised *first*, through increased demand for efficient labour, and this rise of wages, coupled with greater lavishness on the part of the wage-earners, produced a rise of prices as the *consequence*. In smaller towns and inland places, where *custom* still influences wages to some extent, the labourers were partly influenced by the news of increase of wages in the big centres, and appealed to the rise of prices there as a plea for raising their own wages too.

3. The "internal drainage" of the country has been completed by the construction of branch and connecting railways. The great lines are mere arteries, connecting the big towns and ports, and often passing through sparsely inhabited country in order to make a short cut. But in the last 10 or 15 years the net-work of railways has covered every part of the country. There is no isolated nook left where a man may live cheaply. Hence the general rise of prices throughout India; nowhere is the surplus produce left standing to lower local prices. Potatoes are supplied to the military station of Darjiling from the river-side villages of Chapra and Arrah in far-off Bihar. During the Eastern Bengal floods of 1905, Dacca merchants imported rice from Patna. There is

now a wider movement even of indigenous traders, partly from the increased facilities of communication and partly from the extension of horizon and loss of conservatism which time and education have effected."

The economic effects of high prices.—Enhanced prices of Indian produce can naturally benefit only those classes who raise the produce, and even such classes only if the commodities other than home produce which they consume appreciate in a lesser degree. To all other classes of the community high prices must be an evil in themselves, though their effect may be counteracted by other economic factors, such as increase of industry and commercial enterprise and extension of public works and building, which lead to an enhanced demand for labour and higher wages. Our wage-earners have benefited in recent times only in proportion as the development of the country has been *not* agricultural, but manufacturing. Therefore, Morison's view that dear bread is beneficial to India as an agricultural country, has a very slender basis. It is, again, difficult to see how high prices in themselves can benefit the trading classes, as is asserted in the *Moral and Material Progress*, 49th No., p. 124, because the cost-price and cost of living have also increased with the sale-price. The greater prosperity of the agriculturists leads, no doubt, to a larger turnover of business throughout the country.

If prices had risen in India only and not in foreign countries also, the economic consequences of it would have been: (*a*) Contraction of exports from India and stimulation of imports into it in the hope of securing better prices here. This would have turned the balance of trade against India, and caused a crisis in a debtor country like ours. (*b*) The gold in India would have been drained away to foreign countries supplying goods to us but buying much less from us. (*c*) The Indian cost of production would have risen in sympathy with the enhanced cost of living, till Indian industries would have ceased to find a market abroad.

All these would have been *temporary* effects; but as our prices have risen along with world-prices, we have not suffered any of these evils.

How different classes in India have been affected by high prices.—The classes that have benefited are (*a*) *Landowners* (except the permanently settled zamindars and the taluqdars of Oudh, who cannot enhance rents easily or rapidly). (*b*) *Peasants* holding land directly from the State for long periods (in the mahalwari and ryotwari tracts). The price of land has risen with the rise in the profits of agriculture. (*c*) The *labouring classes* are better off everywhere, wages having risen much more than the cost of living, [through non-agricultural causes, as shown above]. The only exceptions to such improvement are domestic servants in large cities and other urban areas in a few circles and wage-earners in certain industries, such as the jute mills of Bengal, the cotton-mills of Bombay Gujrat and Madras, and railway works in S. India and E. Punjab.

The classes that have been adversely affected by the rise are—

(*i*) Zamindars and taluqdars under the Permanent settlement, who cannot raise their tenants' rent easily or quickly. (*ii*) Holders of Government and other securities. (*iii*) Producers who cannot charge higher prices with the increase in the cost of production. (*iv*) Lawyers, doctors and other professional classes whose income depends on customary fees. (*v*) Government servants and men in private service with fixed salaries. (*vi*) Persons dependent upon fixed pensions or allowances. (*vii*) Persons engaged in small hand industries (such as indigenous weavers and paddy-huskers) who are unable to compete with machine-products and therefore cannot raise their prices. (*viii*) Priestly castes, scions of old families, &c. who have been unable to accommodate themselves to the changing order of things, and can neither raise their income nor descend to a lower standard of living. (*ix*) Agriculturists in W. and S. Bengal, Bihar, Chota Nagpur and Bundelkhand. (*Datta*, 184-186.)

Condition of agriculturists.—In Assam their material condition has been improved, as the income from the sale of their surplus produce has increased at a greater rate than the price of the commodities (*viz.*, oil, salt, sugar, cotton cloth, fire-wood &c.) which they buy. But in W. and S. Bengal, as well as

Bihar, Chota Nagpur and Bundelkhand, their cost of living has increased more than their income and they are now worse off than before 1890. In the U. P., Punjab, N. W. F. Province and Sind, after undergoing much suffering by reason of bad seasons up to 1905, they have subsequently improved their lot a good deal. Also in Bombay, but to a lesser extent. In Berar and C. P. this change for the better began in 1900. In the five years 1905-9, the era of famine prices without famine, cultivators in all parts of India (except W. and S. Bengal, Bihar, Chota Nagpur and Bundelkhand) largely benefited by the rise in prices. (*Datta*, 183-184.)

Mr. Datta sums up the result thus:—The material welfare of the country as a whole has increased remarkably, especiuny during the 15 years 1898-1912. There have been a considerable increase in the annual income of India and a general diffusion of wealth in consequence of an increase in the profits of agriculture, the development of the resources of the country, and the growth of enterprise on the part of the community as a whole. India has now to part with much less of her produce than formerly to meet her foreign obligations.

CHAPTER VII.

PROFITS.

Profits of manufacture.—Profits include three elements:

(*a*) interest on capital,

(*b*) insurance against risk, and

(*c*) wages of superintendence.

Where the capital is borrowed, the manager of the business is called the undertaker (in French *entrepreneur*), and the difference between the interest paid to the capitalist and the gross profit earned from the business is enjoyed by the *entrepreneur*.

In India, especially in the handicrafts and petty manufactures, the labourer often works on his own account, *i.e.*, he supplies the requisite labour and capital and also undertakes the risks of production. But in large tows, even before the rise of the British power, there was a class of middlemen or capitalists, who advanced money to the craftsmen, purchased their goods or made them repay the loan in the form of articles manufactured to their order, collected large stores of such goods and either sold them locally or exported them. These capitalists did not themselves employ and superintend labour; still, in one sense they directed the industry and undertook the risks of the business. Few were the men who maintained factories, *i.e.*, directly employed labourers under their own roofs, paying them salaries by the day.

In British India we have a vast development of manufactures on the factory system. But in very few of them is the capital supplied by the manufacturer himself; most often it is borrowed or raised by the issue of shares in a joint-stock company. In such cases the interest (or dividend, as the case may be), has to be deducted from the earnings before we get the undertaker's profit. He often gets a commission in addition to his regular salary.

The efficiency of an industry differs according to the class of men who are the *entrepreneurs*,—their education, ability, keenness in discovering more economical methods, in grading workmen according to their exact individual capacities, and in studying the demand of far-off markets. (*Morison*, p. 5.) These qualities were wanting in the Indian producers of old. Hence, the only industry which could earn good profits was the manufacture of objects of art and allied things. In modern India the *entrepreneur* is more educated and more wide-awake. But as he usually works on borrowed capital, or is the managing agent of a joint-stock concern, his interest in the business is less than if his own capital had been risked in the undertaking. Want of commercial morality and experience, or at least ignorance of business methods, on the part of most managers, has been the ruin of many an Indian joint-stock company. It will be a long time before our investors become wiser in consequence of their losses.

The usual rate of interest being much higher in India than in England, profits have to be higher here. Otherwise, Indian capitalists cannot be tempted to invest their money in manufacture. The evil is aggravated by the fact that our improvident *zamindars* and *ryots* alike are constantly raising loans; and land being the safest form of investment, it competes with manufacture for the capital available in India.

In the old-fashioned Indian manufactures all the profits usually went to the same party. But in most of the modern industries established in India, the three elements of profit are enjoyed by two distinct sets of people: the interest and the insurance* against risk are taken by the capitalists or share-holders and the wages of superintendence by the *entrepreneurs* or managers who in the case of the larger concerns are mostly Europeans, though among the share-holders we find an increasing proportion of Indians.

On the whole, the profits of Indian manufacture have not hitherto been so high and regular as those of usury. Hence manufactures have received

* The insurance of the plant and premises against fire cannot cover the *real* risks of the business, which have to be borne by the capitalists.

comparatively little encouragement among us, while banks are thriving in large numbers.

The profits of the middleman as agricultural money-lender and as commercial agent.—In rural India the *Bania* not only lends money to the peasants, but also acts on a small scale as a speculator and middleman in grain. His loan is repaid by the ryots in the form of grain, and so he first secures his interest, and then, by storing the grain and selling it many months afterwards, he earns the usual profit on trade. There is an immense difference between the price of grain at *harvest* and its price in the *bazar*, months afterwards; where export is keen, this difference is sharply felt even within a week of the harvest being over. Our improvident ryots disburden themselves of their surplus produce within the shortest possible time; then comes the Bania's chance, which lasts till the next harvest.

Happily a change for the better has set in during the last few years. The ryots of the Punjab have learnt to hold back their wheat for months after harvest in the hope of realising better prices. In 1910 they refused to sell their crops so long as to cause serious loss to the Karachi port and the Sindh railway. "The greater competition among traders has also tended to reduce the profits of the middleman, and a larger proportion of the market price reaches the pocket of the peasant farmer. Indeed, it is much more common now than it used to be for the peasant to bring his own produce to market,...instead custom, ing the village shopkeeper to take it at a price part more or less by himself." (*Wilson*, p. 13.)

The ryot, by immemorial custom, clears bazar on to the *Bania* (or *Mahajan*, as he is called in Bengal) by payment in kind at a slightly higher rate than the prices then ruling in the bazar. (Sometimes the rate o repayment is fixed in advance by contract at the time of taking the loan.) This part of the Bania's profit in pure interest. His further gain on the sale of the stored agricultural produce at a higher price between two harvests, is trade profit. The Bania rarely financ es any manufacture. Sometimes wholesale dealen advance money (or raw materials) to petty handicrafts men (such as manufacturers of cloth, shoes, meta vessels, silk stuff, &c.), and take the finished money in payment. Here the former class enjoy a with *interest*, but their further profit is conditional upon the subsequent sale of their goods at a higher price their the cost of production. Chance, therefore, enters case largely into the composition of their *profits* than is the case with the Bania or agricultural money-lendes In other respects these wholesale dealers stand on the same economic footing as the Banias.

Brokers, or middlemen strictly so called, ply their business in jute, grain, and a few other articles. Their work mainly consists in buying from Banias or from tolerably large farmers the produce at harvest and despatching it to centres of manufacture or ports of sbarkation. They run very little risk, as they are run of the sale of their purchases and have previously mtracted with manufacturers or big exporters at helcutta, Bombay, Rangoon or Madras, for the deli-any of a certain quantity at a fixed time. Hence ney are sure of a market and know the limits of the crice which they can safely pay. Where they speculate as advance, they sometimes suffer loss, as happens in he case of jute brokers.

Their second advantage is that they have not to dvance money to the producers; they do not run the Bania's risk, though they cannot make his high profit. the rich exporters at the great sea-ports of India are at constant telegraphic connection with the world's narkets and also command vast resources. They, herefore, naturally enjoy all the profits due to a rise n prices outside India. It takes years for the Indian producer to learn of such a rise and to take advantage of it by raising *his* prices. These rich exporters are only a few in each province and so, at present, they enjoy the advantages of monopolists. Where they same and export, there cannot be the same active competition for Indian produce as when the intending purchasers are a large number of petty exporters. Besides, the enormous resources of the former enable them to crush out their smaller Indian rivals and to dictate (to some extent) their own terms to the Indian producers. If, however, we had *many* rich exporters competing for our produce, the result pointed out by a critic of this book would no doubt have taken place He says, "Such [large] firms are likely to pay highe prices in India for two reasons: (1) their certainty o: a market and knowledge of the price obtainable are Europe and America] enables them to work on smaller margin of profit and to buy more grain to higher prices than if their business were more speculative. (2) The large scale on which they do busines also enables them to work at a lower rate of profit per *maund*. The advantage which such exporters derive from their sources of information and large capital therefore involves benefit to Indian producers also."

Probably this state of things has been already reached in the case of Punjab wheat. "In all the large grain markets of the Punjab, there are agents of exporting firms who study the world's prices of wheat, and buy whenever they think export will be profitable." (*Wilson*, p. 19.) "The greater competition among traders has also tended to reduce the profits of the middleman, and a larger proportion of the market price reaches the pocket of the peasant farmer." (P. 13). In the latter passage Wilson, however, speaks of the price in *Indian* markets.

CHAPTER VIII.

EXCHANGE.

The development of Indian oversea trade.— In the first four centuries of the Christian era, South India had a monopoly of pepper (Sanskrit *pippali*), pearls and beryls (or the aquamarine gem) and did a very extensive and lucrative trade in these articles with Rome through Egypt. Our other exports were also mainly articles of great value in small bulk, such as various kinds of precious stones,—which "held the foremost place" in the Roman market, "there being none preferred to the Indian kind," and spices, indigo, cane-sugar ("honey collected in reeds," as Pliny calls it),—the last two being used as medicines,—silks, muslin and other fine cotton fabrics, and some amount of lac and iron for swords. She took in exchange gold, silver, copper and ironware, and cloth (probably woollen). In the first century A. D., India, according to Pliny, annually absorbed from Europe a little less than half a million sterling worth of treasure, chiefly silver with a fair amount of Roman gold coins. But we must bear in mind that Pliny's India included Ceylon, which was the principal place of exchange for the Eastern trade in those days. (Schoff's *Periplus*, 286-289, McCrindle's *Ancient India as described in Classical Literature*, 102-135, Pliny's *Natural History*, xii. 18 (41) and vi. 26, Merivale's *Romans under the Empire*, ch. 68).

For nearly three hundred years after the establishment of European commercial houses here in the 16th century, India continued to export manufactures mainly. In the middle of the 17th century she supplied to Europe diamonds, pearls, white cotton cloth, muslin, chintz, silk fabrics, especially brocades, carpets, large quantities of spices, drugs (such as borax, opium, &c.,) dyes (indigo, lac, &c.,) sugar, tobacco, and saltpetre (the only raw material of large quantity). Even the steel employed in the famous Damascus blades came from the kingdom of Golkonda. We took in exchange woollen fabrics, "scarlet" cloth (Arabic *saqarlat*, a favourite of the Mughal emperors), metal works, &c., (Tavernier, tr. by Ball, ii. ch. 12; *Storia do Mogor*, ii. 418). But the rapid development of European industries with the help of steam reversed this state of things in the middle of the nineteenth century. Improvements in industrial processes in Europe greatly reduced the cost of production there while the opening of the Suez Canal lowered freights and shortened the period of transit between India and Europe. The opening of the trunk lines of railway has connected our sea-ports with the interior of the country, and made it easy for European manufactures to reach far-off Indian villages, while grain and other bulky goods can be now cheaply brought down to the ports to be drained out of the country. Thus from about 1860 India has become a mere exporter of raw materials and a huge consumer of foreign manufactures. About 1885 the tide just began to turn; thanks to the jute and cotton mills, our export of manufactures has begun to increase, as also our import of raw materials, at a progressive rate.

The following figures show the growth of India's sea-borne foreign trade, including gold and silver and the stores and treasure imported and exported by Government, in *crores* of Rs. :—

Annual average		Imports Rs. *crores*	Exports Rs. *crores*	Excess of our exports over our imports. *crores*
for the decade ending	1844 ...	9·72	13·73	4
" "	1854 ...	14·05	18·75	4·7
" "	1874 ...	44·79	56·61	11·82
" "	1884 ...	57·54	74·49	16·95
" "	1894 ...	83·26	102·66	19·4
" "	1904 ...	105·7	130·96	25·26
" "	1910 ...	146·51	173·15	26·64
" 1910 only	... ...	173·47	217·09	43·62
" 1911 "	... ...	197·52	238·37	40·85
" 1912 "	... ...	228·46	256·85	28·39
" 1913 "	... ...	234·75	256·09	21·34
" 1914 "	... ...	166·74	187·46	20·72
" 1915 "	... ...	149·46	207·71	58·25

Taking the average of the three years 1911-13, our import was 220·24 *crores*, export 250·44 *crores*, and excess of export 30·2 *crores* per annum. In addition to the above we have a foreign trade by land, the value of which is only 4 to 5 p. c. of our sea-borne trade. About 3·5 p. c. of our imports is re-exported by sea.

Analysis of India's imports by sea, 1913—

Merchandise	...	191·31 *crores* of Rs.
Gold and silver	...	43·44 „ „
TOTAL	...	234·75 „ „

out of which 14·88 *crores* worth was imported by Government and the remainder by private persons.

The chief items making up our imports of private merchandise were :—

	Crores of Rs. 1911	1912	1913
Cotton goods	49·56	60·8	66·29
Metals	14·2	15·49	22
comprising			
Copper	2·68	2·37	4·11
Iron and steel	10	11·47	16
Machinery and mill-work ...	4·56	5·85	8·26
Railway materials and stores ...	4·43	6.4	10
Hardware & cutlery	3·12	3·41	3·94
Instruments and apparatus ...	1·3	1·48	1·82
Clothing (other than cotton) &c.			
Woollen goods	3·4	3·05	3·85
Silk (raw & manufd.) ...	3·71	4·78	4·37
Apparel	1·54	1·61	1·71
Boots & shoes	0·55	0·66	0·79

	Crores of Rs. 1911	1912	1913
Railway materials (Govt.) ...		2·54	4
Articles of food and drink.			
Sugar	11·93	14·27	14·95
Provisions	1·93	2·34	2·47
Liquors	1·65	1·82	1·87
Spices	1·54	1·63	1·73
Salt	0·84	0·85	0·87
Tobacco	0·66	0·69	0·75
Oils	4·42	4	4·4
Other things			
Glass-ware & earthenware ...	2·09	2·3	2·59
Paper, paste-board & stationery	1·72	2	2·28
Books	0·45	0·42	0·49
Dyes & colours	2	2·3	2·26
Chemicals & medicines ...	2·18	2·19	2·4
Matches	0·87	0·98	0·89
Coal	0·51	1·16	1·06
Pearl and precious stones ...	0·89	1·08	1·07

Of the total foreign sugar we took, only 9 p. c. was from beet and the rest from cane. Of the mineral oils that reached us from foreign countries three-fourths consisted of kerosene. (69 million gallons against 109 mil. gal. from Burma.)

Leaving out Government transactions and treasure imported by private persons, out of our total imports of merchandise in 1913,

Cotton goods formed (in value)	37 p. c.
Metals "	12 "
Sugar "	8 "
Mineral oils "	2·5 "
Railway materials	6 "

Analysis of India's exports by sea, 1913—

Indian merchandise ...	...	244·23 *crores of Rs.*
Foreign „ re-exported	...	4·68 „
Gold and silver ...	...	7·08 „
	TOTAL	256·12

Government exports have not been included in the above, as they were of negligible amount, only 13 *lakhs* worth in all.

The chief items making up our exports of private merchandise were :—

	Crores of Rs.		
	1911	1912	1913
Raw materials			
Cotton	29·4	28·33	41
Jute	22·5	27	30·82
Seeds (for oil)	26·9	22·7	25·6
Hides (raw)	13·9	11·76	11·72
Wool	2·58	2·63	2·5
Silk (raw)	0·45	0·41	0·24
Articles of food and drink			
Rice	29	32.55	26·6
Wheat	14·14	18·77	14·38
Other grains and pulses	8·26	8·98	4·16
Tea	12·94	13·29	14·97
Coffee	1·34	1·56	1·53
Fruits and vegetables	1·37	0·47	0·61
Provisions	1·08	0·48	0·54
Fodder, bran and cattle food ...	1·71	1·13	0·77
Manufactures			
Jute goods	16	22·8	28·2
Cotton goods	9·77	12·2	12·12
Oils	1·59	0.85	0·98

	Crores of Rs.		
	1911	1912	1913
Lac	2	2·11	1·96
Indigo	0·37	0·22	0·21
Other things			
Opium	13·08	11·22	3·42
Dyeing and tanning materials (excluding indigo)	0·75	0·88	0·83
Metals	1·64	0·77	0·64
Coal	0·77	0·88	0·69
Manures	1·16	0·96	0·94

Of our total exports of merchandise in 1913—

Raw materials and unmanufactured articles formed (in value)	50·1 p. c.
Articles of food and drink	26·5 „
Indian manufactures	22·4 „
Raw cotton	17 „
Rice	11 „
Jute	12·5 „
Tea	6 „
Hides and skins	4·7 „

Our trade relations with other countries, (1913)—

	Percentage of our imports.	Percentage of our exports.	Percentage of our total trade.
England	64	23	40
Germany ...	7	10	9
United States ...	2·6	9	6·2
China	1	2·3	1·7
Japan	2·6	9·2	6·4
France	1·5	7	4·8
Belgium	2·3	5	3·8
Java	5·8	0·8	2·9
Austro-Hungary ...	2·3	4	3·3
Straits Settlements ...	1·9	2·8	2·4

The Indian balance of trade.—During the five years 1911-15 our average annual exports of *merchandise* (both Government and private) exceeded our imports by 64 *crores* of rupees a year. But during the same period we annually absorbed 30·17 *crores* worth of *treasure* on an average. Hence the *net* excess of our exports was 33⅓ *crores* a year; this amount, which is *15 p. c. of the average total* of our *exports* (229 *crores* worth), *is annually drained out of the country*, or in other words we now get no *visible* return for the goods of this value which we export every year. The balance of trade, in the true sense of the term, is against India to this extent, *i. e.*, she parts with about one-sixth more than she gets from the outside world. This is the natural consequence partly of India being a debtor country and partly of her political position, as has been shown on pages 137-141. (See *Ind. Emp.*, iii. 270, *Hunter*, 661, and Gokhale's *Speeches*, 108-111.) A part of the excess consists of the interest on the foreign capital invested in Indian (private) railways and steamer companies, indigo factories, tea-gardens, mills, mines and other industries. (See p. 188.) Another part is made up of the annual savings of European merchants, lawyers, doctors and officials serving in India. But the major portion consists of the Government expenditure annually incurred in England on behalf of India, which is called the Home Charges. Two-thirds of our Public Debt are held in England and the interest has to be paid there.

The Home Charges.—For the five years ending 1913 these charges amounted to 29·77 *crores* of rupees a year on an average, and in 1909 and 1910 they amounted to 27·6 *crores* and 27·9 *crores* respectively. The expenditure in 1913 was thus made up:—

1. *Railway Revenue Account* (*i.e.*, annuities for buying up the shares of railway companies, interest on the debt for State railway capital, price of materials, &c.) also interest on *irrigation* capital, ... *Rs.* 13·67 *crores*

		Rs.
2. *Pensions and furlough allowances* ...		8·4 *crores*
Military	4·52	
Civil	3·88	
3. *Interest on Indian Public Debt* (other than railway and irrigation) held in England		3·22 "
4. *Army expenses in England* (see p. 138) ...		2·24 "
Payments to the British Exchequer for British forces serving in India	1·37	
Transport of troops ...	0·46	
Other charges	0·206	
Payments for warships in the Indian Seas ...	0·209	
5. *Stores purchased* for India		2·25 "
Military and marine ...	1·42	
Civil, P. W. D., telegraph, stationery &c. ...	0·82	
6. *Civil expenditure in England* ...		0·65 "
Secretary of State's establishment, postage, rates, taxes, coal, &c., also miscellaneous ...	37 *lakhs*	
Post and telegraph connections with India ...	18¾ *lakhs*	
Charges on account of other civil departments in India, &c.... ...	9¼ *lakhs*	
TOTAL ...		30·46 *crores.*

[*Cd. 8157, p. 70-71.*]

From the above it will be seen that 19·14 *crores* or about 63 p. c. of the Home Charges (*viz.*, items 1, 3 and 5), represent a payment for which we have already got our money's worth. This portion of the expenditure could have been avoided only if all our public and railway loans had been raised in India and English-made stores replaced by things manufactured in India, both of which suppositions are impossible. (Even a free country like Japan largely buys stores in Europe, because the articles, and in some cases articles of the same quality, cannot be had anywhere else). The Secretary of State periodically urges the Indian Government to buy stores in India as far as possible without any sacrifice of quality or increase of cost. The army swallows up 22 p. c. (or, if we add the military and marine stores, 27 p. c.) of the total. But, so long as the sepoys cannot be trusted with the most efficient weapons or positions of command, and the Indian public cannot be armed for home defence, the British troops are necessary for safeguarding India from invasion, and their pay and pension represents the insurance premium we must annually provide for peace and security. It is, however, a heavy burden. The Special Committee on Home Charges reported in 1889:—

The cost of supplying recruits to India is [now] more than double what it was [just before the Mutiny], and, owing to the short service system, the number on whom the capitation vote is paid is increased....The average cost per recruit sent to India (excluding his clothing and equipment, but including depot-charges for training and hospital, charges for deserters, &c.)

was £40 8s. in 1886....The transport of an adult unit of the army to or from India cost £10 13s. in 1886. The short service system, by causing the whole British army in India to be relieved once in three instead of in 10 or 12 years, has greatly increased the cost of transport. (*Cd. 327*, pp. 95,121,122.) In 1908, over 29,000 soldiers were conveyed to and from India, and the cost of transport was half a *crore* of rupees. (*Cd. 5345*, pp. 220 and 70).

The civil pension and furlough allowances absorb 3·88 *crores*. This amount can be reduced only by the extended employment of Indians in the public service. Political and moral objections are raised by the authorities to the entire replacement of imported public servants by the children of the soil. As for the salary and other expenses of the Secretary of State and his Office in London, the amount is paid by India, whereas in the case of the Colonial Office it is borne by the British Treasury. It, however, forms only 1·2 p. c. of our total Home Charges. (Cf. *Alston*, 108).

Economic effects of the Home Charges.—Whatever the nature of their component elements as analysed above, the effect of the Home Charges now is to compel India every year to part with above 30 *crores* of rupees worth of goods in excess of her imports. The economic consequences of this state of things have been described in pages 141-142. (See also *Ind. Emp.*, iv. 194, *Dutt*, 536, 604, 605, and Gokhale's *Speeches*, 807; and, for the Secretary of State's recommendations for reducing the amount, the Parliamentary *Return on East India Home Charges, Cd. 327* of 1893). That part of the Home Charges which is spent in buying out the English shareholders of Indian railways is a means of the nationalisation of railways, and cannot be called a drain. Similarly, the interest on our sterling debt is the inevitable price of the money which we received in the past, and it will cease when all our public debt is held in India. European countries like Russia and the United States also have to pay interest to their foreign creditors, and in this respect India is not singular. But being connected with the monetary system of Europe they do not suffer any loss through exchange, while India, before 1893, had to bear the entire loss caused by the depreciation of her currency because she as debtor is bound to make payments in Europe. Secondly, Russia and the United States pay interest on their debts with a much larger proportion of manufactures than India does, who has to send out 44 p. c. in raw materials and 31 p. c. in food stuffs. (Cf. *Alston*, 101-109, *Howard*, ch. iv).

How India pays her debt to England.—Every year the Secretary of State for India has to spend 20 million pounds sterling *in England* on our behalf, which must be paid to him out of the revenue of India. At the same time merchants in England have to send money *to India* to buy our produce for export. To avoid this double transport of money, the Secretary of State in Council sells in London documents called "Council bills" (or telegraphic transfers) for which the English merchants pay to him *in gold*, while the agents of these merchants cash the bills *for rupees* at the Government treasuries in India, and buy our raw materials, grain, &c. with the money. When, owing to famine or war, the Indian treasuries are short of money and can pay only a portion of the Home Charges in cash, the Secretary of State sells bills to that amount only and raises the balance needed for his expenses by contracting a debt in England. Sometimes certain sums due to India are paid in England, and the Secretary's drawings on India are reduced to that extent. Very often trade requires more Council bills than are necessary for the Secretary's expenses in England. In such cases he draws bills for the surplus amount, but they are paid in India out of the Paper Currency or Gold Standard Reserve, while their price, paid in London, is afterwards transmitted to India in silver bullion to fill up the gap in the Reserve. Thus the Secretary of State is the greatest exchange banker working between England and India. For example, in 1905 he sold bills for 31 millions, while he required only 3 millions net, (*viz.*, $17\frac{2}{3}$ millions for the Home Charges, less $14\frac{1}{2}$ millions raised by loan in England.) In 1908 his drawings and debt totalled $25\frac{1}{4}$ millions, while the Home Charges were $18\frac{1}{3}$ millions only. Lord Lamington, in a speech on Jan. 20, 1913, held that the Secretary of State should not draw on Indian revenues beyond his actual requirements, as it hampers the employment of capital in India. (*Cf. Howard*, Ch. III.)

The system of India's payment to England operates by means of a long chain: the Indian peasants sell their grain, jute, or cotton to exporters in order to pay the Government revenue and taxes, (*Ind. Emp.*, iii. 271), the Government parts with these rupees to the exporters whose London representatives have paid the equivalent of this money to the Secretary of State who spends the amount in England. Those who look only at the two ends of the chain say that every year we send out of our country food-stuffs and raw materials worth more than Rs. 30 *crores*, the price of which is not paid in India but is spent in England though on behalf of India. They call it a drain. But as has been already shown, the price of these food-stuffs and raw materials would have remained in India and nourished our industries if only *all* our public debt had been locally raised (at the same low rate of interest), all our officers had made India their home and all the stores that a modern government needs could have been manufactured here.

The Indian Public Debt, March, 1914—411 *crores Rs.*

Sterling Debt held in England £177 millions	265·6	"	"
Rupee Debt held in India	145·6	"	"
	411·2	"	"
Analysis of the public debt—			
Railway debt	333	"	"
Irrigation debt	59	"	"

(Both these are capital employed productively)

Ordinary or unproductive debt ...	...	18·3 *crores Rs.*
Initial expenditure on New Delhi	...	85 *lakhs.*

The above method of stating the accounts is unbusinesslike and misleading. The item productive or "public works debt" does not represent debt actually incurred for public works, but only that portion of the national debt which equals "the total capital expenditure which has been incurred by the State on public works, together with the amount advanced to railway companies for capital expenditure,"—*i.e.*, that portion of the national debt which is set off by productive investment of an equivalent initial amount (not the present worth of our railways after deducting depreciation). It must be here borne in mind that some of our railway lines yield no profit and some others, (the strategic railways), are not intended to yield any commercial return. The term "Ordinary debt" is applied to the remainder of our total debt after deducting the "public works debt" for the year. The result is curious. "In any year in which, owing to the use of surplus revenue or deposits for the construction of public works, the capital expenditure of the year exceeds the amount of debt incurred in the year, the effect of this system of classification is to cause a *decrease* to be shown in the amount of the Ordinary Debt,"—*i.e.*, a part of the latter debt is represented as paid off, while it really remains undiminished, and the productive investment of the State merely increases by the use of surplus revenue for capital purposes.

The history of Indian currency.—Before the Muhammadan invasion and for some time after it, gold was the chief currency of India for all large transactions. Copper was used for small change, and villagers and citizens of small towns used shells (*cowries*) in the bargains of their daily life. Silver was coined, though to a much less extent than gold.

The silver *Tanka* was first coined by Altamsh, Sultan of Delhi, in 1233 A.D., and it gradually became the standard of Northern India. In the reign of Sher Shah, 1542, the coin acquired its present weight (180 grains) and the name of *Rupee*. The ratio between gold and silver coins varied from time to time, though both were freely coined by the Mughal emperors. Calculations were made in rupees, though gold was used in making presents or paying tribute. Southern India, being comparatively free from the Muhammadan influence, retained the gold currency till 1818, when it was ordered to be displaced by the E. I. Company's silver coinage.

In 1766 the East India Company tried to establish bimetallism or a fixed legal ratio between gold and silver. Its gold *mohurs* were at first valued at 14 *sicca* rupees. But the new *mohurs* of 1769 were declared equivalent to 16 *sicca* rupees, though the market price of gold was less. The confused state of our currency may be judged from the fact that in 1773 there were circulating in various parts of India 139 kinds of gold *mohurs*, 61 kinds of gold *huns* or South Indian coins (called *pagodas* by Europeans), 556 kinds of silver rupees, besides 214 kinds of foreign coins. Then the East India Company introduced some order amidst the confusion by recognising as the principal standard in its dominions a copy of the *sicca rupee of the 19th year* of the reign of Shah Alam II. (1778) which it minted in Calcutta, while three other rupees were issued by the Company in the provinces and had a local circulation.

In 1835 the silver rupee was declared the *sole* legal tender all over India, the other rupees being withdrawn. Government finally gave up bimetallism, accepted siver mono-metallism, and instead of legally fixing the value of gold coins, left it to the choice of purchasers. Gold *mohurs* and silver rupees (each containing 180 grains, of which one-twelfth is alloy) were henceforth coined, bearing the face of the British sovereign, and this silver rupee was made the only monetary standard of India, while the new gold *mohurs* (valued Rs. 15), though no longer legal tender, were to be coined and issued on demand (for ceremonial purposes). In 1841, officers in charge of public treasuries were authorised freely to receive these gold *mohurs* at their face value in payment of Government dues. (*Ind. Emp.*, ii. 136, 143; *Datta*, 257.)

Currency Legislation.—In January 1853, Lord Dalhousie, alarmed by the fall in the price of gold owing to the gold discoveries in Australia and California, suddenly closed our treasuries to the acceptance of gold coins. In 1864 British sovereigns were authorised to be received in Indian treasuries at Rs. 10 each, (which rate was raised to Rs. 10-8 in 1868). But it had no effect, as silver began to fall rapidly in price and most Continental States demonetised silver in 1872-74. India's trade with Australia and European countries having a gold standard was greatly hampered by the fall in the exchange value of the rupee. The financial burden of the Indian Government, which had to pay sixteen millions *in sterling* in England for the Home Charges, greatly increased as more and more rupees had to be paid to buy the *same number* of sovereigns. For instance,

in 1872 one rupee was worth			1s. 11*d*.
„ 1876	„	„	1s. 8½*d*.
„ 1885	„	„	1s. 6¼*d*.
„ 1887	„	„	1s. 4·89*d*.
„ 1892	„	„	1s. 2·98*d*.
„ 1894	„	„	1s. 1·1*d*.

after which the exchange rose gradually till it reached 1s. 4*d*. in 1899, at which it has remained fairly steady since then.

The rapid fall in the value of "the vanishing rupee" greatly distressed Anglo-Indian officers having to remit money Home, and unsettled our foreign trade by introducing uncertainty as to the standard of value. The Government was driven to levy new taxes to find money for the Home Charges, because "every penny which the rupee falls, necessitates taxation on the people to the amount of one million pounds to meet the charges payable in London." But there is a limit to the fresh taxes that can be imposed on India, and the Government was in danger of turning bankrupt. The last hope of establishing bimetallism by international agreement failed in 1892, when the Brussels Monetary Conference broke up in discord. Then a parliamentary committee under Lord Herschell sat in England and took the evidence of experts on the Indian currency (*Code 7060*). By the Currency Act of 1893, (*a*) from June 1893, the Indian mints were closed to the free coinage of silver for *private* persons but Government was to coin rupees to remedy any shortage of the circulating medium; (*b*) gold, both sovereigns and bullion, was to be received by the Indian *mints* and rupees given in exchange at the rate of £1 = Rs. 15, but gold was *not* yet made *legal tender* to *private* persons; (*c*) sovereigns were to be received in payment of *Government* dues at the same fixed rate. This legislation was clearly meant for a transition stage. Its objects were (i) to stop further increase in the volume of the silver currency, (ii) to induce gold to flow into the country from abroad and discourage the import of silver, and (iii) to familiarise the Indians with the use of the sovereign as currency without forcing it on them. The coining of rupees was absolutely stopped for six years; but exchange rose very slowly, and reached 1*s*. 4*d*., the official rate, as late as 1899.

Meantime a strong body of European traders and tea-planters demanded a return to the free coinage of silver, on the grounds that (*a*) a fall in exchange increases export from India, stimulates production, and gives India more rupees for her produce sold in gold-standard countries, (*b*) tea-planters who sell their produce for gold, but pay their coolies in silver, suffer in proportion as the exchange rises and they get fewer rupees for a sovereign than before, and (*c*) any State regulation of the rate of exchage is opposed to the laws of economics. But the new legislation was an evident success; many of the evils anticipated from it did not actually happen, and most of the experts who in 1892 had opposed the closing of the mints were now as strongly opposed to their being re-opened to the free coining of silver, because such a course would be "disastrous." Another parliamentary committee, under Sir Henry Fowler, took expert evidence in 1898 (*Code 9037* and *9222*) on the problems of Indian currency. By the Act of 1899, (i) sovereigns were made legal tender for the *public*, along with rupees, to an unlimited extent, and (ii) the coining of sovereigns at the Indian mints, which would be legal tender all over the empire, was sanctioned. (*Ind. Emp.*, iv. 518.) Thus the way has been prepared for introducing gold mono-metallism, and the next step, as recommended by MacLeod, would be to cautiously and slowly restrict the amount of rupees as legal tender, in proportion as "India is saturated with gold," till the limit of £5 for silver tender is reached, as in Egypt. (In England silver is legal tender up to £2 only.) As silver is still unlimited legal tender here, we have not yet established pure mono-metallism, but are maintaining a "limping standard" like that of France, Holland, and to some extent of Germany, "that is to say, opening the mints to the free coinage of gold and at the same time allowing the existing rupees to continue as legal tender" without demonetising them. (Schmidt, in *Code 7060* II. p. 76.) Only one metal, *viz.*, gold, is now our standard in international transactions.

The Gold Exchange Standard.—Mr. A. M. Lindsay, of the Bank of Bengal, published a scheme for a gold exchange standard *without a gold currency.* According to it, a large amount of notes or cheap token coins (*i.e.*, rupees) will remain in circulation in India, that is to say, our *internal currency* will remain *silver.* But Government will offer in London rupee drafts for Rs. 15,000 each payable in India at 1*s.* $4\frac{1}{16}$*d.* per rupee, and in Bombay and Calcutta sterling drafts for £1000 payable in London at 1s. $3\frac{3}{4}$*d.* per rupee. By this scheme rupees will be changed into Government sterling drafts and not into gold coins, so that there will be no chance of gold being withdrawn from Europe to India or being absorbed by the people; India will have a *gold* standard *for foreign payments only.* For the conversion into gold a fund of ten millions sterling is to be borrowed by the Government of India, deposited in the Bank of England, and managed by a non-official body to ensure public confidence: "The expense of convertibility to the

Government might be diminished by *forcing the Natives*, by means of a prohibitive duty on silver, to revert to the old practice of melting rupees for the manufacture of silver ornaments,"—*i.e.*, they are to be forced to melt the artificially appreciated rupees and prevented from buying cheap silver bullion!

Mr. Lindsay's proposal, when first published in 1892 and again when made before the Fowler Committee in 1898, was rejected, as Government and its economic advisers held that a gold standard is inseparable from a gold currency. But the Indian Government has now actually drifted into Mr. Lindsay's scheme, unconsciously and by the process of currency development. We now have two currencies, *viz.*, a local currency of silver and notes for purely *internal* use, and a gold currency for *international* or foreign purposes only. In other words, we have adopted the gold standard for exchange only, as advocated by Mr. Lindsay.

This is neither anomalous nor opposed to economic principles. As was first pointed out by Ricardo a century ago, it is wasteful to have an intrinsically valuable circulating medium, and the ideal currency is one in which notes (or cheques) and cheap token coins form the *internal* currency, but are made convertible into gold (the international medium of exchange) at a fixed rate for foreign payments only.

As Mr. J. M. Keynes has shown, "The Gold Exchange Standard [of India] is not, in the currency world of today, anomalous; it is in the main stream of currency evolution...In the last ten years it has become the prevailing monetary system of Asia...It is also closely related to the prevailing tendencies in Europe. Gold is an international, but *not* a local currency" even in England (where cheques form the internal medium of exchange). (Pp. 29, 36.) A gold currency is not a necessary condition of the gold standard. It is an economic truth "that so long as gold is available for payments of *international* indebtedness at an approximately constant rate in terms of national currency, it is a matter of comparative indifference whether it actually *forms* the national currency." (P. 30).

How exchange between India and the world's money-market is maintained.—We have already shown (page 283) how India has in normal years to pay 20 millions sterling to England, and also how our exports exceed our imports by about the same amount, *i.e.*, the Indian *Government* has to make payment of the amount in England, and European merchants in India. The Secretary of State sells, for gold payable in London, *Council bills* (which are sent by post, or *Telegraphic transfers*, which are sent by telegraph), the rupee price of which (at the rate of about 1s. 4*d*. per rupee) is paid in India out of the Government Treasury from the year's revenue, or out of the Paper Currency Reserve or Gold Standard Reserve, as the case might be. This is the normal state of things.

But in famine years or during a monetary crisis in Europe, very little money is sent to India, while the Secretary of State has to spend in England 20 millions of Indian money as in other years. The exchange then becomes very adverse to India; the Secretary of State stops offering his Council bills in London (there being no demand for them), and adopts the converse process *i.e.*, the Government sells, in India, *Sterling bills* or '*reverse councils*' payable in London (at the rate of about 1s. 4*d.* per rupee) and they are cashed out of the English branch of the Gold Standard Reserve, while the rupees paid for them are placed in the Indian branch of the Reserve; at the same time our mints stop coining new rupees, as no longer required on account of the balance of trade being against India. In 1908 eight millions worth of Sterling bills were sold. Thus the exchange or gold value of our local currency (the rupee) is maintained.

The Gold Standard Reserve: its history.—The coined rupee being now very much dearer than the quantity of pure silver it contains, Government makes a profit of about 42 in every 100 new rupees it puts into circulation, (if we calculate from the silver prices of 1912). Its total profit from silver coinage, *plus* interest on the invested portion of the profit, is now (1916) thirty millions sterling. As Government meets the demands of foreign trade by giving rupees in India in exchange for gold tendered in London (*i.e.*, Council Bills) at the rate of £1 = Rs. 15, so conversely, when the balance of trade is adverse to India and money has to be sent from this country to England, our Government ought to be able to pay gold in London for rupees tendered in India (Sterling bills or '*reversed* council bills') at the same rate. Otherwise, the gold parity of the rupee would be destroyed, exchange would fall below the legitimate limit, and the Gold Exchange Standard established by Government would cease to be effective and self-regulating. Whenever the gold price of the rupee is so low that it is profitable to export sovereigns from India to England, *i.e.*, exchange in India falls below *the gold export point*,—the result is that the gold currency is drained out of our country, and the Government of India ought to make its gold in London available for foreign remittances, as the Fowler Committee of 1898 recommended, otherwise our country would become bankrupt in its external or international currency (which is gold).

For this purpose, a fund styled the *Gold Standard Reserve* was created in 1900, when, after six years' inactivity since the closing of the mints, the coinage of new rupees began again on a large scale. It was decided that the net profits of coinage should not be spent as revenue but formed into this Reserve and held in England in the form of sterling securities. In 1906 the *silver branch* of the Gold Standard Reserve was created. It is held in India and consists of rupees, (maximum limit 6 *crores*), so that when a sudden demand for rupees arises through the needs of the export trade, the Government may issue rupees from this Reserve, while the sterling equivalent of the amount is added to the London portion of the Reserve. Thus any dangerous depletion of the Paper Currency Reserve and temporary shortage of rupees in India is avoided.

In 1907 it was decided to invest half the net profit of future coinage in the capital expenditure on railways. This was done for two years only, and then forbidden till the sterling assets of the Reserve should exceed 25 millions. There being little or no new coinage from 1908 to 1911, there was no addition to the Reserve during these four years. In 1912 it was decided to hold a portion of this fund in the form of a "very liquid" or *cash* gold Reserve in England not exceeding 5 millions sterling, because, during the monetary crisis of 1908 the Secretary of State had had to sell his securities in a hurry and at a loss in order to cash the Sterling bills. In 1914, in accordance with the recommendations of the Chamberlain Commission, the silver branch of the Gold Standard Reserve was abolished, by being converted into gold. The Reserve totalled

19 mil. £ on 31 March 1912,
25½ " " 31 March 1914,
28½ " " 30 Sep., 1916. (30 mil. on 31 Dec.)

On 30 Sep. 1916 it was thus held:—

(In England)	Book credit	0·8 mil. £.
	Cash at short notice ...	4·2
	Temporary loans to the Home Treasury balance... ...	2
	Securities	16·4
		23·5
(In India)	Gold...	1
	Temporary loans to Treasury balances	4
		28·5

Indian Paper currency.—In India gold and silver are both legal tender at the fixed rate of £ 1 = Rs. 15. Government did not accept any legal obligation to give gold for rupees, but it has freely issued many millions of sovereigns to the public at the fixed rate in order to teach the people the habit of using gold as currency and to keep a large amount of gold in course of circulation in the country as a means of giving greater stability to international exchange. When our export trade is brisk there is an enhanced demand for rupees, and gold is offered to the Government in exchange for them. But when trade is slack, the rupees return to the treasuries as people (especially import merchants) require sovereigns. This in-flow and out-flow of gold and silver coins takes place largely through the channel of the *Paper Currency Reserve*, or the fund kept for cashing currency notes on demand, and in part through the Gold Standard Reserve. When there is a trade demand for rupees, the rupees go out of the paper currency reserve and gold comes in, while in periods of dull trade the rupees return to the trade centres as there is no more use for them in making purchases, the merchants demand gold to make remittances Home, and gold goes out of this reserve fund. In the former case when the stock of rupees in this fund is greatly reduced, Government buys silver and coins new rupees. Conversely, in the latter case, when the stock of gold is exhausted, Government draws on the sovereigns in the Gold Standard Reserve described above.

Under law Government is bound to hold a reserve against its note issue *equal to their full value*, and only 20 *crores* of the reserve can be invested in securities,—of which not more than 4 *crores* can be securities of the English Government, and 16 *crores* might be securities of the Indian Government. (Act VII. of 1911.) Notes up to Rs. 100 are now "universal" or can be cashed all over India, while notes of higher denominations are legal tender only within the currency "circles" or provinces in which they are issued. (*Ind. Emp.*, iv. 518-522, *Moral & Mat. Pro.*)

On 31 March 1914 our total note issue was 66 *crores*, out of which 50 *crores* were in *active* circulation or in the hands of the public (*i.e.*, excluding the notes held in Government Treasuries and the Presidency

Banks). The total Paper Currency Reserve was thus held on that date:

Sterling securities	4	*crores Rs.*
Rupee "	10	"
Gold in England	9	"
" India	22·4	"
Silver "	20·5	"
	66·11	

Mr. Keynes estimates that the *public* circulation of Rupees on 31 March 1912 was 175 *crores*, against only 120 *crores* in 1900. (These figures exclude the Rupees in the Paper Currency Reserve and the Government Balances.)

Future development of our paper currency.— It will be seen from what has been written above that the distinction between the Gold Standard Reserve and the Paper Currency Reserve has practically disappeared, and that no useful purpose is served by keeping the two funds separate, as they play the same part in the working of our currency system. "The bullion reserve [of the Indian Paper Currency, lodged in England,] is no longer held solely with the object of securing ability to meet the obligation to cash notes in legal tender on demand. It is now utilised for holding gold by means of which the Secretary of State can support exchange in times of depression and maintain at par the gold value of the rupee,...and hence can be hardly distinguished from the resources of the Gold Standard Reserve proper." (Keynes, 51).

The example of other civilised countries shows (as Keynes has demonstrated) that the increased use of notes (or cheques) and replacement of metallic money by them in the case of large payments, is along "the stream of monetary evolution." Hence the use of paper money (and not of sovereigns) should be encouraged by the Government as our ultimate currency ideal. But the Indian system of paper currency differs from that of most note-using countries in this that "the Indian currency is internally absolutely inelastic," *i.e.*, our paper money can be expanded only by depositing an equivalent amount of metallic money in the Reserve, so that the total currency remains exactly the same. We have no credit device for expanding the volume of currency (rupees *plus* paper) temporarily to meet the temporary demands of trade, as our people do not use cheques, and notes cannot be issued without a full money basis, whereas in note-using countries the Central Bank can under law circulate at such times more notes without a corresponding increase in its metallic reserves. (*Keynes*, 56-67.) He, therefore, advocates the establishment of a *State Bank for India*, in order that our note-issue may be associated with the function of banking, and by the use of credit our total circulating medium (rupees *plus* paper) may be expanded at need, and our dependence on the London money market even for short term loans (which compels us to pay a very high rate of interest to cover the cost of remittance both ways), may be got rid of. In the wider use of paper money and not the adoption of a gold currency lies the monetary salvation of India.

Royal Commission on Indian Finance and Currency.—In 1913 a Commission, with Mr. J. Austen Chamberlain as Chairman, was appointed to inquire into the location and management of Indian Government balances, the maintenance of the exchange value of the rupee through the Gold Standard and Paper Currency Reserves, and the financial organisation and procedure of the India Office. The Commission in its Report (*Code 7236* of 1914) arrived at the following conclusions:—

(i) "The history of the last 15 years shows that the Gold (Exchange) Standard has been firmly secured (in India) without the supposed essential condition of the maintenance of a gold currency in active circulation (in the country). The measures already adopted by the Indian Government for the maintenance of the exchange value of the rupee worked well in the crisis of 1907-8."

(ii) "It would not be to India's advantage to encourage an increased use of gold in the internal circulation; the currency most generally suitable for the internal needs of India consists of rupees and notes... The use of notes should be encouraged by Government."

(iii) A mint for the coinage of gold (in India) is not needed for the purposes of currency or exchange; but there is no objection to its establishment.

(iv) No limit can be fixed to the accumulation of the Gold Standard Reserve, but all the profits on coinage should be credited exclusively to this Reserve, and a much larger portion—ultimately one-half,—of it should be held in actual gold. The whole of the Reserve should be located in London, and its Indian or rupee branch should be abolished.

(v) The Paper Currency system of India should be made more elastic. The fiduciary portion of the note issue should be increased at once from 14 *crores* to 20 *crores*, [this was done in 1915], and thereafter fixed at a maximum of the amount of notes held by Government in the Reserve Treasuries *plus* one-third of the note circulation, and the Government should be empowered to make *temporary* investments or *loans* from the fiduciary portion within this maximum as an alternative to investment in *permanent* securities, (which last is the only thing now allowed). The 500-rupee note should be universalised.

(vi) The Government of India should make a regular practice of granting loans to the Presidency Banks from their surplus balances in India against security. In deciding upon the location of *surplus balances* (whether in India or in London), the authorities should carefully consider the possibility of utilising surplus balances for loans *in India*. The amount of the annual rupee loan *in India* should be increased as much as possible, (and India's dependence on the London money market correspondingly diminished).

(vii) The Financial committee of the Secretary of State's Council should always contain at least one member with experience of Indian non-official banking and commerce.

(viii) On the question of the establishment of a State or Central Bank, the Commission was divided; Mr. Keynes and Home financiers generally supported it, while Sir S. B. Broacha, on behalf of the vested interests of the Presidency Banks secured the postponement of any finding on the question.

Is a gold currency suited to India?—In the light of the experience gained during the last 15 years in the working of our present currency system and the recent thorough examination of the subject by Mr. Keynes in his book and by the Chamberlain Commission in their Report, the arguments on the old questions whether India can use a gold currency and whether the closing of the mints was an economically sound measure, now possess a merely academic interest. For the benefit of students of Indian economic history, I shall, therefore, here give a brief summary of them, referring the reader to the 3rd. edition, pages 267-278 for a fuller treatment.

The opponents of a gold currency urge that (1) in India the vast mass of the people make transactions for very small sums, and cannot possibly use gold coins, so that an immense amount of coined silver must be kept in circulation to supply their needs. (2) The Indians have a passion for hoarding, and if gold is made easily accessible to them by the introduction of sovereigns as currency, they will replace their rupee hoards by sovereigns, so that while gold will quickly disappear the market will be flooded with rupees.

(3) The Indians now use paper money in making large payments, but they distrust notes, and if a precious but handy currency like gold is placed within their reach, they will use gold coins instead, and the gold will not be an addition to the volume of active currency of daily use, but merely replace notes, which is no gain but rather a retrogression from the ideal currency system. (*Lindsay*).

(4) The convertibility of existing coined silver into gold on demand must be a condition antecedent to the introduction of gold mono-metallism. But Government would be ruined by the cost if it undertook to convert *crores* of rupees into gold. And yet if Government does not guarantee free conversion, the legal ratio between silver and gold coins in India cannot be maintained.

(5) India has to pay several millions in gold every year as interest on her sterling obligations; and the foreign capital invested in India, when withdrawn during a monetary or political scare, goes out in the form of gold. Hence, during such a scare or even a period of monetary stringency, the country would be rapidly denuded of gold, and the gold standard would break down. A rise in exchange discourages export from India. Hence, the artificial appreciation

of the rupee decreases the balance of trade in favour of India, and reduces the flow of gold from abroad on which MacLeod and other gold mono-metallists build their plans. (See MacLeod's *Theory of Credit*, Ch. vii.)

There is much force in several of the above objections. The ease with which we can now get sovereigns often leads to the making of ladies' ornaments from sovereigns instead of gold-bar as formerly, because a sovereign is a coin of a certain known purity and price and easily ascertainable weight, whereas bar-gold can be assayed only by an expert, and its price fluctuates. This makes no difference in the total amount of gold in the country, but constantly reduces the volume of gold *currency* in the country and causes a pecuniary loss to Government. Sovereigns cannot be a popular currency of daily use in our country, because a sovereign represents Rs. 15, which is too large and inconvenient a unit for the needs of ordinary Indians. Gold coins can come into popular use only in small 5-rupee pieces. The examples of Turkey and (to some extent) Egypt have, however, shown that a gold currency for the big towns, seaports, and foreign trade is perfectly compatible with an internal silver currency for the villages and far inland places.

As for the rupee hoards kept by the Indians, the larger ones will probably be replaced by gold as more convenient and less likely to fall in intrinsic value;

but the smaller hoards, which are far more numerous, will be kept in the familiar and universally usable form of rupees. Moreover, it is a mistake to suppose that hoards are *for ever* withdrawn from circulation; the money is often drawn out and used in time of need or when a safe investment presents itself at hand.

Inquiries made by Government in 1911 showed that in the Punjab and Bombay sovereigns are freely accepted by the peasants as the price of their crops and remain in active circulation as currency. The same is the case, though to a much smaller extent, in the U. P. and Madras. But in the large provinces of Bengal, Burma, C. P. and Assam, the use of gold as currency is negligible. Keynes rightly observes, "In Bengal [and Burma] the slow progress made by gold [in active circulation] is to be explained by the fact that the people of these provinces are much more accustomed to the use of notes, even for the purpose of hoarding....The rapidity with which gold is becoming popularised in the Punjab is probably due in very great part to the fact that notes have never become acclimatised there." (P. 94.) "The sovereign is unsuitable, by reason of its high value, for so poor a country as India...The greater part of the Indian circulation must continue in any case to consist of rupees...It is for comparatively large payments that the sovereign may gradually come into use, and for these it is essentially a rival to the note," which is undesirable. (Pp. 74, 92-94.) This is exactly the view of Lindsay, following Ricardo, and very sound. For remittance and carriage, however, sovereigns can never rival notes. Our note circulation increased by 61 p. c. during the decade ending in 1908, and the demand for paper money is daily growing greater with the extension of our manufacture and commerce, though we are still immeasurably behind the condition of England where credit (or paper money) forms 99 p. c. of the value of all transactions and cash only 1 p. c.

As for the fourth objection, MacLeod has clearly shown that no Government is under an obligation to convert its subsidiary token coinage into gold to an unlimited extent on demand. What the Indian public can fairly demand is that, before gold mono-metallism is adopted internally, they should have a long notice and every opportunity of converting into gold the portion of their rupees which exceeds the amount required for the purposes of a subsidiary and restricted legal tender in daily life.

The answer to the fifth argument is that, as India pays interest on her foreign debt in the form of surplus *exports* of produce, no *gold* need go out of the country for this purpose in normal years. But when a gold currency has been adopted for India, the rupee will no longer be a silver coin, subject to fluctuations of exchange or fall in value with the over-production of silver, but it will be a token coin, representing a fixed portion of gold. Our notes and rupees will "act precisely as if they were bits of gold, by being made convertible into gold for foreign payment" (*Lindsay*). In such a settled state of things, prices in India, even though calculated in rupees, will be really gold prices, and the disadvantage stated in the fifth objection, about an arrest of the fall of exchange inevitably leading to diminished export from India, will no longer operate. As O'Conor says "The advantage of a fall in exchange is entirely *temporary*, because directly there is a fall of exchange, prices are adjusted (to it) and the cultivator gets very little of it. It is either the merchant in England or the merchant in India (*i. e.*, the middleman) who gets the benefit from the fall of exchange occurring during the time the transaction is in progress." (*Cd. 9037*, p. 51.) With a fixed exchange, transactions between England and India will follow a normal course, and such abnormal or transitional profits will not be made.

In summing up the whole case, we must bear in mind that India's monetary isolation can no longer be maintained. For good or evil, she has been joined to the trade of the world, especially of the British Empire. Her silver currency cannot stand; it is a source of weakness to her in view of the rapid fall in the price of silver. Bimetallism, which could have preserved her, is only possible by universal agreement, and the nations of Europe have refused to adopt it. Therefore, India *must* assimilate her currency to that of England and the rest of the civilised world.

Objections to the closing of the mints to the free coinage of silver.—(1) The change has, no doubt, relieved Government of its exchange difficulties, but millions of Indian peasants who had invested their savings in silver ornaments have, at one stroke of the official pen, suffered a depreciation of more than one-third in the nominal value of their only capital, because their ornaments can no longer be coined into rupees of the same weight, but have to be sold as bullion, at 42 p. c. below the price of coined silver. In the famine of 1877 three and one-third *crores* of rupees worth of silver ornaments were sent to the Indian mints to be coined. This remedy was withdrawn from the Indian peasants in 1893. The holders of ornaments have now lost more than one-third of their *credit* in pawning them.

(2) The unnatural and immense difference in value between coined and uncoined silver powerfully encourages the counterfeiting of rupees. One hundred rupees contain 91.6 *tolas* of pure silver, which at the market rate of bullion (about 27 pence per ounce), cost only Rs. 58; so that on every hundred rupees coined there is a profit of 42 p. c.

(3) The artificial limitation of the number of rupees in circulation has turned the rupee into a token money, about 72·5 p. c. above its intrinsic value. Hence, prices calculated in rupees have a tendency to fall, or "the purchasing power of the rupee" has a tendency to increase. There was "a sensible reduc-

tion in the general level of prices during 1898 and 1899," and "a remarkable cheapening of food-grains" in 1898 owing to this cause, as is admitted by Government. (*Ind. Emp.*, iii. 466.) Therefore, the taxes now paid by the Indians represent more commodities than formerly. Similarly, the value of debts contracted in the time of free silver coinage has now increased, as repayment has to be made in the artificially appreciated rupee. Thus, the Indian peasant, the Indian tax-payer, and the Indian debtor alike are sufferers by this currency legislation. [The operation of this economic principle has been retarded since 1900 and prices have been greatly *raised* by other causes.]

(4) The influx of gold into India is increasing, as foreign merchants have to make remittances to India in gold for their purchases, so that while silver has been appreciated, gold has been depreciated in India. Indian commodities now require a higher price *calculated in gold*, and their sale in gold-using foreign countries will be restricted in the same proportion. Both production and export will receive a check. [This objection has been already answered on page 309.]

(5) For the purposes of internal trade, the payment of wages to labourers, and the expenses of daily life, gold can never displace silver in a poor and low standard country like India. If rupees are withdrawn from circulation as more and more gold coins are poured into India, increasing hardship will be felt by the millions of poor Indians from the shortage of the

only currency they know and can use. Government must, therefore, maintain a double currency,—one metal for all home uses and another for foreign exchange. This policy is a violation of economic laws and is bound to fail. [No, as Keynes has clearly proved.]

(6) India's trade with China and other silver-using countries has been disturbed. China is the chief customer of the Indian cotton mills, but as she pays in silver, the closing of our mints has led to the Chinese dollars received by Indian manufacturers fetching merely the price of bullion, whereas formerly they could be freely coined into rupees. Thus, the monetary change in India caused a sudden loss of 42 p. c. to India's chief industry. (*Code 9222, Cd. 7060*, ii. p. 84, Gokhale's *Speeches*, 13, 17, 95, *Dutt*, 585-591). [This loss has been modified only in so far as silver prices in China have risen to adjust themselves to the alterations in the rate of exchange. India is now a gold standard country and stands on exactly the same footing as other gold countries in dealing with a silver country like China.]

Commercial Legislation.—Down to the viceroyalty of Lord Lytton there were duties on many Indian imports and exports. But in the year 1879 an Act was passed repealing the duty on many articles of import, especially cotton goods, though at a sacrifice of eighty *lakhs* of rupees to the revenue. At the same time many export duties were also abolished. Under

Lord Ripon all the remaining import duties, except those on salt and liquors, were removed (1882). For the next twelve years there was no revival of import duties, except a small duty imposed on petroleum in 1888.

But the fall in the exchange value of the rupee and the growth of military expenditure caused a deficit of two millions sterling in 1894. In the March of that year duties were reimposed solely *for revenue purposes* on articles imported into India including silver. *Five per cent.* was the general rate, but iron and steel paid one p. c. only; books, gold, industrial machinery, raw materials, grain, etc., were free. Foreign cotton goods were exempted from the duty. In December, the law was amended, imported cotton goods (both fabrics and yarns) being subjected to the duty of 5 p. c.; but at the same time a countervailing excise duty at the same rate was imposed upon the yarns produced in the Indian cotton mills. As the coarser Indian threads, *viz.*, those below 20 counts, did not compete with Lancashire yarn, they were exempted from the excise.

Act II of 1896 introduced further changes:—(*a*) All cotton yarns, whether imported or manufactured in India, were exempted from the duty. (*b*) The duty on woven cotton goods imported from abroad was reduced to 3½ p.c., the excise on the cotton goods manufactured in the Indian mills being similarly lowered. By making yarns duty-free, the law remitted taxation on Manchester goods to the amount of 51 *lakhs*, while the Indian cotton weaving industry was saddled with taxation, the yield of which gradually rose to 48 *lakhs* in 1911. As the coarser cotton goods of the Indian mills, which competed to a slight extent only with foreign imports in India, were equally subjected to the excise, the duty "raised the price of the poor man's clothing in India without the pretext of relieving the poor man of Lancashire." *(Dutt*, 543.) This duty is a net deduction from the profits of the Indian mill-owners, and for some years after its first imposition restricted their output. The evil was aggravated by the rebellion in China, the closure of the Indian mints to the free coinage of silver, and Japanese competition in the Far Eastern markets. The mill industry of Bombay was sinking when a market was opened for it at home by the Swadeshi movement. (*Ind. Emp.*, iv. 261-265; *Dutt*, 401-416, 537-544.)

In order to encourage the beet sugar industry of Germany and Austria, their governments gave to the exporters large bounties on the sugar exported. This had the effect of artificially reducing the price of beet sugar in India, so that it sold cheaper here than in Germany itself. This unfair competition greatly injured the sale of the cane-sugar of Mauritius, Jamaica and other British possessions, and also discouraged the sugar industry of India which was on the decline. So, the Indian Government in 1899 imposed countervailing duties (in addition to the general import duty of 5 p.c.) on bounty-fed sugar to he amount of the bounty, so as to place all sugars in he Indian market on terms of fair competition. (Act so as of 1899.) The Germans then gave up the system of bounties and escaped from the countervailing buty; but they next tried to evade the law by the 'Cartel system" of combinations to manipulate prices, and a further law had to be enacted in 1902 (Act VIII) to counteract the effect of "Cartel" (*Ind. Emp.*, iv. 264). At present, all foreign countries have entered into coventions with the British Government and dropped their bounties and "Cartel," so that all kinds of countervailing duty on the sugar were withdrawn in 1912. The liquor duty was raised in 1906 and again in 1910; in the last-named year, silver, petroleum and tobacco also were subjected to enhanced import duties, but solely for revenue purposes. The tobacco trade, however, greatly declined in consequence, and therefore in 1911 the rates of duty on all classes of tobacco were reduced by one-third.

The Indian tariff as it stood in 1914.—In addition to the above, *special import duties* are levied on (1) arms and ammunition (for political reasons), (2) liquors and spirits (for moral reasons), (3) silver, 4 annas per ounce (on economic grounds), (4) salt, which pays an import duty equivalent to the excise on salt manufactured in India, *viz.*, Re. 1 per *maund*, (5) tobacco and its manufactures (usually Re. 1 to Re. 1-4 per lb.), opium (Rs. 24 a *seer*), and petroleum (1½ annas per Imperial gallon). Most other goods pay the general duty of 5 p.c., woven cotton manufactures $3\frac{1}{2}$ p. c., iron and steel 1 p. c. In the free list are animals, grain, quinine, machinery, gold, lead sheets for tea-chests, railway materials, books, coal, cotton (raw and yarn), hides and skins, printing presses, type and ink (but not paper), raw wool, manures, &c.

The Indian tariff now contains about 400 different articles. About one-fourth (exactly 23 p.c.) of the total import duty collected in 1913 was derived from cotton goods, 10 p. c. from silver and sugar each, 14 p. c. from liquors, and 7 p. c. from petroleum and metals each. The balance (about 26 p. c. of the total) came from hundreds of minor articles. Some 76 petty articles taken together yield less than ten *lakhs* of rupees as duty. In 1913 our gross revenue from sea-*crores*, imports was 9·2 *crores*, which was thus made up:

Cotton goods yielded	2·11	*crores*	Rs
Liquors	1·32	"	"
Silver	98	*lakhs*	"
Petroleum	70	"	"
Sugar	91	"	"
Other metals	72	"	"
Other articles	2·42	*crores*	Rs

The duty on imported salt and the countervailing excise duty on Indian cotton manufactures are not included in the above figures.

Export duties.—(*a*) At present there is a duty on rice exported from India. This chiefly falls on Burma, where the annual produce far exceeds what is needed for the consumption of the people. The duty is three annas per *maund*, and yielded 144 *lakhs* in 1912, the highest on record, and 126 *lakhs* in 1913.

(*b*) A very low cess of $\frac{1}{4}$ pie per *lb*. has been imposed on tea-exports for financing a committee of merchants formed in order to push on the sale of Indian tea in foreign countries. In respect of this duty, Government acts merely as the collecting agency. Its yield was 4 *lakhs* in 1913. A duty on jute exported from Calcutta was imposed in 1912 for the benefit of the Calcutta Improvement Trust, yielding 11 *lakhs* in 1913. Its rate is 2 annas per bale of 400 lbs. of raw jute and 12 annas per ton of manufactured jute. A similar duty is levied on jute exports from the port of Chittagong.

War changes.—This was the state of our tariff till March 1916, when additions to our custom duties became necessary for meeting the expenses incidental to war. The result of the tariff amendments of 1916 and 1917 was the following changes:

(*a*) The *general* import duty was raised from 5 to $7\frac{1}{2}$ p. c.; the rate of 1 p. c. on iron and steel was enhanced to $2\frac{1}{2}$ p. c.; cotton manufactures, which had stood at $3\frac{1}{2}$ p. c. only, were in 1917 subjected to the general rate of $7\frac{1}{2}$ p.c.

(*b*) The *special* import duties on arms, liquors, manufactured tobacco, sugar and silverware, have been increased.

(*c*) The free list has been curtailed by taxing

imports of machinery, railway materials, food-grains coal, printing materials, &c.

(*d*) Exports were taxed thus in 1916: raw jute cuttings 10 as. and other descriptions Rs. 2¼ per bale of 400 lbs.; jute manufactures Rs. 10 to 16 per ton tea Rs. 1½ per 100 lbs. In 1917 the duties on jute and jute manufactures were doubled.

Protection how justified by the National System of Political Economy.—Under free trade we can buy a thing cheapest, as the products of all countries openly compete for supplying our need. A protective duty raises the price of the commodity and thus harms the consumer, while its artificial stimulus directs capital and labour into a channel naturally less suited to the country and lowers their efficiency. Protection, therefore, inflicts on the country an *immediate loss.* But it is urged by a school of economists whose most illustrious exponent is the German writer List, that this immediate loss is compensated for by the *ultimate* gain of the country, from the growth of home industries and diversity of employment, the stimulation of skill organisation and communications, and the development of national resources, when the country becomes a seat of manufactures under the shelter of protective duties. Therefore, the interests of the individual consumer must be sacrificed to the larger interests of the nation. "Mere accumulation [of wealth] is of minor importance compared with the organisation of the productive forces of society...From the national standpoint of productive power, the cheapness of the moment might be far more than counterbalanced by the losses of the future measured by the loss of productive power." "The *power of producing wealth* is infinitely more important than *wealth itself*. If a sacrifice of *value* is caused by protective duties, it is made good by the gain of a *power of production*, which not only secures to the nation an infinitely greater amount of material goods, but also industrial independence in case of war. Defence is of much more importance than opulence."

The present war has demonstrated the absolute and helpless dependence of India on foreign countries for several of the commonest requisites of civilised life, including medicines, sanitary appliances, artificial manure, railway materials, educational apparatus and even paper and the commonest metal goods. At the same time the closing of the foreign markets at which we have been accustomed to sell our only exports (raw produce) has ruined millions of our peasants and landlords.

Nations, according to List, must pass through three stages in their industrial progress: (1) In the first or agricultural stage they must adopt free trade with the more advanced nations as a means of raising themselves from a state of barbarism and of making advances in agriculture. But the more agriculture is developed the less advantageous becomes free trade.

(2) In the second or educational stage, nations must resort to protection to promote the growth of manufactures, fisheries, navigation, and foreign trade. The import duties should at first be low and be gradually raised. The nation must first of all endeavour to develop those manufactures which produce articles of general consumption. Measures of protection are justifiable only in the case of nations which are naturally capable of developing industries, and "possess all the necessary mental and material conditions and means for establishing a manufacturing power of their own." (3) In the third stage, after reaching the highest degree of wealth and power (by means of protection), nations must gradually revert to the principle of free trade, because at this stage further protection is apt to check progress and lead to decadence,—the exclusion of competition fosters indolence in the home producers. (*List*, xviii-xxiii, 93, 107, 144, Ch. XXVI and XXVII., 313).

Protection, therefore, must be the policy of a transition age and not a permanent thing. When it has achieved its purpose, the protective duty should be abolished, and free trade resumed. The home manufactures, fully developed during the interval, will now sell cheaper than the foreign import and the nation will be benefited as a consumer. (*List*, 117, 313). When this stage has been reached, the continuation of protective duties is positively harmful to the country, as they deprive the home producers of the bracing influence of full and free competition and tend to keep labour and capital inefficient and helpless, like a grown-up lad who has been carried in his nurse's arms ever since his birth.

J. S. Mill also defends protection for the benefit of young industries. "The only case in which protective duties can be defensible, is when they are imposed *temporarily* (especially in a *young and rising nation*) in hopes of naturalizing a foreign industry, in itself perfectly *suitable to the circumstances of the country*. The superiority of one country over another in a branch of production often arises only from having begun it sooner. There may be no *inherent* advantage on one part or disadvantage on the other, but only a *present* superiority of acquired skill and experience...It cannot be expected that individuals should at their own risk, or rather to their certain loss, introduce a new manufacture, and bear the burden of carrying it on until the producers have been educated up to the level of those with whom the processes are traditional...But the protection should be confined to cases, in which there is good ground of assurance that the industry which it fosters will after a time be able to dispense with it." (*Mill*, Bk. V. Ch. X. p. 556).

India and Protection.—The question is whether India can and ought to lay protective duties on foreign manufactures in the hope of encouraging the growth of home industries. Now 62·4 p. c. of our imports come from England, about 7·5 p. c. from the other

British possessions, (making a total of 70 p. c. for the Empire), and only some 30 p. c. or *less than one-third* from alien countries. (Figures for 1911.) No reasonable man can expect a politically dependent country like India to be allowed to impose protective duties on British goods. (See *Views of the Government of India on Preferential Tariffs*, para 10, *Webb*, p. 67.) Even when Britain imposes "a particularly crushing and unfair" duty on Indian tea, tobacco and coffee (*Webb*, 119 and 123), and many British colonies penalise Indian manufactures, India cannot retaliate. The matter, therefore, comes to this that India *can* at best discourage less than one-third of her imports by a protective tariff.

The next question is, *should* India do so? We have seen above that protection is justified by Mill and List only (*a*) as a temporary measure and (*b*) in the case of countries which are naturally suited to the growth of the industry protected. It is not universally beneficial. In the case of India, our chief industries, *viz.*, cotton, jute, tea, and coal, are each more than fifty years old and have attracted a vast amount of capital. They can hardly be called *young* industries. Protection to them *now* will be an encouragement to slack effort and decline of efficiency.

The late failure of several cotton mills in Bombay was due not to the increasing severity of foreign competition, but to bad management, extravagance and unproductive debt by the owners, diminution of effective capital and consequent low rate of return on the total nominal capital, and lack of a reserve to buy raw cotton cheaply far ahead. Mills, under better management, both in Bombay and Beawar, have been earning good profits all this time. In respect of the jute mills of Bengal, with every advantage of European capital and direction, they have hitherto failed to turn out finer fabrics (like those of Germany), because of the inefficiency of Indian labour and the scientific backwardness of their higher staff; and so long as these two defects continue, no protective duty, however high, can transfer the weaving of jute wrappers and coating from Germany to Bengal. Protection alone will not serve our purpose.

We have shown in a previous chapter the organic defects of Indian sugar and paper manufactures. The removal of these defects rather than protection is necessary to foster them. Next to these we have several small industries,—candle works, cutlery firms, cigar factories, soap factories, etc.,—all conducted with small capitals and hand appliances, by a comparatively inefficient because out-of-date process. A duty on imports of these things will merely enrich the existing Indian manufacturers, and act as a premium on inefficiency, at the expense of the general body of consumers. By taking to production on a large scale, the latest machinery and more capable management, these industries can yield profit even now without protection. Many petty industrial ventures which the

Swadeshi movement has called into existence, are backed by so little capital and brain that they cannot possibly succeed ; they are generally managed by men who have failed in other departments of life. New branches of industry, earnestly and competently undertaken, have no chance of failing to secure the home market while the Swadeshi spirit is alive, and it has yet to be proved that any such venture has succumbed from unrestricted foreign competition.

So far as I can see, no case has been made out in favour of protection in India *at present*. On the other hand, there are some special reasons why free trade should be continued. Apart from the general consideration that protection involves an immediate sacrifice of national resources,—which a poor country like India can ill afford to bear,—there is the fact that in this semi-tropical and conservative country, man has a natural tendency to slacken his exertions and let matters follow their wonted course, which is opposed to industrial efficiency and progress. Such a tendency can be fought and kept down only by the freest intercourse with the rest of the world and an ever-present fear of being beaten in competition unless we ceaselessly exert ourselves and adopt the latest improvements. Protection would be a premium on inefficiency and would foster a fatal indolence. Its effect, unless counteracted by the spirit of the people, is always demoralising ;* and we must confess

* "It seems not unnecessary to call attention to the numbing,

with sadness that the Indian people are not like the Germans or Americans.

Secondly, protective duties are easy to impose, but very hard to repeal. By them vested interests are soon created which fight tooth and nail to resist a return to free trade and can always make out a case that protection is still necessary. Witness the long opposition of the English landlords to the repeal of the Corn Laws at a time when a part of the nation was regularly starving. In manufacture the evil effects of protection do not manifest themselves in the same glaring form as in agriculture, and hence free trade in manufactures can be opposed with greater plausibility than the free import of corn.

enervating influence exercised by the protective system. An industry that has been secured against foreign competition is seldom elastic, it is seldom abreast of the times. In a small country the stimulus of foreign competition is indispensable, native competition being, of course, less keen [there]. When people speak of the disadvantages of foreign competition, they would do well not to forget its advantages, not only for the consumer, but also for the producer...It is by no means an easy thing to reawaken the numbed faculties of an enervated body. Even in France, industry was found to be lagging at many points when, in 1860, the protective duties were considerably reduced." (*Pierson*, ii. 189.) "The transition from protection to free trade is always accompanied by losses for some and by temporary lack of employment for a portion of the working classes. There are objections which usually make the legislator hesitate [to sweep away protective duties ever in future]." (*Ibid*, 187.)

Even List wishes to continue a moderate protective duty till his country has reached "the *highest* degree of wealth and power" and can compete on equal terms with the *most* advanced industrial nations of the world,—that is to say, till the millennium arrives! We may, then, be sure that protective duties if they once come, will come to stay and continue to exert for ever their demoralising influence which even List admits. (Pp. 8, 93, 249.) This danger is especially great in India, where the common people have no voice in the administration, where the capitalists (both European and Indian) exert a disproportionate influence on the legislature,* and where the old social system, with its checks and remedies, is undergoing a rapid disintegration which will make the plutocrats supreme for some time to come. It is quite possible for protection to be continued here for the benefit of the rich, after its economic necessity is over, and the silent millions of consumers to be permanently subjected to this indirect tax.

Quite distinct from the promotion of home industries by protection, is the question of *retaliation* or penalising the products of countries which lay heavy duties on Indian manufactured imports. For example, Indian jute manufactures are subject to a duty of 20 p. c. in France, Germany, Austria and the United States of America, and of 32 p. c. in Russia. England

* Two years after the above was published, Lord Cromer made use of exactly the same argument in the *Spectator*.

imposes "a crushing and unfair tax" (in the words of Mr. Webb) on Indian tea and tobacco. Now, retaliation means revenge, and we can indulge in it only in proportion to our power of harming our fiscal enemies, who (*a*) import raw materials from us and (*b*) export their finished goods to India. Our power to tax either of these will be discussed in the section on Tariff Reform. But it should be borne in mind that retaliation is of economic importance only when the *threat* of it removes the disabilities on our produce in foreign countries; when, however, such a threat fails and retaliatory measures are *actually* carried out, the result is a diminution of our production, through a contraction of its foreign market. Unlike protection, it cannot cause new industries to grow in India. But it can increase our revenue somewhat at the expense of the foreigner and thus make some amends for the restriction of the sale of our goods abroad.

Swadeshi means the use of goods made in one's own country. The movement originated more than thirty years ago in the Bombay Presidency. Thoughtful Indian leaders were alarmed at the lack of diversified employment as a protection against famine, the immense preponderance of agriculture with its accompaniment of a low type of civilisation, the absence of arts and industries which might raise our labourers to a higher standard of wages and living, the industrial subordination of India to Europe, the life and death struggle of the infant cotton industry of Bombay against the powerful and long-established mills of Lancashire, and the economic neutrality of a Government that refused to initiate, pioneer or (directly) assist home industries in imitation of the State in Germany. They resolved that the people should try to do what the State declined, and that the voluntary preference of the nation should effect a part of the result that protective duties had achieved in Germany or the United States of America. This spirit animated Ranade, Telang, and many other leaders of the South. When Mr. Viswanath Narayan Mandalik, a Maratha scholar and patriot, came to Calcutta in Lord Ripon's time, his Bengal hosts were surprised at the coarseness of his *dhotis*. To their queries he replied, "I must wear these thick clothes, as my country's mills cannot yet produce any finer fabric."

About a decade afterwards, in the nineties of the last century, a protest against modern luxuries and foreign things in general began to be preached by the orthodox section of the vernacular press. The patronage of home manufactures and the rejection of foreign imports, hitherto based on patriotic motives only, now began to be taught as a social and almost religious duty. England's motive in enforcing free trade on her dependency, after having built up her own industries by relentless protection in the 18th century, was misconstrued in the very manner of List.

(See *List*, 295). The idea, however, was still confined to a select few; Bengal made it universal.

The division of the homogeneous people of Bengal into two mutually exclusive and even antagonistic administrations, against the wishes of the country and with the avowed political object of creating diversity of public opinion between their capitals, roused the Bengali leaders in August 1905 to administer to the nation the vow of avoiding foreign goods and using home manufactures instead. The quick spread of the idea throughout our society was due to the wonderful oneness of life and thought among the Bengali population, irrespective of rank, caste or creed. Alone, among the Indian provinces, Bengal possesses the advantages of having 4½ *crores* of people speaking *one* language, a high percentage of literate people, and several newspapers with a circulation of above 20,000 copies, (each copy being read by a score of people). The movement even affected the genuine Bengali Musalmans of the lower middle class in localities that had no standing source of religious friction,—the reason evidently being that the *lakhs* of hand-loom weavers in Bengal are Muslims and the Swadeshi movement gave them bread after years of steady loss of business and growing starvation.

After a rather stormy career, (due to non-economic causes), "honest Swadeshi" received the approbation of the King-Emperor's representative in the land. It is still far from being universally followed even in

Bengal; but it has got a substantial body of determined adherents, whose number will not *decrease* as the years roll on. It has gained for several kinds of Indian goods a secure market at the very doors of the producers.

From the economic point of view, Swadeshi seems to me to be much better than protection. For one thing, it is entirely voluntary; the State does not, as in Germany or the U. S. A., artificially enhance the price of a commodity. Nobody in India need buy a dearer home manufacture unless he is willing to make the sacrifice of money. Secondly, the fact that there is free foreign competition compels our manufacturers to be ever vigilant in increasing the efficiency of production, because they know that in proportion as they abuse their countrymen's spirit of sacrifice and turn out worse or dearer goods than the foreigner, they will exhaust the nation's patience and lose the home market. The ethical value of Swadeshi is even greater. To hardly one in a million comes the chance of doing a great deed for his country, or sacrificing his all before the nation's eyes. But each one of us, however poor his means, can make a small silent sacrifice for his country every time he goes to market. The poor student who spends an extra eight annas by buying a pair of Indian *dhotis*, denies himself this treat or that which he might have bought for the money if only he had preferred the cheaper foreign *dhoti*,—but he feels that he is making this sacrifice of his own pleasure in order to put bread into the mouth of a starving family of Deccan labourers, whom he will never see and who will never thank him. The wider outlook and spirit of broader sympathy which is fostered by such acts, which provinces together into a nation. The customs-union of the numerous German States consolidated their union into one empire.

Some thinkers prefer protection to Swadeshi on the grounds that unlike protection (*a*) Swadeshi brings no revenue to the State, (*b*) it is generally uninformed and not based upon any clearly thought out policy, and (*c*) the demand which arises from Swadeshi is apt to be uncertain and spasmodic. As for the first objection, it is evident that taxation of foreign goods for revenue and their taxation for protection are mutually inconsistent ideals. In proportion as the yield of the import duty is large, the consumption of foreign goods has been great and the protection of home industries has been ineffectual. A logical protectionist is fully satisfied only when the import duty yields no revenue at all. Then, again, the disadvantage of Swadeshi from the revenue point of view is only temporary; when it has succeeded in establishing new industries at home, the addition to the income-tax from this source compensates the State. Lastly, the revenue raised by protective duties imposes an unfair sacrifice on the consumers of particular goods, as distinct from the whole nation, (*Pierson*, ii. 188,) whereas in the case of Swadeshi such a sacrifice is voluntary. The second objection has some force; but it is not quite certain that a protectionist tariff will always embody ripe political wisdom, or that protective duties will be readily abandoned when no longer necessary for the good of the country. As a practical politician like the late prime minister of Holland remarks, "Protection is a costly specific, and any mistakes made in applying it—*mistakes* which are *unavoidable*—produce very harmful results." (*Ibid*, 188.) The third objection is of no practical significance among a fairly educated and public-spirited community.

Boycott, or the exclusion of any class of commodity, is a mere negation; unlike Swadeshi it *cannot create industries*. An advocate of boycott has asserted, "Boycott creates a gap which Swadeshi rushes in to fill." But it is difficult to see how something can be created out of nothing. If you decline to buy a thing which is not produced at home, you save the money; but you do not thereby encourage a rival home industry. If the conditions are favourable to starting such an industry here, the industry is founded, and you buy the manufacture,—it is a case of preference for home goods, *i.e.*, of Swadeshi, and not a case of boycott. When the Americans boycotted English tea in 1774, they could not thereby create tea plantations in the United States; they simply gave up tea-drinking. Moreover, boycott, like retaliation in trade, is an appeal to the passions, and may cause a diversion of energy into a wrong path. You adopt it to spite your enemy, though it does not benefit you. It is a *political* weapon, not economic.

India and Tariff Reform.—England is a free trading country, while the Continental nations, the United States, and even the British colonies are protectionist. England admits foreign goods free of duty, but her own manufactures are handicapped in foreign countries by having to bear heavy import duties. This has created a feeling of resentment among a certain class of English politicians. They want England to give up the policy of unconditional free trade and lay *retaliatory duties* on foreign imports (or to induce foreign States by the threat of such retaliation to lower their duties on English goods). Secondly, they want to tax imports into England, not so much to protect English industries (which are too well established to need such artificial support), as to *make the foreigner contribute* to the English revenue. It is possible to arrange the tariff in such a way that an import duty, either wholly or in part, may fall on the profits of the producer. In such a case the foreigner will be taxed for England's defence, and the burden of taxation on Englishmen will be proportionately lightened. Thirdly, as the colonies are sometimes as great sinners against England as Germany or U. S. A., the tariff reform party propose a system of *imperial preference* by which England and her colonies will lay lower import duties on each other's produce than on the goods of foreign countries. They hope to knit the empire together by the ties of common interest and common animosity.

The Indian Government, in its despatch of 22nd October, 1903, refused to join in the scheme, on the following grounds:

(*a*) England will refuse to let India impose any *protective* duty on English goods, though the duty be light and foreign goods are taxed at a much higher rate.

(*b*) If the existing duties imposed for *revenue* only are lowered on British imports and enhanced on foreign goods, the loss of revenue will be very great, because we import thrice as much from the British Empire as from foreign countries, and the loss of customs from the former source cannot possibly be made good from the increased taxation of the latter. Besides, in one-fifth of our imports, the competition between British and foreign manufactures in the Indian market is so keen that this preferential duty will enable the former class of goods (paying the lower duty) to displace the latter (which will be taxed at a higher rate), and so the Indian revenue will suffer while the British manufacturer will profit.

(*c*) India is a debtor country and must sell surplus exports worth 6 millions sterling in gold-standard countries, if she is to pay interest on her foreign debt regularly. But a preferential duty against foreign imports may provoke those foreign countries to exclude Indian goods, with the result of forcing India to be insolvent to her European creditors. As the result of Continental reprisals, our exports may fall off, the balance of trade in favour of India may disappear, and India's revenue and credit in the money-market decline; "the result would be disastrous."

But, the Tariff Reformers argue, India has an advantage which no other member of the British Empire possesses: she sends out huge quantities of *raw materials* which England's commercial rivals require for their industries. Our exports are composed of "several products in which India practically enjoys a *monopoly*, *viz*., jute, *til* seed, lac, teak wood, myrobalans, mowra, etc., while in several other articles (such as wheat, seeds, hides, etc.)—in which India competes [in foreign markets] with outside producers,—their remarkable cheapness places us in a particularly strong position; so that we can rest assured that in many important branches of commerce outside nations will be *forced to come to India*, in order to obtain the raw materials necessary to keep their own peoples occupied and their industries prosperous."* (Webb's *India and the Empire*, 88.)

* But the Indian Government is not so confident about our having an effective monopoly in these things and foreign nations being absolutely dependent on us for raw materials. It is "unwise to rely too much upon the hypothesis that India enjoys an effective monopoly in any large number of articles which are essential to the existence of foreign industries." (Despatch quoted, para 15).

Therefore, according to the Tariff Reformers, India can punish the foreign rivals of England by laying a duty on Indian raw materials exported to these foreign countries, (preference being shown to England as a consumer). Mr. Webb admits that if India taxes her export of "jute, the resultant *benefits* would accrue rather *to the United Kingdom* than to India. But that is no reason why India should not" impose such a duty! (p. 99.) It is not pretended that an export duty on Indian raw materials, which must contract their market and thereby injure their Indian producers to some extent at least, will benefit any Indian manufacturer, because most of the foreign manufactures we import are such as "either in kind or quality India does not produce at all." And yet India must impose such an export duty for the benefit of England and her colonies; that is to say, India must be used as a mere tool in England's commercial war with Germany or U. S. A.

Professor Lees Smith has clearly shown that from the nature of England's trade with India, "Great Britain cannot offer any fair reciprocal advantage to India without a substantial rise in the price either of raw materials on which some of her important industries depend, or of food stuffs...India has equally little either to lose or gain from a scheme of preferential tariffs within the Empire. The results for Great Britain ......[will be that] British trade will suffer a staggering blow." He shows that among the ten articles which represent 90 p. c. of the total value of British imports from India, (*a*) preference is a practical impossibility in *raw jute*, *lac*, *tea*, and *jute manufactures*, because in the first three of these India has a practical monopoly of the English market. (Ceylon shares with India the tea supply of England). *(b) Hides*, *oil-seeds*, *raw wool*, and *raw cotton* are necessary raw materials of British manufacture, "of which an appreciable rise in price would not be tolerated" by the English people. (*c*) *Wheat* and *rice* are articles of food "of which no substantial rise in price will be permitted in Great Britain." *(India and the Tariff Problem*, 86-96*)*.

CHAPTER IX.

PUBLIC FINANCE.

The sources of Indian revenue.—(1) The British Indian Government owns land and forests and has Native States politically dependent on it. From these sources it derives an income which is the natural incident of lordship or domain, *viz.*, *rent* from the actual cultivators in certain parts (*ryotwari*) and *land revenue* from middlemen in others (*zamindari*); the sale proceeds of forest produce and fees for grazing in the State forests, royalty for working mines; and tribute from the feudatory States. (2) Government has a monopoly of the sale of *opium* for retail vending in India and export abroad; the income which is derived from this source is the gain of a monopolist. (3) Then, the State undertakes certain commercial services for the public, *viz.*, the conducting of railways, irrigation works, post and telegraph systems,—from which it earns what may be called business remuneration or "fees" in the economic sense of the term. (4) It also exacts payment from all who have to file petitions, &c., in Law Courts, or record commercial transactions in a valid form. In proportion as the payment in these cases exceeds the value of the service rendered by the State to the party, such *judicial fees* must be regarded as a tax and not "fees" in the economic sense. The income from Registration belongs to the same class. (5) Lastly, the Government levies taxes of various kinds on its subjects for the expenses of the administration. (6) It sometimes makes a profit on the coinage of the currency, which is due to the artificially enhanced value of the rupee relatively to silver bullion; but such profits are strictly set apart in a Reserve and do not form part of the fund for ordinary expenditure. As Government has to send the equivalent of above 20 millions sterling to England, it makes a profit when exchange is favourable to India and a rupee fetches more than the fixed rate of 1*s.* 4*d.* Conversely, when exchange is adverse to us, there is a loss under the head of "Exchange." These amounts are usually negligible.

In the financial statement presented to our legislature, the *gross revenue* of Government consists of all its receipts under these various heads, with the exception that the working expenses of the railways and the share of surplus profits paid to certain railway companies are not entered in the gross expenditure but are deducted from the gross revenue, and the railway revenue shown in the accounts represents the net amount received by Government. The *net revenue* is found by deducting the interest charges and working expenses of the railways and irrigation works, the cost of cultivation and manufacture of opium in the British districts, and the charges against other revenue-earning departments (except the cost of collection); these items are treated as deductions from revenue. The receipts of spending departments are not credited to revenue, but treated as deductions from expenditure. The cost of collection in the revenue-earning departments, as well as the cost of national defence, civil administration, public works, and "famine relief and insurance", the interest on ordinary debt, and the price of stores, together form the *net expenditure*. (*Moral and Mat. Progr.*, 48th No., p. 149.) Thus in 1910, the *gross* revenue was Rs. 121 *crores* and the *net* revenue 82 *crores*, while the *gross* expenditure was 115 *crores* and the *net* expenditure 76 *crores*,—the "gross" figures being nearly half as much again as the "net" figures.

Indian Finance in the twentieth century.

	Net income *crores Rs.*	Net expenditure *crores Rs.*	Proportion of land rev. to total revenue p.c.	Proportion of military exp. to total revenue. p.c.	Proportion of opium revenue to total revenue. p.c.	Deficit = − Surplus = + *crore Rs.*
Annual average for 1901-5.	67·81	62·83	40	40·8	7·5	+4.96
Annual average for 1906-10.	73·92	73·08	39·2	39·47	9	+0·81
1911	85·48	79·57	35	34·3	9·1	+5·91
1912	90·54	85·88	38·2	32·4	7·5	+4·65
1913	86·77	83·3	35·6	34·4	1	+3·46
1914	79·77	82·45	38·4	38·4	1·7	−2·68
1915						

Our net revenue (1913) was raised from the following sources :—

			Crores Rs.
I.	*Domain,*	...	34·88
	viz., Land revenue	30·93	
	Forest	3·32	
	Tribute from Native States ...	·61	
II.	*Monopoly and State farming*		
	i.e., Opium sold for export ...	...	·909
III.	*Fees for commercial services,* ...	...	9·57
	viz., Railways	7·18	
	Irrigation	1·89	
	Post office and Telegraph ...	·48	
IV.	*Taxation,*	...	40·91
	viz., Excise	13·18	
	Customs	11·11	
	Stamps	7·89	
	Salt	4·77	
	Income-tax	2·9	
	Registration	·77	
	Provincial rates (=cesses on land) ...	·27	
V.	*Mint and Exchange*	...	·49
	Total ...		86·77 *crores.*

Opium.—The wholesale trade in opium is a monopoly of the State. In British territory it is grown only by licensed ryots who have to sell their entire out-turn of crude opium at the fixed price of Rs. 6 per *seer* to Government agents, by whom it is purified and manufactured into balls in the Government factory at Ghazipur. In accordance with the recent policy of stopping the export to China, Government has been steadily diminishing the sanctioned area for the cultivation of opium; its growth has been stopped in Bihar, and is now confined to a part of the Gangetic valley in the U. P. The quantity of prepared opium required for home consumption (called "excise opium") is made over to the Excise Department and vended through it. [The opium consumed in India is subject to a high duty, which yielded 1·93 *crores* of rupees in 1913 and is credited to the *excise* revenue.] Opium intended for export (called "provision opium") is sold in chests of 140 lbs. each by auction at Calcutta. Opium grown in the Native States of Rajputana and Central India (called "Malwa opium,") cannot enter British territory without paying a heavy duty, (which was raised from Rs. 600 to Rs. 1200 per chest in 1912). The right to export this opium used to be sold by auction at Bombay, and the profit used to be divided between the British Government and the Indian princes according to the terms of their agreement.

But early in 1913 the esport of opium (mainly to China) from Bombay was totally discontinued, and the opium department of Bombay was abolished. The export of Malwa opium has, therefore, ceased.

History of the opium trade with China.—Nearly three-fourths of the opium exported from India used to be taken by China, the remaining one-fourth going to the Malay Peninsula and other countries. By the Treaty of Tientsin (1858) with England, China recognised foreign opium from legitimate article of import. By the additional article to the Chefoo Convention, signed in 1885, it was agreed that in consideration of raising the import duty from 30 taels to 110 taels per chest, the Chinese Government would free the imported opium from the payment of all other duties or taxes (like the *likin* or internal transit duty) while the opium was in transport from the port of entry to the interior of the kingdom; when the chest of imported opium was opened at the place of consumption it would not be subjected to any tax in excess of what might be levied on native opium. Or, in other words, the Chinese Government restricted its power of *internal* taxation on foreign opium, though it was free to terminate these arrangements by giving a year's notice at any time. (*Report of Opium Com. of 1893, Cd. 7313*, p. 137; *Cd. 7723*, p. *132*.)

In 1906 the Chinese Government issued edicts ordering the growth of opium in China to be suppressed within 10 years, and the Indian Government agreed to co-operate with this policy by gradually restricting the amount of opium exported from India to China, *i.e.*, by putting up to auction fewer and fewer chests for export to all foreign countries. Under a new agreement, signed in May 1911, the Indian Government agreed to put a stop to its opium trade with China even earlier, on condition that the growth of opium in China was suppressed before the expiry of the ten years' period; at the same time a further limitation was placed on the number of chests of Indian opium auctioned as certified for export to

Chinese ports. In 1913 the sale (at Calcutta or Bombay) of opium thus certificated for export to China was finally stopped, and the Indian opium traffic with China at last came to an end. Opium is now produced in India, in certain districts of the U. P. only, under a Government monopoly, for internal consumption in India and for export to those foreign countries (such as the Dutch East Indies, the Malay Peninsula and the Straits Settlement) where its use is permitted mainly for medicinal purposes.

By the closing of the China market since 1913, we have lost a net annual revenue of more than 6 *crores* of Rs., derived entirely from foreigners. The total number of chests exported declined from above 80,000 in 1890 to 65,700 in 1907,—44,600 in 1911,—11,856 in 1914,—and 9786 in 1915.

Salt tax.—On the foreign salt imported, a custom duty is levied at our ports and frontier, and on the salt manufactured in India an equivalent excise is levied, but these two sums are included under a separate head, "Salt revenue," instead of being credited to Customs and Excise respectively. This tax was reduced by Lord Ripon (1882) from Rs. 2½ to Rs. 2 a *maund*, raised to the old level by Lord Dufferin (1888), reduced by half a rupee each time in 1903, 1905 and 1907, and raised to one rupee and a quarter in 1916. These successive reductions have greatly lessened the gross revenue from this source, which was 9 *crores* in 1902 and a little below six *crores* in 1916, though the consumption has increased. [We consume about 70 p. c. home-made and 30 p. c. foreign salt. Government itself conducts most of our salt-works.]

The **stamp** revenue is derived from (i) judicial or court-fee stamps which have to be affixed to plaints, petitions, and most other documents filed before law-courts, and (ii) non-judicial or "revenue" stamps which have to be affixed to records of commercial transactions, such as transfer of property, bonds, cheques, bills of exchange, receipts, &c. In 1910 the rate of stamp duties on certain commercial transactions and on probate was raised. (For the merits and defects of this tax, see *Mill*, Bk. V. Ch. V., p. 517, Bastable's *Public Finance*, 3rd Ed., 165, 241, *Pierson*, ii. 537.)

The **Excise revenue** is derived from (*a*) the sale of licences to shopkeepers to vend (and, in the case of country-made spirits, also the distillery fee for manufacturing) all sorts of intoxicating liquors, including the juice of the toddy palm, opium, *ganja*, *bhang*, &c., and (*b*) the excise duty on opium, *ganja*, &c., consumed in India. The import duty on foreign liquors and the countervailing excise duty on India-made cotton fabrics are included in the Customs Revenue and not entered under Excise. For our Customs, see Chapter VIII.

The **Income Tax** (called "assessed tax") before the war was assessed on all incomes of Rs. 2000 or above a year at the rate of 5 pies per rupee of the income, while incomes between Rs. 1000 and Rs. 2000 paid at the rate of 4 pies. In 1914 the total number of persons (or companies) assessed was 332,000, and they paid in all 3 *crores* of rupees. In 1916, a fully graduated Income Tax schedule was introduced: up to Rs. 5000 a year there was no change, but incomes from Rs. 5000 to Rs. 9999 were taxed at the rate of 6 pies per rupee, between 10,000 and 24,999 at nine pies, and Rs. 25,000 and above at one anna. In 1917, a super-tax was introduced for all incomes above Rs. 50,000: the first half *lakh* in excess of the amount is to pay an *extra* anna in the Rupee, the second half *lakh* an extra 1½ as. in the Rupee, the third half *lakh*, an extra 2 as., the fourth half *lakh* an extra 2½ as., and all incomes above 2½ *lakhs* an extra 3 as.

The **cesses on land** (called "provincial rates") are now levied for roads, schools, and dispensaries only in Bengal and Assam. In 1906 the cesses formerly imposed for famine-protective canals and railways (in the U. P., C. P. and Punjab), for the district post, and for the salaries of the village officers and *patwaris*, were abolished, and the total yield of the tax was reduced to nearly one-half. In 1914, the cess imposed for the payment of the rural police in the U. P. was abolished. The rate of the cesses is usually one anna in every rupee of rent or the estimated annual value of land, and they are paid, entirely or half, by the landlord. They are therefore a direct tax. [Municipal taxes and the share of the provincial rates paid to District Boards are not included in the amounts shown in the Imperial revenue, as they are entirely spent by the local bodies.]

The head of revenue marked as "**fees for commercial services**" is liable to extreme variations from year to year. It yielded its first record surplus of 4·61 *crores* in 1906; but two years afterwards, owing to a heavy falling-off in railway earnings and post office income, there was a deficit (the only one in this century)—amounting to 1·13 *crores.* From 1909 the surplus continued to rise till it touched the highest figure yet attained, 9·57 *crores* in 1913. The war brought on a decline *viz.*, to 5·13 *crores* in 1914. There is always a net income from *Irrigation*, which reached a maximum of 1·89 *crores* in 1913, (1·38 *crores* in 1914). The *Post Office* caused a net loss in 1908 and 1909 only, but yielded a profit in all other years, the highest being 47 *lakhs* in 1913. *Telegraphs* caused deficits in 1902-1909 and again in 1911, but supplied a (small) surplus in other years. In 1914 Post and Telegraphs together yielded half a *crore* of net income. The *Railway* surplus first exceeded one *crore* in 1901, rose to 3·46 *crores* in 1906, but was turned into a deficit of nearly two *crores* in 1908. Since then there has been a good recovery, the net revenue exceeding 7 *crores* in 1912 and again in 1913, with a fall to 3·23 *crores* in 1914 in consequence of the war.

Our net expenditure (1913) was thus made up:—

I.	*Interest on* (ordinary) *debt* ...	...	·16 *crore Rs.*
II.	*Military* expenditure ...	...	29·84 ,,
III.	*Collection* of revenue ...	...	10·02 ,,

IV. *Civil* expenditure		42·1	*crore Rs.*
viz., Civil depts. Miscellaneous,	24·78		
civil charges,	7·12		
Civil Public Works,	10·19		
V. *Famine* relief and insurance ...		1·5	"
[VI. *Provincial* balances met exp. of 42 *lakhs*]			
Total ...		83·3	

Under the head "civil departments" (or "*general their*") is included the expenditure on the Secretary of State's office establishment in London, the Viceroy, Governors, Lieutenant-Governors, and their Councils, and other officers down to Commissioners of divisions, as well as courts of law, jails, and the police, education medical and political departments. "*Miscellaneous civil charges*" are made up of pensions, stationery and printthe charges, furlough allowances, territorial and political pensions, &c. The salaries of magistrates and the expenses (other than judicial) of the district administrahead are entered under the head of "collection of land revenue." "*Famine relief and insurance*" consists of the amounts spent on actual relief and on the construction of railways and irrigation works as a protection against famine, about 60 *lakhs* in 1910,—besides a sum spent on "reduction or avoidance of debt" in connection with famine. The capital outlay on our railways and irrigation works is mainly met from loans contracted by the State, partly from the issue of debenture by the railway companies, and partly from the revenue of the year (usually the Famine Insurance fund). Excluding railways and irrigation, our civil public works—*i.e.*, shares, buildings, &c.—are maintained mainly out of provincial revenues, and to a small extent (less than one-seventh) out of the funds of the Imperial Government.

Provincial Finance.—"The Government of India assigns to the Provincial Governments fixed shares of the revenue collected by them under certain heads... [While] opium, salt, customs, post office and telegraph, mint, exchange and railways are wholly Imperial, land revenue, irrigation, stamps, excise, assessed taxes, and forests are divided [between the Imperial and Provincial Governments, according to certain terms decided upon at the 'provincial settlements']. From the revenue so assigned the Provincial Governments are required to meet the whole of the expenditure within their respective provinces under certain heads and a portion of the expenditure under other heads." The revenue retained by the Imperial Government is devoted to meeting the expenditure described in the accounts as Imperial, *viz.*,—the Home Charges, the military expenditure, territorial and political pensions, ecclesiastical charges, and also a portion of the "General Mdministration" expenses. If the Provincial Governments spend less in any year than their income, the saving is added to the *provincial balances* and treated in the accounts of the Government of India as though it had been spent. *Moral & Mat. Progr.*, 47th No., p. 16.)

It is interesting to note the growth of certain sources of revenue and expenditure in recent years, (*in* recent *of rupees*).

	1898	Annual average 1901-5	Annual average 1906-10	1911	1912	1913	1914	1915	1916
Net rev. *crores* Rs.	59·6	67·8	73·92	85·48	90·54	86·77	79·77		
Net exp. ,,	55·6	62·8	73·08	79·57	85·88	83·3	82·45		
Land rev. ,,	26·2	27	29·01	30	34·62	30·93	30·67		
Opium rev. ,,	3·3	5·1	6·72	7·84	6·77	0·90	1·37		
Excise rev. ,,	5·6	7·27	9·51	11·30	12·3	13·18	13·28		
Customs rev. ,,	4·6	5·97	7·56	9·43	10·57	11·11	9·52		
Irrigation rev. ,,	·26	·3	·97	1·20	1·66	1·89			
Railway rev. ,,	—	1·8	1·64	5·68	7·20	7·18			
Police expend. ,,	3·48	4·21	6·03	6·90	6·98	7·29			
Education exp. ,,	1	1·39	2·42	3·03	3·90	4·76			
Medical exp. ,,	1·23	1·04	1·39	1·73	1·99	2			
Civil Pensions exp.	3·93	4·23	—	4·78	4·92	5·10			
Military expend.	25·7	27·6	29·22	29·33	29·34	29·84	30·65	32·76	

Incidence of taxation.—Leaving out of account the income from our export of opium (which is entirely paid by foreigners), the land revenue (which is held by many to be not a tax at all, but only the price of exploiting natural resources belonging to the State), the forest income, the tributes from Native States, the income from commercial undertakings by Government, and the Mint and Exchange revenues, —the total amount raised by pure taxation in 1911 was 36·53 *crores* of rupees, and the *incidence per head of the population of that year* was 1s. 11½*d.* But if the land revenue (1s. 8*d.* per head) be included, the burden of taxation would be 3s. 7½*d.* in 1911 (against 3s. 2½*d.* in 1901).

For a contrast between Indian finance and English, see *Ind. Emp.*, iv. 162; *Bastable*, 256; *Alston* 97-101, 46).

Local taxation.—The rates are very low (except in Calcutta and Bombay), because in most of the towns the municipality discharges the barest minimum of the duties of local government, *viz.*, police, road, and light only. In very few places it supplies drinking water (and that too is mostly the gift of pious founders) or undertakes house conservancy; its support of education is most niggardly, and it is usually contented with maintaining one small hospital. The district boards are equally hampered by the lack of funds and can do little useful work. Except the main artery roads all the other roads of the district, particularly in stone-less Bengal, are mere mud-tracks, and very few rivers are bridged. Education is financed by these boards as far as their scanty means permit, which is far below the need of the vast population.

The usual sources of municipal income are (*a*) octroi duties on goods brought into a town for sale, in the U. P., Punjab, C. P. and Bombay, (*b*) taxes on houses, lands, animals, vehicles, professions and trades, (*c*) tolls on roads and ferries which are farmed out to the highest bidder, (*d*) water and conservancy rates (only where these exist) and lighting rate, (*e*) income from pounds, hackney carriages, and liquor licences within municipal area, (*f*) receipts from markets and slaughter-houses, (*g*) fines, (*h*) grants from local funds, and (*i*) varying annual gifts from Government by way of aid.

In 1912 the total income of the 712 municipalities in India was 8·25 *crores*. In 1911, the average incidence of municipal taxation per head of municipal population for British India as a whole, was 4*s*., (the rate having been 2*s*. 8*d*. in 1899). Our 1126 district and local boards had a total income of 6·10 *crores* (in 1912), and the incidence per head was probably 3½*d*. (against 2½*d*. in 1899.) The income of district and local boards is mainly derived from cesses on agricultural land over and above the land revenue. Since 1908 the accounts of these boards have been excluded from the general provincial accounts, and their funds treated independently like municipal funds, *i.e.*, the proceeds of these cesses are not included in the general revenue. Government makes grants-in-aid to the funds of all boards amounting to about one-third of their income from cesses levied on land. There are sometimes contributions for specific purposes from the provincial funds. The other sources of income of the boards are cattle pound receipts, tolls from ferries and bridges, educational receipts, &c.

The nature of land revenue in India.—A good deal of controversy has raged round the question whether the Indian land revenue is a land-tax or rent. The official writers argue that, as the land in India is ultimately the property of the State, the revenue levied from it is merely the annual yield of a natural monopoly which the State has surrendered to certain individuals, either permanently (as in Bengal) or for 20 or 30 years (as in the other provinces). Hence they deny to it the name of a tax and regard it as only a royalty or compensation paid to the owner for the exploitation of a monopoly. So long as the land-revenue is assessed on the landlord's rent (or on the 'net assets' theoretically regarded as equivalent to rent), it is paid by the landlord out of his own profits, and does not fall on the producer.

It, however, differs from the land-tax of Europe. As Bastable writes in connection with our mahalwari and ryotwari areas, "The State is ultimate owner. The machinery of assessment and collection is compulsory; it is nearer akin to the process of the tax-collector than of the landlord...In strictness [the Government receipts from land] *belong to neither class* [*viz.*, taxes and rent]. They differ most markedly from the rent, either customary or competitive, of a modern landowner and more nearly resemble the dues of the feudal lord. [See also this book, p. 223.] They are just as distinct from the ordinary tax, and are not governed by the canons to which it ought to conform; at the utmost they might be assimilated with taxes on special advantages or monopolies. Where the State dues are frequently revised in accordance with the movement of land values, the approximation to rent is very close; where they are changed in order to suit the needs of the State, they are practically taxation." (*Public Finance*, 173-175.)

The discussion, therefore, is a profitless war of words. (See particularly *Alston*, 45-46, 54-56.) "A distinction between a tax and a rent is merely a matter of *amount;* and if a land-tax is so high as to absorb the rent it becomes in fact rent." (*Campbell.* See *Marshall*, 727 *n.*)

The following advantages are claimed by official writers for the Indian land-revenue: (1) It is the only large branch of the revenue which is raised without enhancing prices or diminishing the general consumption, as it is obtained from the landlord's profits and does not add to the cost of production. (2) It approximates to the "single tax" which is the ideal type of assessment according to many economic writers. (3) Except in the permanently settled parts, India enjoys the advantages of the "nationalisation of land" which is advocated by many philosophers in Europe. (4) It falls on that part of the produce which goes to the *intermediate* rent-receiver and does not touch the pocket of the *actual cultivator*." (*Indian Empire*, iv. 234.) It is true that a *proportionate* tax on rent falls wholly on the *landlord*, as it does not affect the price of agricultural produce, while a *fixed* charge (*i.e.*, monopoly rent) per acre would be an indirect duty on agricultural produce and would raise prices, as it would be levied even on land which yields no economic rent. (*Pierson*, i. 104.) But "the land-tax may be so increased as to check the application of capital to the improvement of the soil. This disadvantage attaches to every land-tax which does not consist in the payment of a fixed sum and which increases with the rent of the land." (*Ibid*, 106.)

The real point at issue between the Indian Government and its critics is one of *fact* and not of principle. Is the land-revenue under the non-permanent settlement a tax on rents only, or is it screwed up so high as to encroach on the cultivator's wages and the interest of the capital spent on improvement? That is the essential question. The official apologists assert that the State takes less than half the 'net assets' and leaves to the farmer not only the wages of cultivation but a substantial profit besides, which equals or exceeds what the State exacts. (*Ind. Emp.*, iv. 217, 222-225.) Such is no doubt the *theoretical* principle of assessment laid down, and it seems to be followed in the Punjab and the U. P. (where agriculture is protected by irrigation and the ryots are thriving) and also in certain parts of Madras, where the average ryotwari holding is 8 acres and a portion is sub-let, showing that the direct tenant of Government enjoys a net rental. But with regard to Oudh, Bundelkhand, the unprotected parts of the C. P., certain Madras districts, and particularly the Bombay Deccan and Gujrat, we have the adverse testimony of those who have observed the *actual* working of the land-revenue system and have been in the closest touch with the people. In these parts, they assert, "the land revenue represents more than the economic rent and trenches on the cost of cultivation." The sober and statesmanly Ranade, who had a long official experience of the indebted Deccan peasantry, came to the conclusion (1892) that "the so-called land-tax [of Western India] is not a tax on rents proper, but frequently encroaches upon the profits and wages of the poor peasant, who has to accommodate himself to a lower standard of life as the pressure increases." (*Essays*, 32.) Mr. Gokhale, the ablest student of Indian economics for the last twenty years, has shown how in the Bombay Presidency "improvements are taxed in spite of statutes and rules at every periodical revision, how lands which can leave no margin for the payment of assessment are assessed all the same,"—how "the increases of land-revenue, especially in the U. P., Madras, and Bombay, are large and weigh with undue pressure on the land." The effect, according to him is to *discourage* all *expenditure of capital on land* and render agricultural improvement an impossible hope. (*Speeches*, 31, 103, 139, 179.) Mr. R. C. Dutt, who combined high scholarship with the ripe and varied experience of a district officer, bore personal testimony to the grinding poverty and hopeless misery of the peasants in the C. P., the Deccan, Gujrat, and certain parts of Madras, and was driven to conclude that the land-revenue in these parts represented more than the entire economic rent. (*Dutt*, 332, 462, 481-'7, 502, and especially 492 *n.*) But it must be admitted that these opinions were formed before the partial relaxation of the stringency of the assessment rules and the more considerate treatment of the ryot in the temporarily settled areas that have been ordered by Government in the last few years. Moreover, during the unexpired portion of the running term of settlement, the cultivators will reap the full benefit of the present high prices of agricultural produce.

CHAPTER X.

INDIA DURING THE WAR.

The war has naturally affected India differently from most other parts of the British Empire. In England and her self-governing Dominions the manhood of the nation has been more or less withdrawn from trade and industry for war purposes, and the manufactories of commercial goods have been turned into munition factories, restricting the output of the former. India, being a Dependency and a preponderantly agricultural country, has not suffered decrease of production in her chief industry, *viz.*, agriculture, through conscription and the consequent depletion of labour. It may almost seem at first sight that she is a neutral country and not a portion of one of the belligerent States.

On closer examination, however, this opinion is found to be false. In as much as India has been, more than any other part of the British Empire, helplessly dependent upon foreign countries for the sale of her produce, the supply of the manufactured goods she uses in daily life, and the ocean transport of both these classes of merchandise, she has suffered loss more than they. The raw materials, which are the only things she can offer for sale, have fallen in price, while the manufactures she consumes have risen in price in consequence of the war, and thus she is a sufferer both as a seller and as a purchaser. At the same time, her utter lack of a shipping of her own and the restriction of her exports by order of Government have prevented her from making the extra profit out of her saleable goods (except gunny bags and indigo) which all neutral nations of the world (and even England and Canada) are making during the present war. If India had possessed a mercantile marine like Japan and had been left free to sell her goods to the highest bidder, she could have compensated herself for the enhanced price of her foreign imports by raising the price of the raw materials she produces.

The outbreak of the war in August 1914 produced the following economic effects:

(*a*) Trade with the enemy countries was at once cut off. They used to take 14·2 p. c. of our total exports (against 23·7 p.c. by England) and send us 9·2 p.c. of our imports (against 64 p.c. by England).

(*b*) Export of materials of manufacture to and import of manufactured goods from the Allied countries greatly decreased on account of the curtailment of their economic production through the diversion of men and capital to the unproductive purposes of war and munition making.

(*c*) Great and growing scarcity of shipping, through (i) the disappearance of the German mercantile marine, (3·3 million tons against 12·4 million tons of England and 1·8 mil. tons of U. S. A.), and (ii) the diversion of 70 p.c. of British and neutral ships to the transport of troops, stores and munitions to the scenes of war. Under this head may be included the temporary insecurity of the Indian Ocean through the ravages of the German cruiser *Emden*. [During "Emden week" in September, 1914, though it was the height of the jute export season, there was no sailing from Calcutta.]

(*d*) The withdrawal of foreign capital from India.

(*e*) Rush to secure gold, cash notes and withdraw bank deposits.

This last was temporary and the scare affected the ignorant few only, though the evil was aggravated by Marwari speculators trying to make a corner in sovereigns and metallic money and trade on the public credulity. This phenomenon, however, was much less widely spread in India than in any other belligerent country and passed away very soon. [A part of the withdrawal from the Government Savings Banks was due not to panic but to the needs of our people, who suddenly lost their usual income from jute cotton and even ordinary trading, and were at the same time called upon to pay higher prices for the goods they consumed. Bank deposits were, to some extent, drawn upon for investment in the cheapened Public Debt.]

The above economic features marked the opening stage of the war. But as the struggle was protracted, they changed in the course of the second year of it, and a sort of adjustment to the new situation has now taken place, of which the following are the noticeable characteristics:

(*a*) A 'state of siege' prevails, *i.e.*, export, import, production and sale are not governed by the free play of economic laws, but by "war ordinances" and made subservient to the needs of the State.

(*b*) There is a phenomenal shortage of shipping, which has absolutely stopped certain classes of export and import, and greatly reduced the volume of others, even where it has not been done by order of Government.

(*c*) Internal transport has been harmfully restricted through lack of materials for renewing and repairing railways and the commandeering of inland and coasting steamers for war work.

(*d*) Certain industries have been killed and all others greatly reduced and made costlier, through the closing of the supply of necessary materials, such as machinery, chemicals, artificial dyes, &c.

(*e*) Abnormal development of a few industries subservient to war, *e.g.*, the manufacture of jute bags, steel and iron, woollen clothing, and leather goods.

(*f*) Inflated profits in the few industries for which India was already equipped, (*viz.*, paper, cotton and woollen mills), and which are enjoying the advantages of a monopoly, except so far as (*g*) operates.

(*g*) The phenomenal advance of Japan (and, to a lesser extent, of the U. S. A.) as sellers in the Indian market. Our imports from Japan rose from 4·4 *crores* of Rs. in 1914 to 7·5 *crores* in 1915. In 1915 Japan sent 83·4 p. c. of our matches against only 44 p. c. in 1913. —

To sum up the whole case, we have suffered in proportion to our dependence on those foreign countries our communication with which has been interrupted either by war or by lack of transport. For example, our food-stuffs have been lowered in price, but not salt, because the 30 p. c. of our salt consumption which comes from abroad (Liverpool) having quadrupled in price, our home salt has grown dearer in sympathy with this rise. [The retail price of salt is now Rs. 3-12 per maund (against Rs. 2-4 in 1913), though the salt-tax has been enhanced by 4 annas only in the interval.]

At present (April, 1917), the whole economic situation in India is dominated by the lack of shipping, reduction of railway service, and coal scarcity, (the price of coal being now 2½ times what it was eight months ago,)—all of which facts (esp., the last two) are seriously affecting our industries.

How Indian producers have suffered loss.— The outbreak of the war greatly reduced, and in some cases altogether stopped, the demand for Indian staple produce in European markets. In the eight months following the declaration of war (Aug. 1914—March 1915) our imports decreased from 166 *crores* (the record of a year ago) to 95 *crores*, a shrinkage of 43

p. c. Imports fell off by 34 p. c. during the same period. The loss fell heaviest on raw jute (17·9 *cr.*) oil-seeds (11·02 *cr.*), rice (9·45 *cr.*), raw cotton (7·55 *cr.*), cotton manufactures (4·11 *cr.*), raw hides (3·91 *cr.*) and jute manufactures (2·49 *cr.*),—the export of which declined in 1914-15 from the level of 1913-14 by the amount of Rupees stated against each within brackets. But these figures under-estimate our actual loss, as the reduction of the quantity exported was accompanied by a fall in price, and the Indian growers received more than proportionately less for what they parted with. For example, the jute crop of 1914 was 10·44 million bales, but as the average price in 1914 was Rs. 40 per bale less than in 1913, the total diminution of the income of jute growers was 41·77 *crores* of Rupees. In 1915, the jute crop was 7·34 million bales and the price Rs. 31 per bale lower than in 1913, so that our total loss was 22·75 *crores* of Rupees. In cotton the total losses in 1914 and 1915 were about 19·76 and 4·56 *crores* respectively, due to the fall in prices from the level of the last year of peace. In Oct. 1913 first class jute had sold at more than Rs. 16 per maund, in September 1914 it went abegging at even less than a quarter of the price. This fall in price made it unprofitable to cut, steep and extract the fibre of the ripe jute in many parts of Bengal in the season 1914, as the labourers did not lower their old rate of Re 1 a day; and the result was that a crop which a year ago might have fetched *crores* of Rupees was left to perish in the fields. This fact reacted on the cultivation in the following years, and the jute and cotton sowings declined as shown below (*in millions of acres*) :—

	1913	1914	1915	1916
Cotton (*all India*) ...	25·2	24·59	17·74	21·21
Jute " ...	2·9	3·36	2·37	

This loss fell entirely upon the Indian producers as the European jute mill owners replenished their stock for 2 years in advance very cheaply during the slump of 1914. When in 1915 raw jute appreciated on account of war demand for bags, the profit went entirely to the brokers. (One Marwari middleman of Calcutta is said to have gained 5 *crores* in one year.)

Our losses in oil-seeds (the large demand for which in France and Germany had ceased), and raw hides and skins, were very high, though less than in jute and cotton. A single sub-division in the Rangpur district suffered a loss of 5 *lakhs* on its tobacco in 1914 on account of the Bay of Bengal being unsafe and the Burma traders refusing to buy the leaf.

The loss suffered by the Indians through the rise in the price of imported goods may be illustrated by the case of sugar. In 1915 we imported 647,700 tons of it, for which we had to pay 16·62 *crores* of Rupees, whereas the pre-war price would have been nearly 6 *crores* less,—which was, therefore, our net loss as consumers. [In the war months of 1914 our loss through the rise in sugar prices was 2·3 *crores.*] Our other osses can be studied in the table given at the end of this chapter. Opium exports, in particular, declined n value by nearly 2 *crores* between 1913 and 1915.

How India has benefited by the war.—There the been a rise in the prices of articles which are in special demand in Europe in war-time,—such as wheat, tea, indigo, woollen stuff, dressed leather, gunny bags, and tobacco, and the rise has benefited India in so far as Government has not interfered with their sale. But as regards wheat, the Government of India on 28 December 1914 restricted wheat export to British possessions only and even there up to a maximum of 78,000 tons a year. It also began to purchase and export wheat on its own account (amounting to 82 p. c. of our total wheat export in 1915,—Rs. 6·89 *crores* worth out of 8·44 *crores* worth). Tea prices have risen in England, but the enhanced British duty on it has curtailed India's profit. As the result of the disappearance of synthetic indigo, the vegetable indigo of our country now commands a monopoly price in Europe, and yielded an extra or war profit of 1·20 *crores* in 1915. But the whole of this amount went to the European planters and not to the peasants, though the latter have borne the entire loss of the depreciation of our jute and cotton. Jute manufacture received a tremendous impetus during 1915, which has been rightly called by Mr. Shirras an *annus mirabilis* for the industry. "War demands from the

French, Russian and British Governments, for sand-bags, grain-bags, gunny cloth &c., were so considerable that the trade entered on an unique period of prosperity." But this war profit was shared solely by the European managers and share-holders of the jute mills, and not by the jute growers nor by the labourers. "The disappearance of the Continental demand [for raw jute] and the absence of freight gave the Calcutta mills a complete hold on the market in raw jute for a long period....Another factor which favoured the mills was the good supply of labour. The stoppage of railway and other large projects owing to war, released a large mass of labour which drifted to the Calcutta mills"; and there was, in consequence, no rise in wages. The export of gunny bags doubled in a single year (1915). The total value of our jute manufactures exported rose from 28 *crores* in 1913 to 38 *crores* in 1915. The price of the shares of several jute mills trebled in 1916.

Raw cotton (food for cannon) and coal appreciated in 1915 and 1916 on account of military needs. The former, however, has not yet recovered its pre-war price-level.

War and the cotton industry.—"Some Bombay spinning mills went into liquidation in September 1915 on account of the general depression in the industry following the outbreak of war and owing to the difficulty of financing mills which during 1914 had suffered from the fall of yarn prices in China."

(*Shirras*, 35). The stoppage of chemicals and dyes, which used to be supplied by Germany, affected the output of our cotton mills. But in spite of it, a satisfactory revival took place *in 1915*, when for the first time the value of *our home production of cotton goods exceeded that of imported goods.* In 1914 the imported foreign yarn and cloth had been worth 3·65 *crores* more than our mill production, but in 1915 the latter outstripped the former by 2·56 *crores.* Scarcity of coal caused by the shortage of railway stock is now (1917) the most serious problem for our cotton mills.

Prices and Wages.—In addition to what has been stated above on these two points, we may note that on the outbreak of the war grain prices (esp., that of rice in Burma, the chief exporting province) fell, while everywhere cotton, oil-seeds and hemp realised poor prices. *Wheat* was the only exception; its price was rapidly forced up by the war and the rise continued in spite of the limitation of export from 28 Dec. 1914 by Government order. So, in March 1915 the Indian Government undertook its "wheat deal," *i.e.*, it purchased the exportable surplus in India and placed it in the London market on its own account, private wholesale trade or export of the grain being forbidden. This scheme was abandoned in May 1916, and wheat is now allowed to be exported privately on permits from the Customs Department, on condition that Government decides the maximum quantity to be exported in each season and also by each individual firm. The movement of wheat prices since the outbreak of the war, (taking the July 1914 price level as 100),—Sept. 1914 (102), Oct. (110), Dec. (125), January 1915 (134), Feb. (145), March (121),—the decline continued till it reached 93 in July, when a rise set in which culminated in 102 in Nov. 1915 and January 1916, with a fresh fall which touched 91 in March 1916.

For three months after the outbreak of the war the price of most imported manufactures did not rise, as there had been over-trading and accumulation of large stocks (esp. piece-goods) in the preceding year, and the decline in the prices of raw cotton and jute greatly diminished the purchasing power of the Indian people. The Durga Pujah market of Sep.-Oct. 1914 was the dullest and least profitable seen for a generation. Holders of imports were eager to convert their goods into cash on the outbreak of the war and very wisely decided not to scare away the unexpectedly impoverished customers by raising prices. But from November a rise began in the price of imported goods which has continued since then (with special severity in the case of chemicals, medicines, metals and metallic ware) as the following comparative table will show:

PRICES.	JULY 1914	MARCH 1915	MARCH 1916	MARCH 1917
Wheat	100	132	90	
Rice	„	108	108	
Raw jute	„	64	90	
„ Cotton ...	„	72	102	
Java sugar ...	„	174	183	
Liverpool salt ..	„	206	394	
Tea	„	117	107	
Oil-seeds	„	83	82	
Jute manufactures ...	„	96	144	
Cotton „ ...	„	95	121	
Metals	„	112	168	
Corrugated sheets ...	„	128	210	
Indigo	„	386	372	

The outbreak of the war was followed by retrenchment in railway construction, public works, private house building and in the growth of mills and business firms. This led to a considerable amount of unemployment. In Bengal during 1914-15 agricultural wages suffered from the low jute prices and the poor paddy crop, and also in Bihar and Assam where the rice harvest was defective. The unemployment was very wide-spread, though for a time only, in the cotton trade, and in a lesser degree in the jute industry. Wages did not rise in any industry (except breweries and tea-gardens) during 1914 and 1915. Notwithstanding the heavy war orders in the jute and wool industries and the extra demand on paper mills, mines, cotton mills and the rice industry,—there was no rise in the pre-war rates of the wages paid, (except 3 p. c. in the sizing and weaving departments only.)

Exchange, freight &c.—Ocean freights in March 1915 were from 3 to 4 times the pre-war rates, and had risen to 9 or 10 times by March 1916.

On 3rd August 1914 the Government of India announced its readiness to sell *Reverse Councils* if necessary up to one million sterling a week. The sale of *Council Bills* in London naturally declined; it fell to the unprecedentedly low figure of £7·7 mil. in 1914 (against £31·2 mil. in 1913), and £20·70 mil. in 1915. Reverse Councils were sold to the amount of £8·70 mil. in 1914 and £4·89 in 1915. The issue of gold to private individuals in India was stopped from 5 August 1914. The import of gold (net) declined from 23·33 *crores* in 1913 to 7·64 *crores* in 1914 and was stopped by the Home Government in 1915-16. The net imports of silver were 13·03 *crores* 1913, 8·88 *crores* 1914, and 4·82 *crores* 1915.

Public Finance.—The great falling off in the export of our staples and consequent loss of purchasing power by our people in the first few months of the war, threatened a commercial crisis. In Bombay, in particular, there had accumulated heavy stocks of piece-goods in which a large amount of capital was locked up. Any forced sale by the merchants to pay their liabilities, would have ruined them. At the same time none would venture to buy the raw cotton at a fair price and save the ryots from starvation.

To avert this double catastrophe, Government placed a large portion of its Treasury balances at the disposal of the trade, through the Presidency Banks, and the situation became remarkably easier in consequence.

The war involved the Indian Government in heavy financial liability in spite of its retrenchments in civil departments and public works and railway construction. The comparative figures of *gross* revenue and expenditure are given below *in millions sterling*:

	1913	1914	1915	1916	1917
Gover Revenue ...	85·20	81·15	82·62	96·83	98.85
„ Expenditure	82·89	82·94	85·26	89·45	98·81
British or deficit	+2·31	−1·78	−2·64	+7·39	+·03

The increase of taxation has been described in Chapters VIII and IX. In addition, our Public Debt has been increased, both in England and in India.

In March 1917 the Government of India decided to make a free gift of 150 *crores* of rupees to Great Britain for the war. This amounts to an incidence of Rs. 6·1 per head of the British Indian population, man woman and child, rich and poor alike, and represents one-fifth of the total annual national income of India and nearly two years' public revenue. It will involve on the Indian Exchequer an interest and redemption charge of 9 *crores* of rupees a year for 30 years to come. The previous war contributions in kind made by the Government of India to England, had exceeded 73 *crores* by the end of 1916, besides 5 *crores* subscribed by our people to various war funds.

IMPORTS.		1913	1914	1915	1916
Net gold	... *cr. Rs.*	23·33	7·64	—1·11	
„ silver	... „	13·03	8·88	4·82	
Cotton goods	... „	66·29	48·99	43·27	
Woollen „	... „	3·85	1·88	0·95	
Dyes ...	... „	1·41	·71	·45	
Sugar ...	... „	14·95	10·52	16·61	
„ (quantity),	... *mil. cwt.*	17·93	11	12·85	
Hardware and cutlery	... *cr. Rs.*	6·43	4·29	4·08	
Iron and steel	... „	16	9·76	9·19	
„	... *mil. tons*	1·01	·6	·42	
Copper	... „	·74	·51	·11	
„	... *cr. Rs.*	4·11	2·77	·74	
Quinine	... „	·15	·12	·16	
„	*thousand lbs.*	117	89	95	
Matches	... *mil. gross*	13·89	15·41	18·30	
„	... *cr. Rs.*	·89	1·12	1·38	

EXPORTS.		1913	1914	1915	1916
Jute, raw,	... *mil. tons*	.768	.505	.6	
"	... *cr. Rs.*	30.82	12.91	15.64	
" manuf.	... "	28.27	25.82	37.98	
Cotton, raw,	... *mil. cwt.*	10.62	10.34	8.85	
"	... *cr. Rs.*	41.04	33.48	24.92	
" manuf.	... "	12.12	8.01	9.61	
Oil-seeds	... "	25.67	14.65	10.12	
Raw hides	... "	11.72	7.81	9.79	
Manuf. leather	... "	4.25	4.75	5.63	
Indigo,	*thousand cwt.*	10.9	17.1	42	
"	... *cr. Rs.*	.213	.9	2.07	
Opium	... "	3.42	1.76	1.47	
Coal	... "	.69	.52	.73	
"	... *mil. tons*	.72	.59	.8	
Tea	... *mil. lbs.*	289	300	338	
"	... *cr. Rs.*	14.97	15.52	19.98	
Rice	... "	26.6	17.15	15.45	
"	... *mil. tons*	2.45	1.56	1.36	
Wheat	... "	1.2	.7	.65	
"	... *cr. Rs.*	13.13	8.32	8.44	
Total grain, pulse and flour	"	45.14	29.04	29.07	

Under the stress of war, in order to maintain the exchange, the Government of India took power to increase the invested portion of the Paper Currency Reserve in 1915 by 6 *crores* of Rs., in 1916 (Act IX) by 6 *crores* more, and in December 1916 by 24 *crores* more, (making a total of 50 *crores* against 14 *crores* up to 1914). On 25th January 1917, we had a note issue of 83·40 *crores* of rupees, which was thus secured :

Securities in England	32·82 *cr. Rs.*
" " India	9·99 "
Silver in England	0·13 "
Gold " "	11·17 "
Silver in India	16·68 "
Gold " "	12·52 "
	83·31

The introduction of one-rupee paper money is now under contemplation.

BIBLIOGRAPHY.

[In this work when any reference is given, it merely indicates that the reader will find the same subject treated in the work referred to. In the following Bibliography, I have put *an asterisk against the books* which an economic inquirer will find *most useful.*]

* *Indian Empire.*—The first 4 vols. of the new ed. of the *Imperial Gazetteer of India.* Vol. III is *indispensable* to the student of Indian economics, as it has distilled the essence of a large number of blue-books. Vol. IV. supplies the most correct and authoritative information on the government, finance, public works, etc., of India. (Statistics obsolete.)

* *Statement exhibiting the Moral and Material Progress and Condition of India during the year*......presented to Parliament (Wyman & Sons, London). Issued annually, about 15 months after the year under review. It summarises the contents of all our periodical returns and reports, and no student can do without it. [The 48th No., for 1911-12 and the 9 preceding years is very useful; *Cd. 220*].

* *Statistical Abstract relating to British India*, presented to Parliament, 49th No. [*Code 8157.*] Invaluable for reference. (Wyman & Sons, 1916).

* *Statistics of British India*, Pt. I. Industrial, Pt. II. Commercial. (Suptdt. Govt. Printing, India). Replaced, since 1913, by *Statistical Abstract for British India.* Vol. I. Com., II. Finance. (Govt. Pr., Calcutta.) * Noel Paton's *Notes on Sugar in India*, 3rd ed., 1911, (Suptdt. Govt. Pr.)

Prices and Wages in India, 30th issue, 1913. (Superintendent, Govt. Printing, India). Full of detailed statistics.

Minutes of Evidence...Indian Currency Committee, (Eyre & Spottiswoode, 1893), *Code 7060-II.*

* *Minutes of Evidence...Indian Currency Committee*, Pts. I. & II. (Eyre and Spottiswoode, 1898-99), *Code 9037* and *9222.*

* *Review of the Trade of India*, (Suptdt., Govt. Printing), issued annually. *Review of the Industrial Position and Prospects* ...published for each province. *Technical and Industrial Instruction in Bengal*, and other official papers published in India.

Among blue-books published in England, I have also consulted *Factory Labour in India*, 1907 (*Cd. 3617*); *Labour Commission Report*, 1893, Vol. II. (*Code 6795*-II); *Reports of the Famine Commissions*, 1898 and 1901; *East India Home Charges Return*, 1893 (*Cd. 327*); *First Report Opium Com.* 1894 (*Cd. 7313*).

* K. L. Datta's *Inquiry into the Rise of Prices in India*, Vol. I. Report (Govt. Pr., 1914), most useful. *Report of Committee on Co-operation.* (Simla Govt. Pr., 1916).

* Nicholson's *Report on Agricultural Banks*, 2 vols., Dupernex's *People's Banks for Northern India.*

Journal of Indian Arts and Industries (Griggs) contains good accounts of old Indian handicrafts. Baden Powell's *Short Account of the Land Revenue in British India*, 2nd ed.

* Jones's *Peasant Rents* (reprint by Macmillan).

Seton-Karr's *Cornwallis* (Rulers of India series).

* Morison's *Industrial Organisation of an Indian Province.*— One of the best special treatises; it indicates the right line of economic research in India. [Quoted as *Morison.*] The same author's *Economic Transition in India* contains interesting essays. * Howard's *India and the Gold Standard* (Thacker Spink & Co., 1911) gives a very lucid, informing and accurate account of our currency and its operations, as well as of several connected subjects. * Alston's *Elements of Indian Taxation* (Macmillan, 1910) is a short but indispensable exposition of the principles governing Indian taxation and the effect of the fiscal system. Lees Smith's *India and the Tariff Problem.* * Keynes's *Indian Currency and Finance* (Macmillan, 1913). Chamberlain Commission Report (*Code 7236* of 1914).

Among general works on economics, I have consulted Mill's *Principles* (People's ed., 1888), Marshall's *Principles*, Vol. I., Pierson's *Principles*, 2 vols., Macleod's *Theory of Credit*, Gide, the *Statesman's Year-Book*, Mulhall's *Dictionary of Statistics*, 4th ed. (1899), Webb's *New Dictionary of Statistics* (1911), List's *National System of Pol. Econ.*, tr. by Lloyd, (Longman, 1904), Cunningham and McArthur's *Outline of Eng. Industrial History*, (Cambridge), Cunningham's *Growth of Eng. Indus.*, Vol. II., Leone Levi's *Hist. of Br. Commerce*, 2nd ed.

On the Indian side we have Ranade's **Essays on Indian Economics* (2nd ed. 1906), Gokhale's **Speeches* (Natesan, 1908), R. C. Dutt's *India in the Victorian Age* (2nd ed. 1906), Prof. V. G. Kale's *Indian Industrial and Economic Problems* (Natesan, 1912). * Jack's *Economic Life of a Bengal District*, (Oxford, 1917).

* *Indian Year-Book*, 4th year, 1917 (Bombay), and two quarterly journals of Economics published at Calcutta and Allahabad.

* *Indian Trade Journal*, weekly, (Govt. Pr., Calcutta.)